Miles Booy studied film, television and literature at the College of St Mark and St John in Plymouth, before doing post-graduate work at the University of East Anglia. He lives in Stafford with ιd son. He has a PhD, so you can call him 'The Doctor'.

INVESTIGATING CULT TV

Series Editor: Stacey Abbott

The **Investigating Cult TV** series is a fresh forum for discussion and debate about the changing nature of cult television. It sets out to reconsider cult television and its intricate networks of fandom by inviting authors to rethink how cult TV is conceived, produced, programmed, and consumed. It will also challenge traditional distinctions between cult and quality television.

Offering an accessible path through the intricacies and pleasures of cult TV, the books in this series will interest scholars, students, and fans alike. They will include close studies of individual contemporary television shows. They will also reconsider genres at the heart of cult programming such as science fiction, horror, and fantasy, as well as genres like teen TV, animation, and reality TV when these have strong claims to cult status. Books will also examine themes or trends that are key to the past, present, and future of cult television.

Published and forthcoming in **Investigating Cult TV** series:

The Cult TV Book edited by Stacey Abbott
Dexter: *Investigating Cutting Edge Television* edited by Douglas L. Howard
Investigating Alias edited by Stacey Abbott and Simon Brown
Investigating Charmed edited by Karin Beeler and Stan Beeler
Investigating Farscape by Jes Battis
Love and Monsters: *The* Doctor Who *Experience, 1979 to the Present* by Miles Booy
Torchwood Declassified: *Investigating Mainstream Cult Television* edited by Rebecca Williams
TV Horror: *Investigating the Darker Side of the Small Screen* edited by Lorna Jowett and Stacey Abbott

Ideas and submissions for **Investigating Cult TV** to
s.abbott@roehampton.ac.uk
philippabrewster@gmail.com

Miles Booy

LOVE AND MONSTERS

THE *DOCTOR WHO* EXPERIENCE
1979 TO THE PRESENT

I.B. TAURIS

LONDON · NEW YORK

Published in 2012 by I.B.Tauris & Co Ltd
6 Salem Road, London W2 4BU
175 Fifth Avenue, New York NY 10010
www.ibtauris.com

Distributed in the United States and Canada
Exclusively by Palgrave Macmillan
175 Fifth Avenue, New York NY 10010

ISBN: 978 1 84885 478 9 (HB)
      978 1 84885 479 6 (PB)

A full CIP record for this book is available from the British Library
A full CIP record is available from the Library of Congress

Library of Congress Catalog Card Number: available

Printed and bound in Great Britain by T.J. International, Padstow, Cornwall

MIX
Paper from
responsible sources
FSC
www.fsc.org   FSC® C013056

'It begins with things like Dalek cakes, and it ends up with people trying to write scripts.'

– *Who* scripter Rob Shearman

'No self-respecting *Doctor Who* fan throws stuff away.'

– *Who* novelist Peter Anghelides

CONTENTS

ACKNOWLEDGEMENTS/
NOTES ON SOURCES

This book is the product of both memory and research. I joined the *Doctor Who Appreciation Society* in 1983, aged 15, as part of a boom in membership which followed the BBC's Easter-weekend convention at Longleat that year, left the society some years later and have hung at the margins of fandom ever since. What that means, and the baggage which it brings, is part of the story which follows. No two *Who* fans' experiences are the same, but this was far from atypical. If anything written here about fandom's issues and experiences exaggerates or overemphasizes anything, I can only plead that it was probably because I, and my (often similarly aged) fan friends felt particularly acutely about the issue at the time. That said, research has hopefully ironed out the distortions of memory. Primary research materials for this book have been *Doctor Who Magazine*, (published by Marvel, then Panini), the Appreciation Society's newsletter *Celestial Toyroom*, and their 1980s rival *Doctor Who Bulletin* (later *DreamWatch Bulletin*, and more familiarly DWB). These publications often appear in the chapters which follow as the objects of study, analyzed for the interpretive techniques they used and the readings of the programme which they put into circulation. They are also, however, important primary sources of information and history about the development of fandom itself. This reading was supplemented by a wealth of other fan materials, publications which perhaps only reached a handful of issues.

Fanzines of all sorts constitute a vast resource of cultural interpretation which traditional archivists have never stored and come
to terms with. In the absence of such archives I am obliged to those
who lent or donated fanzines to me for this project, and to those who
sold me merchandise via eBay. Within fandom, it should be noted,
the issue of fanzine archiving is beginning to be addressed. There
have recently evolved a number of fanzine preservation projects,
though none to my knowledge commands large-scale support as
yet. Self-publishing and online databases have allowed some editors to reprint their fanzines' content in a longer-lasting form.
Access issues aside, fanzines present specific problems of quotation.
I have attempted to provide full citations for everything quoted,
but, although striving for professionalism in many ways, 'zines do
not always provide full publication information. Since most solicit
contributions from the readership, an editorial address is normally
provided, though even this has not proven universal. Thus, publication information given in the footnotes is as thorough as I have
found possible. I have also, on occasion, chosen to omit the name
of the writer. Many things were committed to print in the heightened atmosphere of 1980s *Who* fandom, and one or two of them
are reprinted here as examples of the prevailing mood. However,
not everyone stands by the bluntly stated opinions of a generation
ago, and perhaps they don't wish to be identified with them now.
Consequently, in many instances full source details are given (with
the qualifications above), so that researchers who really need to
locate a cited piece can find it, but with no author named. By the
turn of the century, of course, the centre of fandom had shifted
online, a medium which presents its own referencing problems.
The long-running *Outpost Gallifrey* site – for a decade the online
home of fandom – closed down in 2008, and its forums, so full of
information, interpretation and, yes, invective, are now lost.

Any modern work on *Who* stands on the shoulders of decades'
worth of prior research. A book of this sort would be impossible
without the episode guides, production histories, analytical studies
and interview compendiums which have preceded it. Where specific facts are taken from these books, full references are given, but
much of what has been debated or uncovered is now simply the air
which *Who* fandom breaths. It is hard to remember now, but there
was a time when a four-page explanation of what a script editor

did constituted cutting-edge research. At times this book holds those prior interpretations at critical distance, but it is also formed by them – as, indeed, to a staggering degree, was I. In seeking to contextualize prior research, I'm obliged to Jeremy Bentham, David Howe, Stephen Walker, and, especially, Andrew Pixley for their recall of the conditions under which it was conducted. Similarly, Nigel Robinson clarified some points concerning 1980s Target books whilst John Tulloch and Keith Miller answered my queries about the publication of *Doctor Who: The Unfolding Text* and *The House That Jack Built* respectively. I asked a number of questions online and I'm thankful to those who took time to respond. David Booy allowed me to peruse his copies of *Doctor Who Adventures*.

Sergio Angelini, Giovanni Antonelli, Karl Johnson and Tim Small commented on the manuscript at various points in its drafting, and I'm obliged for their observations and insights. All errors of fact or interpretation remain, sadly, mine. The proofreading of Paul Scoones and Matthew Kilburn has saved me some blushes. Of course, the best corrections I had to make were reducing the number of missing episodes by two – who'd have thought? Longer term intellectual debts are to Cindy Hamilton, Nigel Morris and Steven Marchant – fine people, all of them, whose only flaw is their lack of interest in *Doctor Who*. Editorial and production staff at I.B.Tauris and NewGen Publishing and Data Services have taken care with my project and I'm thankful to them. I'm obliged to Stacey Abbott and Philippa Brewster for commissioning this book, and allowing me to fill my house with even more *Who* books and magazines under the guise of research. Whether my wife, Samantha, is as thankful about that is another matter, but she has supported the writing of this book with patience and good humour and it is to her and our life together, that it is dedicated.

INTRODUCTION

Octover 1979 saw the release of issue one of *Doctor Who Weekly*, a 28-page hybrid of magazine and comic which came complete with free transfers. The young David McDonald – better known now as David Tennant – realised instantly this was a better purchase than *Spiderman and Hulk Comic*. Russell T. Davies bought his every week from a Swansea newsagent with the unlikely name of Billy Hole.[1] Like the hero it celebrates, the publication has regenerated several times in the intervening years, but has avoided cancellation and is still with us. *Doctor Who Magazine* is now a glossy, 84-page extravaganza with closer access to the personnel and creative processes behind the revamped series than any media magazine has ever previously offered its readership. On the downside, it costs significantly more than the original 12p and you don't get transfers anymore.

The release of *DWW* was due to Dez Skinn, a UK comic professional who was alert to the possibilities of magazine tie-ins. He had previously devised *House of Hammer*, a magazine combining strips derived from the films of the Hammer film studio with articles about their production. Upon moving to the UK branch of Marvel Comics, he had launched *The Hulk* into his own comic to tie-in with the then-popular television series. He saw in *Doctor Who* a property which could be similarly developed. His comic/magazine would be similar to *House of Hammer*, but aimed at a younger audience. He knew who to hire to work on the comic strips, but needed people to write features on the programme's history and icons. He would need the help of organized fandom, and so he brought on board senior members of the amateur *Doctor Who Appreciation Society*. And, so, like some pop culture Pandora, he opened the box ... [2]

This book is about what happened after Skinn first broke down the barrier between amateur and professional, how his keen eye for *Doctor Who*'s commercial exploitation was speedily taken up by others, and how the programme's Appreciation Society became a recurrent part of tabloid coverage of the show. I seek to trace the evolution of fan discourse from the second half of the 1970s through to today, and to tell the story of how the programme, the spin-off products it generated and the fandom who loved it so (if sometimes in monstrous ways) grew closer together. In 1975, when the Appreciation Society was formed, the show, its fans and its spin-off products were discrete entities with few sustained points of connection. Fandom – such as it was – was invisible to the general public and merchandising was mostly aimed at schoolchildren. By the time the programme was cancelled in 1989, the merchandise lines had been completely appropriated by fans, first as consumers who wrenched the products away from the general children's market towards their own concerns, and then as producers themselves. In the 1990s, in the absence of a television programme, the fan-written but professionally published *New Adventures* novels became the show's semi-official continuation. At that point, the three once-distinct areas of 'show', merchandise and fandom had merged completely. Later still, some of these products would help set the agenda for the revamped series.

Early Fans

This is not a history of *Doctor Who* fandom. A lot of internal politics and some notable personalities unconcerned with the relationship show/fan/merchandise are not present. The long history of *Who* fandom in Australia barely registers in what follows and American fandom features mainly as a problem/threat to the British way of doing things. Similarly, there were 'Doctor Who fan clubs' before the DWAS, but they don't feature either, and the earliest days of the Appreciation Society itself are only fleetingly covered. There is a feeling within fandom that a history is needed, now that the DWAS and the activities which stemmed from it constitute 35 years of unbroken activity and thought, but this is not that book.

All of those qualifications aside, this study does take an historical approach to its subject, both because of the nature of the project and because an historical element is so often missing from those academic accounts of fandom which exist. Such accounts have been insightful, but tend to be written in the present tense, as if what fans 'do' is what they always did. Even those commentators who acknowledge historical dimensions to the question rarely have the space to explore them. In order to discuss how value judgements work in the fan community, Alan McKee asks 'Which is the best *Doctor Who* story?'[3], but the fans' answer has changed over the years. A poll conducted in 1983 concluded, typically for the time, that it was a Jon Pertwee story, 'The Daemons', an adventure which wouldn't make the cut a decade later when it was being openly ridiculed as derivative, repetitive and padded in some influential sections of fandom. In another piece, McKee asks 'Why is *"City of Death"* the best *Doctor Who* story?'[4] It is a question to which the simplest answer might be 'It isn't'. It is only since the late 1980s that this 1979 story came to be held in such high regard, and – if we are to be pedantic – it has never to my knowledge won a 'Favourite Story Ever' poll of any significant size. Earlier academic research, by John Tulloch and Manuel Alvarado in the early 1980s, uncovered only qualified praise for the story when prominent fan Ian Levine 'grudgingly admitted that he "liked 'City of Death'" ... It was certainly the best in that lamentable season'[5] McKee, who in a previous non-academic incarnation, won a 1986 short story writing competition in *Doctor Who Magazine*, surely knows all of this, but he represses it from his analysis.[6] From the mid-1990s onwards sophisticated fans would refuse to accept the terms of the 'best story ever' question, arguing that no one single story encapsulates all of the show's values. (They would then vote for something which was broadcast when they were eight.)

Beyond the question of acting as an addition or corrective to such historical views, delving into the past of *Who* fandom raises issues which do not face the modern fandoms which are so often the subject of academic analysis. What was fandom like before the internet? How did consensus form when lead times on fanzines were so long? How were the programme details recorded for posterity in the age before video recorders? Where did interpretive authority lie in a programme without an auteur-creator to guide it through all its history? These are questions which do not require answers when the objects of study are *Buffy* fans or X-philes. Modern programmes are created in an environment where fan audiences are welcomed, and often courted, as a key component of an audience which is conceived as a coalition of different interests. *Doctor Who* fans, by contrast, became visible only after the programme had been running successfully for nearly two decades, and its specialised reading position threatened to drag to the cultural margins a programme which the BBC preferred to position within the mainstream (as 'family entertainment', or part of 'Saturday evening on BBC1').

Consequently, an analysis of *Doctor Who* and its most impassioned fans must necessarily distance itself from much that is common across the study of other fandoms. A fan of left/liberal political views might enjoy a self-image as someone who subverts the products of, for instance, the Fox Network. It is significantly harder to feel that working against the expressed intentions of the BBC – a licence fee-funded broadcaster with a public service remit and a host of private-sector enemies – is the same sort of political act.[7] It is similarly difficult to champion fan 'resistance' when this manifested itself in highly personal attacks upon production staff and performers who were doing their jobs in, as the 1980s continued, increasingly difficult situations.

Studies of fan culture became central to debates within Cultural Studies during the 1990s when it was promoted as an instance of active interpretation by the audience, a 'poacher' community producing its own meaning from corporate product. This conception of fan culture is open to several criticisms. For Matt Hills, such accounts lacked any acknowledgment of the conflict within fandom. For Sara Gwenllian Jones, they overstated fans distance from consumerist economic patterns and failed to account for the ways in which the allegedly deviant readings of fans are recuperated back into the corporate strategy.[8] They are both right, and to this list of gaps must be added the way in which the 'poacher' paradigm underestimates the conservatism of interpretive practice in many areas of *Doctor Who* fandom, where appeals to authorial intention – revealed across the huge array of interviews to which the modern fan has access – can be a strong objection to wider interpretations. Thus, when one fan proposed that the 1976 Tom Baker story 'The Deadly Assassin' was not just a rip-off/homage of the film *The Manchurian Candidate* (the normal interpretation), but also drew on the imagery of the Kennedy assassination, the article drew this sharp retort which sought to push the story's interpretation back into the traditional mode: 'Tim Ryan's "American Dream", although fascinating, unfortunately misses one vital point – namely that it wasn't just fans who drew the link between "Deadly Assassin" and *The Manchurian Candidate*, but [script-writer] Robert Holmes himself, who once admitted in an interview that the movie had been his inspiration for the story.'[9] Such forceful renunciations of new interpretations based solely on authorial statements of intent are certainly rarer now than they were when that declaration was made nearly 20 years ago. However, *Who* fandom remains a place where the most common way of explaining the textual features of a given episode is to research the relevant BBC procedure or personnel. Like many other fandoms, explanations based on personal intervention are privileged over wider, cultural factors.

This, however, is to talk only of organized fandom. Much *Who* devotion has taken place outside organized lines. There was no such thing as fandom when the programme began in 1963, but there were fans, however invisible. The 14th episode (broadcast 22/2/64, the first part of the seven-episode 'Marco Polo' story) is one of 106 missing from the BBC's archive, having been wiped in the early 1970s when black-and-white television was no longer thought to be of commercial or aesthetic interest. However, that episode – like the 105 others – survives as an audio soundtrack, recovered from tape recordings made by enthusiastic viewers who had decided, as early as February 1964, that this programme was something special, something worth recording using the only equipment at hand. They then kept the recording for 20 years before the BBC showed any interest in it. I think we can call these people fans. In 1968, as part of its ongoing audience research, the BBC recorded the opinions of viewers about Patrick Troughton's 'The Dominators', and one respondent self-identified themself as 'a Doctor Who fan of many years standing'.[10] All of this occurred during the period when the programme had very little back story, when not even the Doctor's race had been revealed. It is often suggested that texts which attract fans often do so because of their power to immerse readers/viewers in a well-worked-out internal continuity, but that is not a feature of 1960s *Who*. It attracted a following anyway.

The William (Doctor Who) Hartnell Fan Club was created in 1965, and was run out of Hanley in Stoke-On-Trent. The club went through various organizers, mostly offering information about the cast, signed photos, information on upcoming storylines, and memories of the past. It changed its name, for obvious reasons, to *The Doctor Who Fan Club* when Patrick Troughton took on the title role. During Jon Pertwee's era, responsibility for the club passed to Edinburgh-based Keith Miller – 14 when he took it on – and membership escalated to the point where the production office itself had to take responsibility for reproduction and distribution of the news-sheets which Miller had assembled. When membership topped a thousand, many of them overseas, this became a drain on production office resources and incoming producer Philip Hinchclffe was less keen than his predecessor, Barry Letts, to support the club in this way.[11]

The Doctor Who Fan Club left little mark, although some copies of its materials do remain. The club's opinions made no impact upon either later fan debates or the production of the programme. Its members never partook in many of the activities which the DWAS would regard as normal (such as holding conventions, appearing in local newspapers, and demanding the producer's resignation/head on a plate). This would all change with the formation of the *Doctor Who Appreciation Society,* from which direct lines can be drawn to modern-day fandom. In one crucial respect, however, the DWFC was emblematic of things to come: its interest in the past. Whilst Jon Pertwee was glad that a club existed he felt it should primarily concern the current cast and stories, even going so far as to encourage another fan to set up a rival club in this style, something which was subsequently vetoed by Barry Letts. At other times, in other ways, however, such as a 1970s request that the covers of novelizations not feature the image of any Doctors apart from the then-current Tom Baker, the production office would, for its own purposes of branding (not that anyone was using the term then) also seek to privilege the programme's present.

Fans have had other priorities. There are no general rules, but in the UK most children watched the show from the age of four or five upwards. Fandom, by contrast, was an older affair, particularly in the pre-internet world. The costs of fanzines and/or travel to conventions, the vocabulary used and the places in which fan materials were advertised (e.g.: mid-1970s horror magazines) carried with them a wealth of implicit minimum age barriers. Most fans came to fandom carrying up to a decade's worth of memories which they obviously wished to compare and share with others. The present was more-or-less accessible in that it could be remembered (and later videoed), but the past was something desperately in need of recovery and it always seemed to be somehow better than the present. John Nathan-Turner, producer of *Who* throughout the 1980s, argued that 'The memory cheats.' This became his rejoinder to the hordes of teenaged fans who knew that the show was objectively better when they were seven.

For all of these reasons, it is necessary to be careful when making assertions about fan activity or views, since enthusiasm for the programme manifested itself across Britain in different ways. The DWAS never numbered more than three and a half thousand, though a number of active fans might be counted beyond that, particularly by 1985. UK comics and science fiction fandoms would have counted many amongst their number with significant enthusiasm and knowledge of the programme. The UK in the 1980s also boasted a more generalized 'media fandom', closer to the famed US model in its activities. Although often focused on other programmes, *Doctor Who* was a reference point. Beyond all of this activity was a large group of people (the young Russell T. Davies, for example) who partook of none of these activities, but did read *Doctor Who Magazine* (a major conduit through which fan thinking/research on the show reached a wider audience) and the novelizations of television stories. By the mid-1980s, when these novels had retooled themselves in line with fan preferences and expectations, they routinely had a first print run of 50 to 60 thousand. That's a lot of *Doctor Who* experience – or, rather, a lot of different experiences – for one book to chronicle.

In seeking to do just that, the current history starts in the late 1970s. Chapter one sets the context for the appearance of *Doctor Who Weekly*, considering the cultural place of the programme itself, the state of the market for *Doctor Who* products and the creation of the *Doctor Who Appreciation Society*. This chapter necessarily covers a relatively lengthy six years – the majority of Tom Baker's record-setting seven-year term in the title role – because it outlines the position from which subsequent events (the massive shift in the way in which *Doctor Who* was viewed and merchandised) started. The high ratings achieved in the era, and the success of these episodes in North America, meant that the period would be an inescapable reference point in subsequent debates. Merchandisers would be drawn to the imagery of the era (notably its blue, diamond-shaped logo) even when it had been replaced onscreen with newer, fresher models; public nostalgia would recall it fondly, and for some fans it would form the gold standard against which later episodes would be found wanting. The chapter concludes with analysis of *Doctor Who Weekly* itself. Although this deceptively simple product sat on the racks with other children's comics, it was cannily marketed to several groups, a sophisticated exercise for 1979, somewhat ahead of its time.

Chapter two covers the period 1980 to 1982, the period during which *Doctor Who Weekly* became *Doctor Who Monthly*, now very much a magazine rather than a comic. The new format favoured articles over comic strips and refocused its target audience away from primary schoolchildren. This allowed writer Jeremy Bentham to bring fan concerns to the fore. He was aided and encouraged in this by the programme's ambitious new producer, John Nathan-Turner. I relate this to the visually excessive style of production which Nathan-Turner oversaw, a vast escalation of the visual spectacle which, whatever the jokes about dodgy effects, had always been part of the programme. The early 1980s saw a massive boom in the membership, activities and public profile of *Doctor Who* fans, as well as seeing the rise of an American fandom beloved of the UK media for its fancy-dressing and sheer size. The impact of these factors is the subject of chapter three, covering the period from 1983 to 1984 when the show celebrated its twentieth anniversary, when merchandisers brought forth an array of products heretofore unseen, and fans thought the programme would go on forever.

They would, of course, have such illusions rapidly dispelled. Chapter four considers events during the short, controversial tenure of Colin Baker as the Sixth Doctor. The consensus which reigned across *Who* fandom was shattered under the pressure of his starkly different portrayal of the character and of the BBC's decision to suspend the show for 18 months (effectively meaning no transmission during the 85/6 television season). This became full cancellation in 1989 after Sylvester McCoy had been the Doctor for three years. McCoy's portrayal, and the script editorship of Andrew Cartmel, were regarded by many fans as a creative renaissance, but there could be no return to earlier success in the ratings. The lightly metafictional tone of the programme in its last three years would influence the form of the novels which appeared after the cancellation and which, featuring McCoy's Doctor, would claim to be the official continuation of the series. This period is covered in chapter five.

The year 1996 saw the brief return of the Doctor to television screens, played for one night only by Paul McGann. The TV movie failed to inspire a full series, but, as chapter six discusses, the period after its transmission brought about significant shifts in the way in which fans, academics, journalists and writers – and some fans by this point were academics, journalists and writers - found ways to ride the cultural zeitgeist and talk warmly about the show, its place in British cultural history, and their fan experiences in mainstream media without experiencing public ridicule. The late 1990s also saw a shift in merchandising as the BBC concentrated more products in-house and branded them with a uniform logo. This experience would stand them in good stead when the programme returned triumphantly to the screens in 2005, becoming a merchandising powerhouse. Chapter seven considers this most recent moment in the programme's development in the light of the history outlined in this book.

I have not appended to this book a full table of transmitted *Who* stories. Many readers will already own more than enough of those. Those who don't can easily find one on the internet or in print. However, so that those unfamiliar with the broad terms of the programme's historical development can contextualize some of the information discussed, each chapter is prefaced with a list of stories transmitted during the period under discussion (some of which are referred to in the main text) as well as a paragraph **in bold** outlining the major onscreen events, significant changes of production personnel and other notable events.

The book, then, begins in the period when Tom Baker was the Doctor, and works forward from there. However, one incident of the late Pertwee era deserves a mention. Scottish fan Keith Miller became the first person to breach the barrier that separated fan work from professional by having a story printed in *The Dr. Who Annual 1975*. Miller wrote serialized stories for the *DWFC Mag* in the early 1970s and then-*Who* producer Barry Letts, thinking them better than the stories used in the annual, encouraged him to submit to the publisher, World Distributors. Miller submitted two, 'The House That Jack Built' and 'The Seeds of Doom'. Having been accepted by the publisher, the stories were then passed to the programme's production office for approval, whereupon the second was rejected for being too similar to an upcoming production (presumably 'The Seeds of Doom', 1976). 'The House . . .' was named for and inspired by an episode of *The Avengers* which Miller particularly admired, sharing the theme of escape from a madhouse. He would never submit again, and thus the story would be his sole professional *Who*-related credit. Offered a toehold in the *Who* merchandise market, he declined to follow it up and carve a niche as a full- or part-time writer of *Who* materials. He wouldn't be the last person to act in that way, but this book is mostly about the people who made a different choice.[12]

BLUE DIAMOND

The Fourth Doctor – Tom Baker
Season Seventeen (01/09/79 – 12/01/80)
Producer: Graham Williams. Script Editor: Douglas Adams

Destiny of the Daleks (4 episodes)
City of Death (4 episodes)
The Creature From the Pit (4 episodes)
Nightmare of Eden (4 episodes)
The Horns of Nimon (4 episodes)
Shada (Would have been 6 episodes. Abandoned mid-production, due to industrial action at the BBC)

Between December 1974 (when Tom Baker donned his scarf for the first time) and March 1977 (the end of his third series), *Doctor Who* regularly attracted over 10 million viewers, sometimes appearing in the top 20 programmes for the week – something which hadn't been true since the Dalek-fueled ratings highs of William Hartnell's second season (1964/5). Reviews were similarly good and press interest was high. *Doctor Who* was produced at this time by Philip Hinchcliffe and script-edited by Robert Holmes. After three years of high ratings, but also ongoing complaints from Mary Whitehouse and the National Viewers and Listeners and Association about the levels of horror and violence, Hinchcliffe moved (or *was moved*, it has never been clear) to a post-watershed crime series, *Target*. Holmes remained for another six months then returned to freelance writing. Incoming producer Graham Williams was ordered to tone down horror and violence in the series, whilst inflation required him to make episodes with substantially less resources than his predecessor. Ratings declined to around eight million, but the show was still a staple of the BBC's autumn/winter Saturday evenings. When *Doctor Who Weekly* debuted (it was cover-dated October 17th 1979, but released a week earlier), the show was glorying in unrepresentatively high ratings (the programme's highest-rating ever is 16.1 million for 'City of Death' episode four) because of a union dispute on ITV which caused the network to cease transmission for nearly three months.[1] The high ratings of the early Baker era might explain the high number of fans who entered fandom six to seven years later when membership of the Doctor Who Appreciation Society jumped from 1,000 to a still negligible 3,000, a tripling which affected fandom's debate and quality judgements for over a decade. This chapter both sets the context for the release of *Doctor Who Weekly*, and outlines the baggage which that huge influx of fans brought with them.

Doctor Who: The Merchandised Reading

However visible it would later become, active *Doctor Who* fandom has always constituted a small percentage of the audience for a television series the ratings for which never fell below 3.1 million (its nadir, in 1989) and were regularly 8 to 9 million in the late 1970s. What was it like watching *Doctor Who* at a time when no one had heard the term 'cult TV' and certainly wouldn't dream of applying it to a popular family series? Fans have written their own nostalgic accounts of getting through the week waiting for the next episode, and of how Saturday itself could seem to stretch endlessly. These are, by their nature, hardly typical. More representative, I think, is the diary kept at the time by young Andrew Collins and published decades later with a postmillennial gloss.[2] When *Doctor Who* gets a mention – and it gets several – it is usually as part of a list: 'we watched *Play Away* and *The Mouse Factory*, *Tom & Jerry*, *Dr. Who* and *New Faces*' (p. 118); 'We changed the poster board. We've got the Dr. Who, Hitler, Keep Mum She's not so Dumb, and Tommy gun posters up.' (p. 127) 'Weetabix gave away premium gifts ... *Asterix* characters, *Star Trek* or *Dr. Who'* (p. 147). This, I think, indicates the mind of the young *Who* viewer at the time – it was integrated into the broader childhood experience, and was perhaps no more important than the other items on the list. August 1978 finds Collins reading the novel *Doctor Who and the Auton Invasion*, so like thousands of others he interacted with the programme outside of its transmission slot through merchandise.

The 'merchandised reading' of *Who* in the 1970s was wildly uneven. Often aimed at primary school children, comic strips, jigsaws, books and toys reworked the programme as a very basic adventure story, shearing it of its themes and complexities. The Doctor would routinely be referred to as 'Doctor Who' as if it were the character's name (it is not, that is the title of the programme). In/on merchandise, the programme might be referred to as *Dr. Who* (as in *The Dr. Who Annual*), whereas the televised version has never used the contracted form. The Doctor would also be shorn of his ethical nature, routinely blowing up or killing aliens without a thought or scruple. Daleks, themselves often reduced to the status of simple killer robots, would be depicted in garish primary colours which rarely bedecked their on-screen counterparts.

Even when they were not consciously skewing their product towards pre-teens, liberties would be taken with the text as merchandisers sought to produce the cheapest product possible. This entailed paying the BBC only for rights to the series' title, the character/likeness of the actor playing the Doctor and the TARDIS (the Doctor's space/time ship. The acronym stands for Time And Relative Dimension in Space). Extra payments were required for the rights to the characters of the companions and to the actresses/actors for the rights to reproduce their features. Rather than make these payments, many companies – the creators of the comic strips which had run in *TV Comic* before *Doctor Who Weekly*, for instance – created new companions. Some of them looked like their TV equivalents, but others were younger – schoolchildren, even – in line with the perceived audience of the merchandise. Similarly, rather than licence the rights to existing villains, new monsters were mostly devised. Some of these were designed to look quite like Daleks to the eyes of children, but not to the letter of the law.

This arrangement was necessary because of the nature of UK television scripting contracts. *Doctor Who* was produced, script-edited and designed by BBC employees who, in return for regular employment, forewent all copyright over their work. It was mostly written, however, by freelance authors who (as non-BBC employees) retained the commercial rights to all new characters and monsters which they created. Thus, the estate of the late writer Terry Nation retains copyright of the concept and name of the Daleks, but the BBC has control of the design because that was devised by staff-worker Raymond Cusick. This is true of most of the programme's iconic monsters. Such a situation was an unhelpful complication to manufacturers of early *Doctor Who* products who would have liked their licensing agreements with the BBC to cover all the programme's imagery (although some were unaware of these limits and used characters and monsters for which they assumed they had paid). In later years, the diffusion of copyrights presented an opportunity to those with whom the BBC would not deal, and without it much of the creativity discussed in the second half of this book would never have happened. The wide range of the subculture generated by the programme owes much to the fact that there are surprisingly large chunks of it over which the BBC has no legal control. It also had implications for what would later be termed 'canonicity'.

Foremost amongst *Doctor Who* merchandise were the novelizations of old and recent episodes published by Universal-Tandem, beginning in May 1973.[3] Although the style was standardised in the late 1970s, the earliest books were written by various writers to varying lengths and styles. Gerry Davis, Brian Hayles, Barry Letts and David Whitaker were just some of the programme's writers who adapted their own work for the printed page. They worked freely, expanding the stories or changing details as they felt necessary. The most substantial example – and certainly the one most often evoked within fandom as an example of the novels' divergent continuity – occurs in the book *Doctor Who and The Daleks*, David Whitaker's adaptation of the second story.

Whitaker was *Doctor Who*'s first script editor, the man in charge of scripts at the production office. That some of the earliest spin-off writing devolved to him is hardly surprising. Given the task of writing the first ever novel based on the series, he did not assume that the reader knew how two humans came to be travelling with the Doctor and his granddaughter Susan – as shown in the programme's opening episode – and so created his own, very different version of the events by which they came to do so. On screen, they were two teachers – Ian Chesterton and Barbara Wright – who forced their way into the TARDIS whilst investigating Susan, a school pupil with a strangely advanced grasp of science but a lack of common cultural knowledge. In the book, which is told from Ian's perspective, he is a frustrated schoolteacher who has just failed to get a private sector research job, and who is stopped from driving home when an intense fog falls across London. Barbara, an office worker who does private history tuition on the side, is also stranded, having insisted on taking her pupil, Susan, home, Together they stumble upon the TARDIS. The novel, alongside Whitaker's other book, *Doctor Who and the Crusaders*, contained a romance between Ian and Barbara which was never shown on screen.

Other changes in other books were smaller, perhaps unnecessarily so. On screen, in 'The Ribos Operation' (1978) the Doctor's new Time Lady companion Romana had described his achievements at the Gallifreyan academy as 'scraping through with fifty-one per cent at the second attempt', whilst the novelization amends this to his receiving a Double Gamma (in contrast to her own Triple Alpha). What is gained by such amendments? Very little, I think. Other additions in other novels are more obvious in their intended effect. Budget considerations alone have meant that *Doctor Who* has rarely shown massive galactic wars, but has dealt instead with the small groups of survivors who lived through such battles. Novelizations such as 'Pyramids of Mars' and 'The Horns of Nimon' added prologues in which the planetary carnage which could never be shown on screen exploded across the page. The former tidies up the large amount of loose ends and plot inconsistencies which pepper the script, as well as containing a touching epilogue in which, years later after leaving the Doctor and settling back on Earth, companion Sarah Jane Smith visits the town where the story is set and looks through the local newspaper's archives to see how the events of the adventure were reported.[4]

Many writers declined to novelize their stories, allegedly because the money was poor compared to scripting television. They may have come to regret their short-sightedness. The books themselves would sell into the mid-1990s, long after the invention of home video had rendered their original use as a record of the programme obsolete. In the new millennium, the BBC began to reissue them as talking books read by the programme's stars. Artists who worked on the covers in the 1970s were similarly preparing for the future, though they did not know it at the time. In the 1990s, the same work could be sold to fans as postcards and quality 'prints', and some of it was reused as covers for *Doctor Who Magazine.*

The shifting values in the market for *Who* products can be read from the different packaging which the novels would take over the years. The original 1970s editions were careless in areas where care would later be taken. Even so small a fragment of text as the first 11 words on the back of the 1973 edition of *Doctor Who and the Crusaders* yields several such moments. 'Back on Earth again, *Tardis* lands DOCTOR WHO and his friends ...' begins the cover blurb. In later years, that would be *the* Tardis, and TARDIS itself would be capitalized; the Doctor would not be called Doctor Who, and the chummy 'his friends' is language unlikely to recur later (when 'companions' became the recognized term). More bizarrely, the original cover for *Doctor Who and the Daleks* depicted a pink TARDIS. Story titles were changed if the original was felt to be insufficiently exciting. 'Doctor Who And The Silurians' became *Doctor Who and the Cave Monsters*, the brief 'Robot' was given added excitement as *Doctor Who and the Giant Robot*, and 'Colony In Space' became the more apocalyptic *Doctor Who and the Doomsday Weapon*. When they were reprinted in the 1990s, and aimed at fans who wanted a product that matched the television episodes, all the 'and the's were dropped and the titles matched to those onscreen. Thus, 'The Cave Monsters' was switched back to 'The Silurians', and the 'Giant Robot' shrunk back down to being merely a 'Robot'. The covers underwent several revampings down the years, but by the new century nostalgia, and a widespread acceptance amongst fans that these stories existed in multiple forms, meant that the BBC's audio books would reuse 1970s artwork, and that original book titles (*Cave-Monsters, Giant Robot, Doomsday Weapon*) would return. The books would return to printed form in 2011 when the BBC reissued six of the earliest titles in paperback. Sales must have been healthy as more titles have been scheduled for 2012.

The audio books and the reprints offer an overdue opportunity to rediscover books which have sat on fans' shelves or in their lofts for decades. What we find there can surprise, for authorial signatures are not always limited to the 'facts' as established by the subsequent decades of fan research.

The modern fan picture of Troughton/Pertwee–era script-writer, Malcolm Hulke, for instance, is dominated by his historical materialism. A 2002 review of his 1973 story 'Frontier in Space' begins 'Malcolm Hulke was a committed Marxist; so comfortable in his beliefs that he had a humanist funeral, with no religious elements.'[5] Pertwee-era script editor, Terrance Dicks, a friend and colleague to whom Hulke was something of a mentor, frequently mentions his left-wing views. The DVDs of his stories frequently come with extras exploring how these left-wing views are reflected in his writing, notably in villains motivated by corporate greed or nationalistic politics.

There is much in Hulke's book *Doctor Who and the Doomsday Weapon* which tallies with this view of the author. The story concerns the conflict between the ruthless Interplanetary Mining Corporation (who wish to rip the raw materials out of the planet Uxarieus, leaving it ecologically devastated) and a group of colonists who seek to settle there, living at subsistence-agriculture level. Fandom has always regarded highly the stark view of twenty-fifth century Earth from which the colonists are fleeing. It is a brutal world where powerful corporations choose their employees' marriage partners. Workers who live in huge tower blocks pay for the novelty of travelling to the roof just to sit on concrete in the sunshine, or go on simulated indoor 'Walks' where they jog on the spot surrounded by the smells and images of long-extinct animals and plants. None of this is in the televised version. Less commented upon by fans is the fact that, although this dystopia is one where books have been long been abandoned, the colony's leader, Ashe, having returned to this dead art form in search of agricultural information, has stumbled across a Bible (not named as such):

> a copy of something written thousands of years ago, and was largely
> about someone called God ... the strange language fascinated him.
> It contained four versions of a story about a man who sacrificed his
> own life for the sake of others. It was this part of the book which most
> interested Ashe, because it was so difficult to understand. (p. 137)[6]

This excellent addition to the story is used to motivate Ashe's
own self-sacrifice for the good of the colony at the story's conclusion, an action which the televised version simply accepts as
a generic given (heroes self-sacrifice in adventure fiction, everyone knows that) that needs no explanation. Whilst the programme
has been analyzed for its religious themes and imagery on several
occasions in print (and many more in the pulpit) such evocation
of the Bible occurs nowhere on screen, and exists only in Hulke's
novelizations, where a seam of such imagery runs through several
titles. In *The Sea-Devils*, the Doctor reveals that his speech at the
trial of his arch-enemy the Master contained the words *redemption*, *saved* and *believe* (p. 12), he passes the village of Belial ('the
name used by your poet Milton for one of the fallen angels' – pp.
17/18) and hears the Master bid Jo and the Doctor farewell with
the words 'may God be with you' (p. 28). In *The Green Death*, the
BOSS computer's attempts to brainwash Dr Bell into doing what
he knows is wrong sets off a moral conflict in his mind which is
articulated in terms of Christian slogans: 'Murder ... save lives ...
no unauthorized personnel ... Thou shalt not kill ... exterminate
... Jesus saves' (p. 87). In the same book, Jo lists 'Jesus of Nazareth'
amongst the impractical dreamers who changed the world (p. 19)
and she 'prayed silently' (p. 120) once Professor Cliff Jones is near
death. Mike Yates, meanwhile, objects to BOSS's plan to enslave
the world because 'God gave man the right of free will' (p. 129).
A later novel, *Doctor Who and the Dinosaur Invasion* begins with
the fate of hapless drunkard Shuggie McPherson, who recites the
Lord's Prayer as he dies (p. 10). Later, the Doctor explains time
travel, evoking 'the time of the birth of Jesus' (p. 42 – this shortly
after an encounter with a medieval labourer has produced several
Christian references), and Sarah is said to 'pray' as she takes her
life in her hands (p. 112). It concludes with the villains being flung
into the past, Sarah's questioning of which causes the Doctor to

stop off at London's *Foyle's* bookshop to find a copy of the Bible ('You know, there's a book you might try reading sometime' – p. 140) and read her the Old Testament book of *Ezekiel* chapter one verses five-six, as a sign of how strange things occur: 'Also out of the midst thereof came the likeness of four living creatures. And this was their appearance; they had the likeness of a man. And every one had four faces, and every one had four wings' [7]

Such moments of authorial flourish – so divorced from the television series they adapted – would become rarer in the late 1970s as the product became standardised. Illustrations vanished from the inside of the books, along with the maps which had enlivened *Doctor Who and the Cave Monsters* and *Doctor Who and the Day of the Daleks*. Externally, the books adopted the programme's then-current diamond logo (an obvious point now, but far less common then – *The Doctor Who Annual* didn't adopt it until 1979, and it was only at that point that it ceased to use the contracted form: *The Dr Who Annual*). Target preferred recent stories over older ones, so a BBC directive requesting that pre-Baker Doctors not adorn the front covers was of little inconvenience. A number of the original authors dropped out. Terrance Dicks, leaving the programme's script-editorship at the end of the Pertwee era to return to freelance writing, picked up the slack, often producing a book a month. This, more than anything else, determined the style and size of the books. Page counts stabilized around 120 pages of text, shorter than previously, and each book was usually divided between 12 chapters. A six-part adventure has two chapters per episode and a four-part adventure has three chapters per episode. Even the chapter titles became repetitious. David Howe and Tim Neal calculated that 16 of the books feature chapters called '(The) Escape', ten have one called 'Capture(d)', and '(The) Sacrifice' occurs 11 times.[8] (Arguably, such repetitions originated in the formulaic nature of the show.) The books of the late 1970s efficiently retold the plotlines, but added little, and they were readable by eight year olds. The language of the dialogue was often dumbed-down. In 'Robot' on television, the Doctor begins his consideration of his new appearance with the words 'as for the physiognomy ....' The book prefers 'as for the face ...'. Similarly, descriptions of recurrent characters and situations became repetitive. Tom Baker's Doctor was 'vaguely Bohemian', the noise of the TARDIS was a 'wheezing, groaning sound'.[9]

By 1980, teenaged or older readers who still loved *Doctor Who*, but who had grown out of books like this, would become critical of their limitations. A decade later they would learn to laugh affectionately at them. In the mid-1970s, however, the books were crucial because they could be returned to daily, a contrast to the fleeting existence of the television broadcast. Consequently, the rituals of buying the novels – the bookshops you visited, perhaps always on a Saturday, wondering, in those pre-newsletter days if a new book would be out – are as significant a part of many fans' nostalgia for *Who* in this era as the programme itself. Mark Gatiss' novel *Last of the Gadarene*, published in 2000, is a novel aching with nostalgia for 1970s *Who*, and he prefaces it thus:

> And during the eternity between seasons we always had the Target books. They gave us exciting versions of stories we had seen, and glimpses into a strange and mysterious past where the Doctor had been *someone else*. Whenever I was off school, my medicine of choice was always *Planet of the Daleks* (and maybe oxtail soup), because it took me light years away from my four walls and into the Doctor's universe.[10]

He spoke for many. The importance of the books gave Terrance Dicks a visibility beyond anyone working on the actual programme. Fans sporadically refer to him as 'Uncle Terrance', the only *Who* celebrity to be awarded so familiar a nickname.[11] The length of the relationship between the television series and its novelizations (Target or the companies it evolved into would hold the *Who* franchise until 1997) resulted in the unprecedented situation whereby the books themselves contributed some of the most famous words in the *Doctor Who* vocabulary. Terms such as *Time Rotor* (the column that rises and falls at the centre of the TARDIS console), *incarnation* (referring to the different Doctors as manifestations of the same persona), *chameleon circuit* (the device which, if it worked properly, would camouflage the TARDIS' exterior) and the notion that the Sontarans are clones arose in the novels, and were later used in the television series once their usage by fans and other viewers had become accepted.[12]

For all the retrospective fondness now bestowed on them, the novelizations of the late 1970s diverged from the fan view of the series which was emerging at the time. This, for instance, is the period during which fans came to view Robert Holmes as the

pre-eminent writer of the series. Holmes had worked on the programme since Patrick Troughton's day, but was felt to have come
into his own writing for Pertwee and Baker. His witty scripts, often
with satirical elements, caused fans to view him as a purveyor of the
programme's most sophisticated delights; a master with language,
a pricker of official pomposity, the creator of larger-than-life characters often paired off in double-acts, and the owner of a dark sense
of humour. This sophistication, however, did not always fit well into
Target's range. Thus, his story 'The Ark in Space' was not released
as a novel until May 1977, over two years after its transmission. At
a time when Target prioritized recent stories, this was a significant
gap (the previous story, Baker's debut 'Robot', had been on the
shelves within three months of transmission), and an even longer
hold up occurred four years later, when another Holmes script 'The
Sun Makers' was transmitted in December 1977, but not released as
a book until November 1982, Target having apparently shied from
its allegorical levels.[13] Notoriously amongst fans, this book blunts
Holmes' gleefully bloodthirsty vision. It concludes when the workers of Pluto revolt and throw the chief tax gatherer from the roof
of a skyscraper. On screen it is done with cheers and no regret,
but to the novel Dicks adds: 'The crowd shuffled off the roof, a
bit shamefaced. There was a general feeling things had got out of
hand, gone a bit too far. But there wasn't very much that they could
do about it now. From the top of a thousand-metre building, it's a
very long way down.'[14] Those stings of conscience amend Holmes'
story towards the sort of morality that might be thought suitable
for eight year olds and show how, just as the emergent Doctor Who
Appreciation Society was acclaiming Holmes as the programme's
'grandmaster', Target were finding it sporadically difficult to fit his
vision of the show into their format.

Be it the entry of Ian and Barbara to the TARDIS, colonist
Ashe's grappling with the gospels, the conscience of the rebels
against the Sunmakers, or simply the dumbing down of the language in the dialogue, the programme's history was slightly different if you followed the novels rather than the television series.
However, this was not the only way in which Target came to be
the guardians of the programme's history. A more self-conscious
effort at providing such a history was their publication of *The
Making of Doctor Who*.

Behind the Scenes

Doctor Who fans would become rapacious collectors of knowledge of their chosen programme's production. In the twenty-first century, there is no contribution so small or long ago than its agent won't be tracked down, interviewed and their recollections analyzed. However, *Doctor Who* generated an unusual amount of reports about its construction long before fandom emerged. In the 1970s and 1980s, the BBC recurrently used coverage of the programme's production (from *Blue Peter* through to late-night fare such as *Late Night Line-up*) to demonstrate its own resources and cleverness. By the early 1980s, Mat Irvine was the semi-official face of the BBC Visual Effects department, a frequent guest on magazine programmes showing off technical tricks and props. As such appearances suggest, although *Doctor Who* lacked the prestige of costume dramas it was consistently used by the BBC, just as historical serials were, to promote the imagination and skills of their design and costume departments. This reached its peak with the Radiophonic Workshop (the branch of the BBC dealing with electronic music and non-naturalistic sounds) which became so associated with the programme in the mind of the British public that the rest of their broad range of work was neglected and remains underappreciated to this day. This was most famously the case of her majesty Queen Elizabeth II, who, when introduced to the staff of the Workshop in the early 1970s said 'Ah, Doctor Who'.

From this background emerged *The Making of Doctor Who*, the first attempt to deal with all major aspects of production. The book was initiated by the publishers Pan, who approached the BBC. Then-script editor Terrance Dicks was enthusiastic, but he was too busy to take on the project, so Malcolm Hulke took on the majority of the writing with Dicks also contributing. It was published in 1972 by Piccolo, the children's imprint of the prominent paperback publisher Pan. When Target published a second edition four years later, Dicks overhauled the text considerably. Whatever fans might feel about the shorter, more standardized novels which the company – and Dicks – was producing at the time, Target did a good job of anticipating, or moulding, the fan taste for certain types of information. A comparison of the first and second editions – the Piccolo version, and the Target one – amply demonstrates this.[15]

For much of its word count, Hulke's original version playfully entered the fictional world of the programme. The First and Second Doctors' adventures were recalled in the form of a long report to the Time Lords (notionally a document prepared for his trial before the Time Lords at the end of Patrick Troughton's time as the Doctor), and those of the Third Doctor were presented as the reports of the military/scientific team he worked for during his exile on Earth. In the Time Lord document, the Doctor was even given a name, an abstract scientific formula. Hulke entertained a wide range of critical questions, ones which would never be dominant in fandom. His chapter 'Could it all be True?' considered the science of time travel and life on other worlds, and cited *Ezekiel*, which, as with the Doctor and Sarah Jane, Hulke thought readers might like to read for themselves. The Reverend John D. Beckwith AKC was given three pages to discuss theology in the article 'Honest to Doctor Who'. Beckwith's reading of the programme's philosophical core was common at the time: 'Good in the end triumphs over Evil'. If that sounds an uncontroversial interpretation, we shall see later how others developed.[16]

Dicks' rewrite dispensed with much of this. He kept solidly to the question of the programme's production and threw out the scientific and theological chapters. The fictional formats in which the accounts of the Doctor's adventures were recounted were scrapped, replaced by a division of the stories into discrete units with title, writer credits and the number of episodes. It looked, in short, just like the numerous episode guides which came after it. Whilst the first edition's back cover enticed readers with the promise of reliving or discovering the programme's fictional content ('What happened when Doctor Who was put on trial by the Time Lords? Why did he agree to help UNIT?'), the second edition held firmly to its remit to treat the programme as a constructed artifact ('Here it is … the story behind one of television's most successful, longest running shows'). Hulke's version is playful and wide-ranging. It reads like no other history of the programme ever written. Dicks', by contrast, is quite recognizably an early model for the many volumes on the show's production which would follow.

The short-term impact of *Making Of …* were some impressively precocious criticism. Fan/writer Lance Parkin remembers being unimpressed with the opening story of season 15 – 'Horror of Fang

Rock' (1977) – which he felt was poor: 'I realized why. I saw the end credits and noticed the producer was different [from the one mentioned in *Making Of*] ... I knew what a producer did and that he was in charge, so if it had changed, it was because the new producer had said it should'.[17] Not bad for a six year old. Longer-term implications are explored in the following chapters. However, whilst publications like *Making Of* ... could give some information, volumes on *Who* were repetitious because all reference works were compiled from the same BBC paperwork. A fan might read the plot summary of Patrick Troughton's 'The Mind Robber' (1968) in the *Radio Times' Doctor Who Tenth Anniversary Special*, published in 1973, and learn this.

> The Tardis arrives in the Land of Fiction, a huge white void where fiction appears as reality. The travellers are hunted by White Robots and encounter mechanical soldiers. Jamie gains entry to the Citadel of the Master, an aged gentleman who wants to retire from rule and insists the Doctor takes his place. The Doctor refuses, so the White Robots capture Jamie and Zoe. In the following battle of wits Dr Who calls up champions from fiction to defeat the Master, and the time travellers escape.[18]

Turning to *The Making of Doctor Who* (1976) would provide no extra knowledge, because its summary reads as follows.

> The TARDIS arrives in the Land of Fiction, a huge white void where fiction appears as reality. The travellers are hunted by White Robots and encounter mechanical soldiers. Jamie gains entry to the Citadel of the Master, an aged gentleman who wants to retire from rule and insists the Doctor takes his place. The Doctor refuses, so the White Robots capture Jamie and Zoe. In the following battle of wits the Doctor calls up champions from fiction to defeat the Master, and the time travellers escape.[19]

Certain small shifts – the central character is no longer referred to as 'Dr Who' and TARDIS is now capitalized – reflect the way that the language of the programme was reaching a standard form, but apart from that it is identical. In 1981, Target would publish *The Doctor Who Programme Guide* by French fan and media journalist Jean-Marc Lofficier. As the next chapter outlines, things were beginning to change substantially by then, and the book's listing of production crew, transmission dates and guest cast continued the process of treating *Who* stories not as fiction to be imagined as real, but as a television programme which should be researched for the history and aesthetics of its production. Its plot summaries, however, were somewhat familiar.

> To escape a lava flow the TARDIS jumps out of Space and Time, and arrives in the Land of Fiction, a huge white void where fiction appears as reality. The travellers are hunted by White Robots and encounter mechanical soldiers. Jamie gains entrance to the Citadel of the Master, an aged gentleman who wants to retire and insists that the Doctor takes his place. The Doctor refuses, so the White Robots capture Jamie and Zoe. In the following battle of wits the Doctor call up champions from famous Earth fictions to defeat the Master. Meanwhile, Zoe finds the true Master of the Land: a giant computer. They manage to overload the machine and escape.[20]

Some new details, but essentially the same. *Who* was generating reference books, but often they repeated themselves. Progress towards detail was agonizingly slow.

This was the situation in 1979. *Doctor Who* the programme, the merchandise and the fan base remained largely distinct from one another. The production office approved merchandise, but its touch was light, and the resulting products roamed well away from the style of the television programme. A few fans with writing ambitions were submitting story ideas to script editors, but that had so far yielded nothing firm, and the show's writing team was solidly composed of television professionals with track records in the medium (and one young, emerging talent, Douglas Adams). Television scriptwriters could adapt their scripts for Target, but few did and this was mostly the preserve of Terrance Dicks. Outside of the small Appreciation Society, there was no notion of fans as a target audience for merchandise, and thus no opportunity for articulate fans to market their specialist knowledge. That knowledge itself was limited because home video was only now becoming a domestic presence and would not become a normal part of the UK home for another half a decade. *Doctor Who Weekly*'s complex marketing plans, and its year-long birth pains, would change everything.

Doctor Who Weekly

When Marvel Comics released *Doctor Who Weekly* it was the consummation of a flirtation which had been on-again, off-again throughout the decade. Between February 1971 and August 1973, the *Doctor Who* comic strip had left its traditional home in *TV Comic* for the more sophisticated *Countdown* (later *TV Action*). Aimed at an older audience, this comic allowed longer, more complex stories and the artists – Harry Lindfield, Frank Langford and Gerry Haylock – drew from the same wells of pop art as did the more avant-garde of the artists on American Marvel comics (Neal Adams, Jim Steranko, etc). American comics themselves were also a fleeting influence at Target, notably in the brief stint of artist Peter Brookes, who completed the cover art for four novels in 1975: *The Giant Robot*, *Terror of the Autons*, *The Green Death*, and *Planet of the Spiders*. Each of these depicted a distinct scene from the story (with a smaller scene inset) rather than montages of diverse images favoured by the books' original artist Chris Achilleos. Brookes drew black lines around the edges of characters and objects, giving the look of a pencil-and-ink comic strip.[21] Even when Brookes left, and Achilleos returned, the comics influence sporadically remained. His cover for *The Three Doctors* drew heavily on Jack Kirby's front cover for *Fantastic Four* no. 48 (powerful villain Omega stands in for the planet-consuming Galactus, the faces of the Doctors are positioned as were those of the FF), and *Dinosaur Invasion* featured a large-lettered comics-style sound-effect on the front cover, the (now infamous in fandom) *kklack!* of a pterodactyl's snapping jaws. This style of cover was a short-lived experiment, however, and when Target began to rejacket the books in 1978, 'The Three Doctors' was first up, followed by 'Dinosaur Invasion' and Brookes' quartet of covers. However, Brookes' sense – conscious or otherwise – that *Who* and Marvel comics shared an audience was an astute one and it foreshadowed the release of *Doctor Who Weekly*.[22]

The *Weekly* was launched in October 1979. The publication itself was a hybrid of children's comic and magazine, and there were successful models of both upon which it drew. The 1970s had seen a variety of UK titles based around fantasy and science fiction. *World of Horror, Monster Mag*, and *Monster Fantasy* all previewed upcoming films, provided historical accounts of past films and gave career overviews of genre practitioners. Before taking up the editorial position at Marvel, Dez Skinn himself had launched *House of Hammer* and *Starburst. House of Hammer*, in particular, with a chatty editorial, 'answer desk' (to readers' questions), comic strips extrapolating further adventures for characters derived from Hammer films and articles on fan collecting would seem particularly familiar, even down to the paper stock, to anyone aware of the magazine that *DWW* would evolve into by summer 1981. In the comics market, *2000AD* demonstrated how sophisticated storytelling and social satire could be packaged in a humorous fantasy version of its own production (the comic was supposedly edited by a green-skinned alien called Tharg, with his army of art and script robots, just as *DWW* was notionally edited by the Doctor himself). *Star Wars Weekly*, Marvel UK's other big tie-in title, provided much of *DWW*'s format: the 28-page length, the 12p price tag and the glossy cover (which were then rare on Marvel UK comics, having been mostly phased out as a cost-cutting measure). *DWW* was so plugged into this preexisting network of SF/fantasy publications that it received mail citing them even before publication commenced, in a letter it reprinted in issue 10: 'you've already produced two revolutionary fantasy mags – *House of Hammer* and *Starburst* ... thanks for being an innovative publisher in these days when most comics are grossly plagiaristic.' The correspondent, clearly older than anyone else featured on the letters page, was a fantasy fan from Haywards Heath called Matthew Waterhouse.[23]

Such responses show just how carefully constructed a product *Doctor Who Weekly* was. With Tom Baker and a Dalek on the front cover, free transfers and quizzes including coded messages warning of alien invasion, *DWW* must have looked to many like business as usual, with young children targeted as the major audience. The letters page reflected back an image of the readership, printing photos of them bedecked in scarves and holding cardboard K9s. There are more girls represented than later stereotypes would suggest. Under the surface, however, it was a more complex affair. Older fans/readers were amply catered for with the comic's coverage of the series' early days. It aimed to retell the stories from the first episode in order, a project which necessarily skewed early issues towards the Hartnell era. Tom Baker graced the covers of the first five issues, often with the programme's other primary icons (Daleks, K9, Cybermen), but soon older Doctors and monsters started to appear. Issue 15 featured a stunning full-colour cover of Hartnell outside the TARDIS – manna from heaven for fans starved of such imagery, but perhaps an unusual image on the children's comic racks.

Beyond this dual appeal to older and younger readers was the other target audience: the emergent constituency of comic fans. Whilst previous Marvel UK editors had been happy to remain anonymous, Skinn began to appear not only at the increasingly frequent UK comic conventions, but also in the pages of his own comics. At Marvel he authored a column ('Sez Dez') which promoted the company's publications. His model in this was Marvel US's creator/mascot Stan Lee, but his agenda of making clear who was at the top, and creating a visible persona, anticipated the way John Nathan-Turner would promote both the programme and himself upon becoming producer of *Doctor Who* in 1980.

Skinn's ambition was to reverse the usual process whereby Marvel UK comics simply reprinted American material. He wanted to initiate new work, and sell it to the USA. A number of original strips began to appear, particularly in *Hulk Comic*, in 1978, but that comic's size and style didn't lend itself to work suitable for republication in the standard US Marvel comic. When Skinn created *Doctor Who Weekly*, he made sure its comic strips would work both in the UK market and the US Marvel formats. He hired Pat Mills and John Wagner, stalwarts of *2000AD* who had been unsuccessfully submitting script ideas to the *Doctor Who* production office, to write it and Dave Gibbons to draw it.

Since a US Marvel comic featured 17 pages of story, the earliest stories in DWW were 34 pages long, divided into two 17-page sections. For UK publication, those 17 pages were further divided up across four issues in a five/four/four/four page pattern. The genius of the strip's construction is the way that this division was anticipated and structured. Thus, the last frame of every five/four page section ends with an exciting image/plot point which serves, in the UK editions, as a cliffhanger: *The Iron Legion* episode one – the Doctor gets blasted by an energy weapon as he runs to the TARDIS, *Iron Legion* episode two – he is thrown into an alien arena to face a creature called the Ectoslime, etc., etc. Artist Dave Gibbons composes the images of every fourth page in such a way that UK editions can replace the top left hand corner with a plot recap without losing any vital narrative information. The US editions just print the pages straight through, devoid of recaps and 'next issue' slogans, and it flows very well.

The Iron Legion, the first Marvel comic strip, is the point where the *Doctor Who* comic strip first began utilizing the full range of comic storytelling devices (largely as inherited from Marvel, DC and *2000AD*). A partial list of the devices used to create mood and communicate information would include the following: depicting the monsters in shadow or total silhouette; jagged borders for panels of special drama; wide panels for panoramas of scale; close-ups for small details; panels devoid of background image so that the foreground might be emphasized; fuzzy, television-shaped images which do not simply record the world as it happens, but instead show the media coverage from the games, and using consecutive panels to cut between the contrasting action of a British sweet shop's interior (where the Doctor shops for jelly babies) and its exterior (where a robot Roman approaches). Whilst none of these devices may be particularly significant in themselves, their presence en masse represents the first full immersion of the *Doctor Who* comic strip in a sophisticated vocabulary of storytelling which was equal to that of the techniques used in making the television episodes. Whilst *The Iron Legion* and its ilk were no doubt devoured for their plots alone by an initial readership of nine year olds, they were also stories which could be rewardingly read and re-read by those with an interest in the processes and aesthetics of comic strip storytelling itself. Thus, *Doctor Who Weekly* wasn't just aimed at ten year olds. It was also niche-marketing to the newly emergent phenomena of UK comic's fandom. In 1981, *Doctor Who Monthly* (as it would become) would win an Eagle, UK comic fandom's award for Best Comic Magazine.

This concern with creating a more sophisticated *Who* comic strip than had ever existed before was also apparent in other areas, notably its strict attention to continuity details and its capturing of the exact mood of late-1970s *Who* as Graham Williams was producing it. As regards continuity, the comic sets its stall out in the first issue with a sequence which plays on the fact that Time Lords have two hearts. In the story, a robot legionary who encounters the Doctor becomes confused by the contradictory data it receives: only one human visible, but two heartbeats registering. As to the tone of Williams' *Who*, Dave Gibbons' drawing of the Doctor himself, a somewhat caricatured figure all flashing grins and flailing scarf, took its cue from the heightened humour of the television series in this period, as did some of the dialogue. The Doctor's references to 'Gallifrey comp' and being 'a spotty teenager for fifty years' would, if they'd ever have been uttered on screen, have joined Romana's 'time tot' quip in 'Shada' in the fans' hall of disdain.

The Marvel comic strips would be worthy of note if this was all they achieved. As the first products to take pains to get the continuity right and attempt to replicate the distinct style of the late-1970s programme (rather than some generalized spirit of the show) the strips are an important evolution in the *Doctor Who* product. Atop all of this, the strip had its own social realist agenda to follow, something it wasn't taking from the programme itself. When the TARDIS materializes in issue one, it does so outside a village newsagent, whilst a running joke has the Doctor repeatedly attempt to take the TARDIS to Benidorm for a holiday, and he sings 1974 novelty hit *Y Viva Espana* when he thinks he has got there. These are small touches, but significant ones at a time when the programme's idea of Earth normal was Parisian art galleries and Cambridge colleges. Issues 19 to 26 presented *The Star Beast*, the highpoint of the strip's social realism. The story is set in a northern steel-mill town called Blackcastle, and Sharon, the new companion who debuts in this story, is black, granting the Doctor a coloured companion 27 years before the television series did. She enters the story as a happy schoolgirl, but ends up screaming at the Meep, the story's villain, 'I hate you, you're horrible'.[24]

If you only know the television series, then the insertion into *Doctor Who* of overtly emotional material is the big development of the 2005 reboot. In fact, the quest to produce this sort of *Who* – one with a greater amount of emotional content than the classic series ever managed to consistently achieve – is a long one, stretching right back to the Ian/Barbara romance which David Whitaker inserted into the very first novelizations. *Doctor Who Weekly* escalated efforts to wring emotional material from the programme's format. In addition to the Doctor's adventures, a second comic strip told stories about the programme's favourite monsters. Without the Doctor to act as a moral centre, and perhaps aware that the readership might be rooting for the familiar villains rather than their newly created (usually humanoid) adversaries, these stories take place in an altogether harsher universe. Alliances are fragile and opportunistic, authority is useless or corrupt, and heart-breaking loss – the emotion which revamped television *Who* most consistently returns to – stalks the characters, notably the two deemed sufficiently popular to return for second stories: Abslom Daak, Dalek Killer and Kroton, a junior Cyberleader. Daak is a hard-drinking, leather-wearing, chainsaw-wielding serial-killer straight out of the *2000AD* school of anti-heroes. A convicted murderer, the sentence for his crimes is to be instantaneously transported to a Dalek world, where, with a life expectancy of two hours, he must kill as many of the creatures as possible. Here, Daak finds unexpected redemption as planetary liberator but his new love, Princess Taiyin, is cut down by the one Dalek who survived his savage assault. In subsequent stories, as he makes his way through Dalek space, he carries her in a cryogenic unit, though she is beyond medical help. Kroton is a Cyberleader whose conversion from human hasn't fully taken, causing him to question his orders, and to respect the non-logical responses of human beings. In his first story ('Throwback: The Soul of a Cyberman', *Doctor Who Weekly* 5–7), he aids heroic human rebels who fight against their Cybermen conquerors even though their defeat is assured, but ends up adrift in a fuelless craft in space, caught between two worlds and able to live in neither. His tragedy becomes more complete in issues 23 to 24, when his ship drifts into a time vortex, there encountering a leisure-cruiser. With the ship stuck in time, and the passengers having nothing to do but enjoy themselves with pleasures long since gone stale, Kroton is confused again by a variety of human emotions, this time less admirable ones. His technical skills release the craft from the time vortex, but it has been there over 600 years, and the crew age instantly to dust as they re-enter normal space, leaving the lonely Cyberman friendless again. These were sophisticated emotions to be writing about and the stories stand comparison with anything else going on in UK comics at the time.[25]

The fusion of comics culture with *Who* worked because, although it would later take on a mammoth life of its own, in 1979, *Doctor Who* fandom wasn't easily separated from SF fandom or comics fandom. All were finding their feet in the specialist bookshops cropping up around that perpetual crucible of British subcultures, Tottenham Court Road (notably the original *Forbidden Planet* which opened in Denmark Street) and comics fandom would boom alongside *Who* fandom in the early 1980s. Once a month, *Who* fans mixed with the wider SF culture at the One Tun pub in Saffron Hill, London. Tom Baker and Terrance Dicks were frequent guests at SF conventions – indeed, *DWW* printed photos of Baker at one in its second issue. At the Comic Marts held monthly at Westminster Hall, *DWW* writers and artists signed autographs, answered questions and did sketches. In 1980, Marvel hosted its own 'Film and Fantasy' convention, where, amidst the other events, BBC special effects man Mat Irvine and sound technician Dick Mills demonstrated their skills, whilst scriptwriter David Martin signed copies of his new 'Adventures of K9' books aimed at young children. A petition circulated to save the robot canine from being written out of the television series. At this point, *Who* appreciation was a junior member of the various cult fandoms. Literary SF fandom had a much longer history and serious links with the major writers. Comics fanzines were more sophisticated than their *Doctor Who* equivalents, being frequently printed on A4 paper (*Who* fandom preferred A5), a format which encouraged longer articles. Those lengthy pieces could be written because the comics, unlike television shows in the pre-video age, could be read and reread until their stylistic secrets had been cracked. *Who* fandom was learning fast, though, not least because many fans were acquainted with the comics world, and because home video was on the horizon.

Doctor Who Weekly, then, was a sophisticated and multifaceted marketing ploy. It was not, however, a successful one. The actual sales figures seem lost in the mists of time, but it is certain that after a successful launch, sales soon dipped, sliding, according to some estimates, towards the 20,000 mark. When Skinn took an unexpectedly extended holiday in America, editorship passed to Paul Neary, who shifted the magazine towards a younger audience. Artwork covers were introduced, alienating those fans for whom photographic content – particularly the colour cover – was the main attraction. New features aimed at junior-school children were introduced, such as *Fantastic Facts* (unlikely out-of-this-world stories sourced from *The Fortean Times*). The *U.N.I.T Hotline* page debuted in April 1980, treated the world of the series as if it were real, and offered readers the chance to join up in the fight against alien invasions. It printed *Know Your Enemy* files on old monsters which could return to Earth with evil intentions any minute: ('Cut the files out and keep them in a safe place – they must not fall into the wrong hands ...'[26]). However, when this new direction failed to stimulate sales, Marvel sought further reorientation. A shift to monthly publishing (from issue 44, cover-dated September 1980) enlarged the magazine, meaning that the comic strip (the most expensive pages to produce) accounted for slashed its monthly pagecount, thus reducing publication costs. It also, though this did not become apparent until later in the year, allowed for longer articles. *Doctor Who Monthly* aimed itself not at the generalized children's market, but at the more distinct group, the fans. But, who were they? And what was their take on the programme?

Fandom

In 1975, the formation of an Essex-based fanzine, *TARDIS*, had led to more substantial communication between *Who* fans than had previously been the case. Consequently, a group established itself at Westfield College in London. In 1976, this became the national *Doctor Who Appreciation Society*, absorbed *TARDIS* into itself, and became the centre of *Who* fandom for a decade.

The differences between the DWAS and *Doctor Who Weekly*'s vision of the programme's followers was in some respects huge (some members who fancied themselves more sophisticated referred to the comic as 'the weakly'), but in other areas was not so large. In 1979, the society's magazine *TARDIS* was running a series of articles, *Astronomy of Doctor Who*, in which writer Gavin French studied a planet from the programme's past, outlining its geography and history as depicted in the series (or, more likely, the novelization), expanding on what was only hinted at in the story, and inventing where appropriate: 'Huge fortunes were made by many of those who traded with Voga and their accounts at the galactic banks grew larger with each trip to the planet. As Voga's gold did not need to be registered, many swindles took place which would otherwise have been impossible'.[27] This sort of fictional expansion wasn't far removed from the U.N.I.T. Hotline.

Even when *TARDIS* treated the programme as a fictional artifact, with home video still not widespread the analysis remained basic. It printed reviews in its *Teleview* section sent in by readers. Tim Dollin piece on Parisian art thriller 'City of Death' was 468 words long, well over half of which summarized the plot ('But in episode three we learn that the count is not actually travelling through time himself … .'[28]) The review concludes 'Full marks to the production team,' but mentions no one specifically. Though video was available to some at this point, this is a representative review from the pre-video age, attentive to record plotlines and characters before they faded from memory.

However, if reviews were brief, they could be damning. It became an oft-repeated mantra in the 1980s that this was an 'appreciation society' and not a 'fan club'. As such, it 'appreciated' the show for what it was – which, in some people's view was not much. Barely had the Society gone national than its president, Jan Vincent-Rudzki, reviewed the 1976 story 'The Deadly Assassin' with scorn and concluded by asking 'What has happened to the magic of *Doctor Who*?'[29] The sentiment, right down to the nebulous language such as 'magic', would be recycled for years, and the reasons are not hard to find. Whilst fandom formally barred no one from entry, its methods of operation effectively excluded the youngest viewers. Active fandom requires the freedom and money to travel to conventions, and small-circulation fan-produced materials aren't cheap by pocket-money standards. Active *Who* fans were, almost by definition, past the age which most people in the UK thought the show was aimed at and chiding it for childishness was partly a symptom of disappointment that it had refused to grow up with them. Vincent-Rudzki's attack on 'The Deadly Assassin' kicked off a cycle whereby new stories would be critically mauled then later re-evaluated as new fans, who'd thrilled to these episodes when young, entered fandom. 'Assassin' finished bottom of the DWAS' annual poll of the season's stories in 1977, but was later acclaimed a 'classic' and in 2009 was voted the twentieth best story ever (out of 200) by readers of *Doctor Who Magazine*.

The criticism of 'The Deadly Assassin', and the other stories of the 1976/77 season might have developed into a broader critique of producer Philip Hinchcliffe and script editor Robert Holmes, but that they left their jobs, replaced by Graham Williams (producer) and script editors Anthony Read and Douglas Adams, who became the objects of scorn across much of the Society

Teleview was edited by executive member John Peel, who made appropriate (as he saw them) comments at the end of each piece. Peel was at what might then be regarded as fandom's cutting edge in that he had an acute sense of the programme as a constructed piece of art/culture which could be critiqued for its aesthetic qualities. Anyone familiar with the mid-late 1980s (when, with criticism of the programme rampant, the Society would attempt to remain neutral and its officers would sometimes use their positions to chide those whose view of the show had become so negative) might be surprised to find that the society's magazine led the critical charge against the late 1970s production team. 'After a shaky start to this season, the usual degeneration seems to have set in,' Peel appended to a generally positive piece on 'The Creature From the Pit', before reviewing 'Nightmare of Eden' himself.

> There seems to be a very strange idea that flits currently about the
> Dr. Who office that the show is for kids and can therefore be treated
> as casually as anyone pleases, since kids will watch any old rubbish ...
> Perhaps I'm wrong, but I doubt it. I have this awful feeling that this is
> exactly how they do decide on these terrible stories ... unless – no,
> it's not possible, really – unless ... maybe they actually think that this
> rubbish ... wait for it ... maybe they really and truly think that this
> rubbish is good?'[30]

The charge that *Doctor Who* was being made for children (and the use of the more dismissive term 'kids') cut to the heart of fan anxieties. Unlike their foreign brethren, UK fans could enjoy the fact that their programme was an acknowledged part of the cultural mainstream, a reference point in everyday conversation. The downside of this was the fact that much of the public thought it was for pre-teens. *Who* fans, conversely, would spend the late 1970s and 1980s seeking parity for the programme with other prestigious, adult dramas – partly to validate their own ongoing interest. That

Doctor Who was made by the BBC's Drama Department, not the Childrens' Department, was a routinely cited article of faith, one of fandom's most repeated mantras right up to the programme's cancellation in 1989.

The aesthetics of Graham Williams' time as producer seemed to undercut this fan ambition. Having been told to reduce the horror and violence after pressure-group complaints earlier in the decade, Williams sought to fill the consequent gap with humour. 'Humour' in that sentence covers a whole range of material. 'The Horns of Nimon', derided at the time and labelled by some fans as 'the worst story ever', contains, for instance, lines of substantial wit, such as this Freudian pun: 'He lives in the Power Complex', 'That fits'. However such lines, often delivered speedily, and perhaps obscured by domestic noise when watched in the family home, passed fans by. They were similarly unimpressed by the self-reflexive humour which permeates season 17 ('How is it,' the Doctor asks in 'The Horns of Nimon' 'that wherever I go in the universe there are always people like you pointing guns or phasers or blasters?') which was seen as childish, particularly when it was felt to puncture the drama by pointing up the illogical weaknesses of the prime villains (as in 'Destiny of the Daleks' when the Doctor taunts his foes about how they cannot climb after him). If the genuine wit at work here passed fans by in 1979, Tom Baker's clowning made a more lasting impression. Baker would talk much in newspaper interviews about children, whose opinions and openness he clearly valued. He made an effort to insert material they might find interesting or amusing, and his public claims about doing this enhanced a view that the show was being made for eight year olds.

Not until the 1990s, when the show had been cancelled for several years, did fandom learn to live peacefully with *Doctor Who*'s pre-teen audience, though they had once, of course, numbered amongst it. As the 1970s became the 1980s, John Peel's views echoed and repeated across fandom. Prominent fan Ian Levine, asked about the Williams era by academic researchers, objected to the programme becoming '*Fawlty Towers* in space' and the quote was well circulated.[31] In other contexts, Levine might have enjoyed *Fawlty Towers* – it was a popular show at the time – but he felt it an inappropriate source of generic comparison with *Doctor Who*. As we'll see, fandom in the late 1980s and 1990s came to embrace a wider view of the programme's aesthetics, to the point where many would argue that *Fawlty Towers* was an appropriate thing to aspire to. That was in the future, though, and fans stuck to stricter generic rules as the 1980s began. The couple of thousand fans who joined the society in those years entered an environment where the received wisdom was that Graham Williams' time as producer was a comical low-point. A twentieth-anniversary poll run by the society in 1983 asked members to rate the 20 stories which had won individual season polls, and whilst the top three showed an even spread – with Pertwee, Baker and Troughton all represented – the bottom trio were all from the Williams era.[32]

Given the informal barriers to entry, it was rare that the programme's innocent pre-teen fans and their production-conscious, respect-seeking elders in the *Appreciation Society* collided – rare but not unknown. Gareth Roberts, later a writer on the revamped series, joined the DWAS, aged 11, and his memories of attending a convention amply demonstrate how youthful enthusiasm for the present contrasted with the *Society*'s yearning for an idealised past. Roberts recalled how, as the convention approached, he had

> thought it was gonna be people talking about how jolly *Doctor Who* was. Instead it was people complaining that Graham Williams was rubbish, and I didn't even know who he was ... The highlight of the convention was the screening of [the show's opening episode] *An Unearthly Child* for the first time since 1963. I was thoroughly bored by it. So help me God, I would much rather have seen [the most recent story] *The Armageddon Factor* again.'[33]

Lance Parkin, the young fan who'd declared Williams to be rubbish at the age of six, would surely have felt more at home.

I have said that a cycle exists whereby stories which debut to scathing criticism are subject to re-evaluation. The Williams era was often derided for its poor production values (the scrappiness of its monster costumes, a general cheap look). A decade later the episodes had found their champions. Stories, like 'The Horns of Nimon', once ridiculed as childish would later come to be regarded as containing some of the programmes most sophisticated moments. Even those who still disliked the stories were less scathing because, by the late 1980s, information about how the programme's budget was slashed in real terms more-or-less as Williams took over had become public. This set an economic context for the perceived failings. Of course, since the programme was regularly attracting viewing figures of over eight million people every week in 1979, even after ITV came back on air, it is fair to say that not everyone agreed with the fans' criticisms.

One man, broadly speaking, did, however. And when he replaced Williams as producer, everything changed.

JONATHAN AND JEREMY

The Fourth Doctor – Tom Baker

Season Eighteen (30/08/80 – 21/03/81)

Producer: John Nathan-Turner. Script Editor: Christopher H. Bidmead

The Leisure Hive (4 episodes)

Meglos (4 episodes)

Full Circle (4 episodes)

State of Decay (4 episodes)

Warriors' Gate (4 episodes)

The Keeper of Traken (4 episodes)

Logopolis (4 episodes)

K9 and Company (28/12/81)

Producer: John Nathan-Turner. Script Editors: Antony Root, Eric Saward

One-off drama intended as pilot for a proposed series, in which Sarah Jane Smith (played once more by Elisabeth Sladen) receives a gift from the Doctor (who doesn't appear) of K9 Mark III.

The Fifth Doctor – Peter Davison
Season Nineteen (04/01/82 – 30/03/82)
Producer: John Nathan-Turner. Script Editors: Antony Root, Eric Saward

Castrovalva (4 episodes)
Four To Doomsday (4 episodes)
Kinda (4 episodes)
The Visitation (4 episodes)
Black Orchid (2 episodes)
Earthshock (4 episodes)
Time-Flight (4 episodes)

In 1980, the regional broadcasters which made up the ITV network acted to uniformly screen the American import *Buck Rogers in the Twenty-Fifth Century* against *Doctor Who*, the ratings for which took a serious dent despite displaying improved production values of its own. For season 19 onwards, the programme was rescheduled twice-weekly in weekday slots, ending the affectionate link between the programme and Saturday nights. In the short term, this solved the ratings problem ('Time-Flight' episode one was the twenty-sixth most watched programme of the week). Season 18 itself was one of the most 'hardcore' science fiction series in the whole of the programme's run, though its visual design was extensive and eclectic, presenting alien worlds in a number of styles. Tom Baker departed, and whether he left of his own accord or failed to have his contract renewed remains unclear. K9 and Romana similarly left. Season 19 threw off most of the SF trappings of the previous year, drawing instead upon a broader notion of family adventure. In Davison, the show introduced a physically younger, more vulnerable Doctor to match the younger, more vulnerable companions. One of the latter – a teenage boy called Adric – was killed by the Cybermen. Overseeing all of this was a new producer, John Nathan-Turner. No one knew it then, but Nathan-Turner would produce the show for a decade until its cancellation, becoming so associated with the programme that finding other work would be difficult.

Upon his death in 2002 he received an obituary in the London *Times* for no other reason than producing *Who*. A *Who* celeb in his own right, Nathan-Turner would feature in the press and make television appearances promoting the show. He was the first producer with a nickname, and (probably) the only one who ever received death threats. The new style of excessive visual display that he brought to the show encouraged interpretation and analysis, and they exploded well beyond the fan arena in this period. Welcome to the world of JN-T.

The New Style

When season 17 ended in January 1980, *Doctor Who* was a recognizable quantity. It was a solid part of BBC One's Saturday early evening. Its spin-off comic confirmed it as a family programme which skewed towards the young and the male, though adult appreciation was known to exist based on its unpretentious wit and imaginative adventure format. Two years later, when the nineteenth season finished transmission, all of this was untrue or disputed. *Doctor Who* had changed.

The primary agent of that change, the man who was, at this point, in sufficient control of things to initiate changes directly or encourage them elsewhere, was the new producer, John Nathan-Turner. Whilst previous producers had backgrounds in writing or directing, Nathan-Turner had worked his way up the BBC after a short career in theatre as a stage manager and actor. (In the later controversies over his time on *Who*, Nathan-Turner would alienate writers and directors, but seemed to retain the loyalty of performers). He applied to the BBC, and was taken on as a floor assistant, a position in which he worked on many programmes including Patrick Troughton's penultimate *Who*, 'The Space Pirates' (1969). Promoted through the ranks – assistant floor manager, production assistant – he became production unit manager, and in this capacity he worked on *Who* throughout Graham Williams' period as producer, managing the show's budget. Upon Williams' election to leave, Nathan-Turner became producer. This background determined the strengths of his decade in charge. He knew the BBC system and understood how to work it, resulting in a staggering increase in production values, which, in his opening season, contrasted strongly with the year before.[1]

Whilst the fans' view of *Doctor Who* circa 1979 (its alleged silliness, the childishness of K9) might have been at odds with that of much of the general viewing public, it tallied with that of the new producer, who rung the changes accordingly. The first story of season 18 was 'The Leisure Hive' and its beginning (i.e.: the moment of Nathan-Turner's entry to the series) remains one of the most incredible shots in the programme's history. The camera, positioned near the seafront at Brighton, begins with an image of the pier, then pans to the right past beach huts and deckchairs for 1 minute and 40 seconds before resting on the TARDIS and the sleeping figure of the Doctor, slumped in a deckchair. There are other lengthy takes in the programme's history, but they all bustle with activity, multiple extras, multi-level sets (e.g.: the second shot of 'Warriors of the Deep' [1984] episode one), or else they are relatively impressive effects (as in the opening of 'The Trial of a Time Lord' (1986)). They are all, in short, showing something off. The opening of 'The Leisure Hive' does nothing of the sort. Nothing else in the programme has ever drawn so much attention to its own duration. Over two decades later, in the DVD commentary, script editor Chris Bidmead likens it to the work of Italian art cinema director Antonioni (an obvious reference point for the cine-literate), though he laughs as he says it, the laugh of a man distancing himself from his comments even as he makes them.[2]

Whatever we make of Bidmead's nervousness, it is a shot which begs interpretation, and mine is this. It is a punctuation mark, a massive sign of separation between the immediate past, which Nathan-Turner sought to leave behind, and the new series. For the next five years, *Doctor Who* would be peppered with similarly visually striking set pieces. The highlights include the following: the end of 'Full Circle' episode one when the marshmen creatures arise from the mud in striking slow motion photography; 'State of Decay' superimposing a bat over the vampire Aukon as he declares 'my servants will find them'; the slow motion photography and setting of 'Warriors' Gate', a white void where the only landmarks are a ruined castle and some stranded spacecraft; the pre-credits sequence (then rare on UK television) which opens 'Castrovalva'; a shot in 'Kinda' which begins with Tegan in medium close-up, then travels through her eye into her consciousness (rendered in black and white); the slow mixing between scenes in 'The Caves of

Androzani', and the fast-cut, pacey editing of 'Earthshock', a story which contained a greater quantity of shots than any *Doctor Who* story before it. The ending of the opening scene of 'The Leisure Hive' also deserves a mention because it concludes as audaciously as it began. The camera draws back and back into the sky. The Doctor and his companions on Brighton beach become smaller, though Romana's monologue remains at a constant audible level, and the starfield of the title sequence surrounds it. The image of the beach retreats to the centre, finally becoming invisible, and we pull further back through space, and the next shot is the distant planet Argolis. It should also be noted that 'Hive' director Lovett Bickford recurrently composes its images in depth, more so than any other *Who* story past or present.

This is just a handful of the programme's foremost visual flourishes during these years. All of these moments foregrounded the programme's own narrational processes in a way which it had rarely encouraged before. A subtler, but almost weekly, instance of the programme's new visual stylishness occurs as the opening credits are replaced by the narrative itself. Graham Williams and his directors had simply cut from the title sequence to the action, but Nathan-Turner's era more often sees a mix from the one to the other, the forward-moving stars of the titles remaining visible for a second as the story begins.

We're entitled to ask where this new visual stylishness came from, and it might be relevant that Nathan-Turner was a fan of studio-era Hollywood. This is normally discussed in connection to his large collection of studio-endorsed fan magazines, and his alleged desire to run *Doctor Who Magazine* along similar lines, but we can wonder if it also influenced his total overhaul of the programme's visual style. Before Bickford, for instance, composed 'The Leisure Hive' in depth, did he and Nathan-Turner enthuse about the Hollywood masterpieces of the forties which shot their images in this way (Orson Welles' *Citizen Kane*, William Tyler's *The Best Years of Our Lives*)? Did they, whilst shooting on Brighton beach, discuss Antonioni's *Il Grido*? On the DVD commentary, Bickford doesn't respond to Bidmead's reference to the Italian director, so is that an interpretation which only appeared later? Often overlooked in questions of the visual look of 1980s *Who* is that Nathan-Turner was himself the owner of a keen eye. In 1989, he oversaw a second unit shooting underwater sequences for 'The Curse of Fenric', and the resultant footage is generally reckoned crucial in the creation of mood in a highly regarded story. In 1983, working to a shot list from director Peter Moffat, he directed the massacre of the Cybermen for 'The Five Doctors'. That is a widely acknowledged highpoint of the story, and whilst the sequence's effectiveness is mostly created in the editing suite, Nathan-Turner's imagery, such as the decapitated Cybermen falling to the floor, is impressive.[3]

As the DVD discussion of the opening shot of 'The Leisure Hive' makes clear, the excessive new visual style seemed to imply something beyond the simple telling of a story in a straightforward manner. It invited interpretation, and this same invitation was extended by the titles of stories. With Nathan-Turner's arrival, the practice of titling also underwent an overhaul. The 'X of Y' titles ('The Seeds of Doom', 'Destiny of the Daleks', etc.) which had been standard throughout the Baker era were replaced by shorter, allusive (and often elusive) titles, frequently only a word ('Meglos', 'Logopolis') or two ('Full Circle', 'Warriors' Gate') in length. Hereafter, 'The X of Y' titles would be used primarily with returning monsters ('Attack of the Cybermen', 'Warriors of the Deep'), or for self-conscious returns to the styles of the mid-seventies ('The Caves of Androzani', 'The Curse of Fenric'). The new, more poetic titles ('Full Circle', 'State of Decay') often had to be shoehorned into the script through unlikely dialogue ('Tell Dexeter we've come full circle'; 'I've never seen such a state of decay') and seemed to hint at levels of meaning beyond this rather pedestrian use. Such story titles welcomed interpretation, even requiring direct translation on some occasions; 'Logopolis' is Greek, 'city of the sign'; 'Kinda' evokes 'kinder', the German for children; 'The Visitation' evokes both a visit (by aliens) and a plague whilst the Mawdryn of 'Mawdryn Undead' is derived from the Welsh 'dyn marw' meaning 'dead man'.

These titles were just one strand of a concern with wordplay and visual allusion which peppers *Who* in the early 1980s. If 'The Leisure Hive' briefly homaged Antonioni, the visuals of 'Warriors' Gate' more extensively referenced Jean Cocteau's *Orphee* and *La Belle Et La Bette* and the white void coin-spinning of Tom Stoppard's play *Rosencrantz and Guildenstern are Dead* (a popular A level study text in the 1980s, seemingly always in rep somewhere in the UK at the time). Shakespearean quotation or paraphrase abounded, culminating in 'The Keeper of Traken', an Elizabethan tragedy transposed to an alien planet. 'Castrovalva' was named after a print by M. C. Escher, and incorporated elements of that artist's famously paradoxical imagery, whilst 'Kinda' evoked Christianity in its Edenic imagery, Buddhism in its character names and the novels of Joseph Conrad in its themes of colonialism and dreaming alone. In 1983, 'Terminus' would take its visual cues from Norse mythology and medieval leper imagery. More pedestrianly, some character names were anagrams (companion Adric = Dirac, a scientist who theorized about black holes; Tremas is Master). If there's one piece of critical theory that ever *Who* fan can recite (because it would come from an academic textbook on the show and was subsequently incorporated into the dialogue of a 1987 episode) it is that 'the semiotic thickness of the text varies according to the redundancy of auxiliary production codes'.[4] In plainer English: the variety of interpretations you can possibly take from an episode of *Doctor Who* varies depending on whether the multiple areas of production (costume, props, set design, writing, performance style, etc.) work towards a single unified theme or expand, via their allusions and/or extreme stylization, into a wealth of potential meanings. Nathan-Turner's stylistic revolution saw the programme consciously seeking to expand its semiotic thickness.

Unravelling the intended resonance of this new aggressively stylized programme raised a number of interpretive conundrums for fandom. What is *Doctor Who*'s relationship to these prior texts, beyond plagiarism? What is the status of the end credits? A number of the character names in 'Kinda' are symbolic, but those names are only given in the end credits. Moreover, where does interpretation end? 'Kinda' is one of the programme's most ambitious and abstract stories. On an alien planet, Deva-Loka, the Doctor's companion Tegan is 'possessed' by a force called the Mara which calls forth the feelings and characteristics which she normally represses before manifesting itself as a giant snake. The snake is finally defeated by a circle of mirrors (on the rather hopeful basis that evil can't stand its own reflection). The next story to be transmitted, 'The Visitation', begins with a scene set in 1666, then another of the Doctor in the TARDIS console room, before we cut to the room Tegan shares with Nyssa. This scene begins with a shot of Tegan applying lipstick, and the camera then moves to reveal that what we've seen is not Tegan, but her reflection in a mirror. The camera holds the angle as she agonizes over her recent experiences: 'My mind was ... occupied, taken over ... something called a Mara.' We hold the shot, seeing both the back of the real Tegan's head and the reflection of her face as she talks. The scene (shot by a completely different director some weeks prior to filming on 'Kinda', since *Who* stories were frequently recorded out of transmission order) could be a visual link back to the earlier story, but, even if so, what was it meant to signify?

Whilst fans puzzled over these enigmas, behind the scenes, producing the programme at this level was causing tensions. John Tulloch and Manuel Alvarado, academics writing a book about the programme's history for use on Media Studies courses, had access to the crew of 'Kinda', and were allowed to record production conflicts which were ruled out of bounds in other coverage. They recorded the frustrations felt not just by the ambitious writer, who found his abstract spiritual story crashing up against the generic limits of a family adventure show, but also by BBC staff who found the avant-garde nature of the script presented them with little chance to display their professional skills in the usual manner. Effects man Peter Logan, for instance, found the story's emphasis on character over action frustrating because it left him with little to do. 'I feel cheated. Cheated because I feel that my assistants could do just as well with some of the hardware that was necessary as I could. I feel that I am really superfluous because I'm not really applying my mind in what is required.' He preferred the more traditional SF/adventure storytelling of 'Destiny of the Daleks' (1979).[5] Similarly, a number of the directors found that their visions were not matched by the BBC's own ambitions or resources and weren't invited back. For Lovett Bickford, it was a matter of money ('The Leisure Hive' went well over budget). A more spectacular bust-up occurred over 'Warriors' Gate' director Paul Joyce's refusal to keep within standard BBC shooting practices, something senior production team members felt was endangering the story's completion. He later expressed the view that the production team were 'if not completely intellectually bankrupt, were operating to the limits of their mental overdrafts',[6] but this went unknown outside the BBC at the time. There was, at that point, nowhere to go public with his complaints. This would change.

The New Criticism

The value of all the allusion, influence and wordplay crammed into 1980s *Who* varies. Some of it is utterly trivial. Others are tied more deeply to the themes and images of the stories which they are part of. Their presence en masse, however, gave the impression of a programme which required minute attention and contained an adult level. Fans could use this to back up their claims that the programme was not a children's show, but was instead a legitimate site for mature enthusiasm. Taken together, the arty atmosphere and fans' desire for the show to be viewed as respectably adult may explain the curiously long shelf life of the unlikely rumour that 'Kinda' was really scripted by playwright Tom Stoppard.[7]

However, if the programme had created a new style which openly invited interpreters to read it, who were those interpreters to be? Although the final answer – *Doctor Who Monthly* and the fans – is obvious in retrospect, the list of candidates at the time was surprisingly long. Nathan-Turner's promotion to producer coincided with massive interest from British publishers in issuing books about the details of the programme's production. Of the 14 serials which make up seasons 18 and 19, the production of three of them were followed by people writing books on the series. 'The Leisure Hive' was trailed by Graham Rickard for his book, *A Day With a Television Producer*; 'The Visitation' was covered in *Doctor Who: The Making of a Television Series* and studio recording of 'Kinda' was attended by academics John Tulloch and Manuel Alvarado.

These books were for diverse audiences. Rickard's book was aimed at primary school libraries whilst *Unfolding Text* would stretch undergraduates. All three books were parts of longer series, aiming to introduce its audience to a range of issues (e.g.: volumes in the 'Day With ...' series covered a number of professions). If they hadn't been written around *Doctor Who*, they might well have been written around other series. We don't know what commercial calculations made *Who* the focus of these projects, but the marketing of each reflects the trajectory of *Who* products in the early 1980s. *Television Producer* was aimed at primary school children, had a low-key release in November 1980, and passed many fans by; *Making of a Television Series* was a mainstream publication which couldn't help but be part of the marketing circus surrounding the show when it was released in July 1982 (with a paperback a year later), and *The Unfolding Text* – discussed further in chapter four – was released to coincide with the programme's twentieth anniversary and offered at a discount to fans through the DWAS. This rush of publications revolutionized fan understanding of the programme's production, and made information which was once inaccessible very familiar. In 1980, for all that fans understood about the programme's place at the BBC, few knew what the production office looked like. By the end of 1982, that office, its occupant, the photos from old stories which decorated it, and the mighty whiteboard which dominated one wall, and upon which Nathan-Turner kept track of production, were all well-known. There are 13 photos taken in or around the office in the Rickard book alone.[8]

Photos taken from Rickard's book – depicting the Brighton beach location shoot for 'The Leisure Hive' – were reprinted in *Doctor Who Weekly* issue 31 (cover-dated 14th May, 1980. Pages 8–9). The accompanying article gave a brief description of the producer's job in hyperbolic terms; 'Rumours of a strange new force at large behind the spacey scenes of *Dr. Who* sent me hurrying down to the BBC to discover the truth for myself. John Nathan-Turner, the bold new producer with ideas and the power to get them into the series, is the fighting force behind *Dr. Who*'. The 'me' in that sentence was assistant editor Jenny O'Connor, but most of the magazine's articles were written by Gordon Blows and, predominantly by Jeremy Bentham, head of the Appreciation Society's Reference Department, though most of the readership would have been unaware of that fact since the authorship is nowhere credited. Nathan-Turner himself, intent on the work at hand, and wrapped up in a large coat against the March cold, could hardly appear more different to the images which would proliferate in the years to come (in which he would wear a large smile, jeans and a colourful Hawaiian shirt). The article constituted a significant break with the magazine's previous, sporadic coverage of production which concentrated on the traditional areas of *Who*/BBC craftsmanship (special effects, alien sounds). For *Weekly* readers, however, this was also information without context. Nothing explained the stills, no further information came in the next issue, or the next ...

And so things might have stayed if the comic had remained weekly. As outlined in the last chapter, however, the financial economies of the magazine's production forced it to a different schedule and it became *Doctor Who Monthly* in the summer of 1980, gaining 16 extra pages. Article length expanded, and type shrank to fit more text in. The magazine was consciously repositioning itself as a more adult concern. Jeremy Bentham brought fan concerns to the fore, whilst Nathan-Turner took a far greater interest in its content than his predecessor. From our post-millennial perspective (when *Doctor Who* magazines hit the shelves with cover imagery tied to that very week's transmission) it seems bizarre that *Doctor Who Weekly* debuted during the seventeenth season, but only with the eighteenth issue, in February (when the season was over), did a still from that series first feature on the cover. We might applaud the economic innocence of the times, the small hold that synergy – a word no one was using then – had over the decisions that were made, but it wasn't to last.

Coverage of season 18 would be very different. Covers featured the story currently in transmission (the magazine's monthly schedule being roughly equivalent to a four-part *Who*), and previews inside the magazine printed photos and tantalizing plot summaries. 'Star Profiles' appeared – part-interview, part career summary of actors and writers on the programme. As the season unfolded on screen, the magazine was developing, almost by the month, its range of opinions and its sense of historical debate. By modern standards, the article 'Architects of Fear' in issue 48 is hopelessly naive, but it takes a theme (what makes the programme scary?) which it traces over the course of the show's history, and acknowledges the opinions of various groups from the National Viewers and Listeners Association, through professional psychologists to the BBC itself. It takes a stance, broadly supporting the use of fear-inducing material and regarding the programme-makers as acting responsibly, but within that it acknowledges mistakes. For instance, it describes the killer policemen of 'Terror of the Autons' (1971) as 'a grave error of judgment which both Barry Letts and Terrance Dicks admitted to'.[9] The piece is slight, but it is easily recognizable as an example of the sort of article which would come to dominate the pages of the magazine, and it was through articles like this that many readers were introduced to the issues which would come to define fandom.

In Winter 1981, for instance, Bentham publicized the depleted state of the BBC archive, and shortly after this episode two of the

Patrick Troughton story 'The Abominable Snowmen' was returned. Coverage of the episode's return provides a snapshot of the gulf that separates fandom then from now. The search for missing episodes is one of contemporary fandom's biggest concerns, and should one be rediscovered it causes banner headlines across the front of *DWM* and is publicized across almost all BBC news outlets. The return of the 'Snowmen' episode, by contrast, was not headline news in the February 1982 edition of *Celestial Toyroom*, the DWAS' newsletter, but featured instead in the *Trivia* column, beneath the news that the Forbidden Planet store in London sold posters for the Peter Cushing Dalek movies and that official BBC postcards of the programme's current cast were now available.[10] That seems incredible to modern eyes, but BBC postcards – issued for every series regular – were something fans zealously collected at a time when quality photographs were a rarity, whilst an episode returned to the archive was unlikely to ever be seen. This was prior to home video. The mere existence of an episode wasn't an issue. Opportunities to view those which were safe in the BBC's archive was. Early 1980s *Who* fanzines displayed significantly greater interest in the possibility of repeats of those early stories already in the archive than in the recovery of missing episodes.[11]

Whilst the *Monthly*'s previews of new stories for season 18 were simply plot synopses with tantalizing questions ('Who are the marshmen and why are they so hostile towards the inhabitants of the Starliner?' asked issue 47's preview for 'Full Circle') by season's end, the reviews began to look deeper, with Bentham often using the programme's big visual moments as hooks upon which to hang a wider theory of television aesthetics.

> It is often said that if you notice the director's handiwork in a production then something is wrong with the story. On the basis of 'Full Circle' I would dispute this. The slow motion rising of the Marshmen from the lake was a cinematic play but it made for one of the best episode endings in a very long time.[12]

Nor was the magazine shy of handing out criticism where it felt it was warranted. Thus, in the same season overview, 'Meglos' was dismissed in two sentences as

> the tale of the cactus with a megalomaniac desire to control a doomsday weapon and thus rule the Universe. In all honesty

> I could find little in this story to recommend it. The plot lacked
> originality and the majority of the production values verged on
> the tacky. (p. 27)

Whilst the programme was transmitting, attention was focused
on the episodes on screen. The nine-month gap between seasons 18 and 19, however, gave Bentham time to step up his crash
course in television production. Old writers and production staff
were interviewed. Articles such as *Behind The Scenes Report:
Script-Editing* explained the ins and outs of the various production
jobs.[13] In his interviews and star profiles, Bentham would trace
whole career paths, showing how people like Nathan-Turner or
director Peter Grimwade had worked on *Who* in a number of positions over the years. He was outlining a model of the Corporation
in which the creatively ambitious could carve out a career, beginning at the bottom and working their way up to the senior creative positions. More than anything else, to hundreds of readers
this made a career in television seem a possible reality. Years later,
Neil Harris, by then a columnist for the same magazine, would
capture something of the intellectual excitement generated by
these features.

> I wasn't simply reading, I was devouring, absorbing and, most of
> all, learning. It was the magazine which made me a fan. I was no
> longer merely someone who watched *Doctor Who* and enjoyed it ...
> it didn't patronize its readers. Which meant that when I was asked
> at school 'what do you want to be when you grow up?' I answered,
> 'I want to be a script editor'.[14]

Harris hasn't yet achieved that goal, but other readers did enter
the industry. The career progression which Bentham outlined was
largely gone by the end of the 1980s, as the BBC was forced to
downsize, outsource and employ more people on temporary contracts, but there was still time for some fans to jump on-board.
Richard Marson entered as a floor assistant (in which role he worked
on 'Remembrance of the Daleks' (1988)) and ended up, over a decade later, as producer of *Blue Peter*.

Moreover, whilst preparing the first season of the revamped
series, Russell T. Davies, himself a reader from the first issue, would
acknowledge that the writers on postmillennial *Who* had learnt

good habits from reading these very articles. Contrasting their will-ingness to rewrite scripts with a reticence seen elsewhere in the industry, he argued that Steven Moffat, Mark Gatiss, Paul Cornell and Rob Shearman were

> taught by *Doctor Who*. Since they were kids, they've been reading the wise words of Mr. Dicks and Holmes and Saward and Cartmel and Whitaker ... They know that rewriting is vital, because their own fandom taught them so. All those years of reading fanzines and websites and DWM have paid off.[15]

Indeed, Cornell can be found on the letters page of issue 70 (November, 1981) tut-tutting obliquely 'still haven't done anything about that letters page, I see' and arguing that Bentham should inter-view Nathan-Turner more often. Perhaps the most interesting aspect of the letter is Cornell's plea for a poster 'just of Sarah Sutton (Yes, I know I ask every letter, *and I'm going to keep on asking, so there!*)'[16]. The same month found him airing the same concerns as his column, 'Paul Cornell's Zero Room', debuted in the fanzine *Cygnus Alpha*: 'Paul [West – the editor] asked me and I was glad to oblige, but even, I, notorious Sarah Sutton fan, couldn't write 1,000 words on her alone ....'[17] Apart from occasional British film references which perhaps gave away his preferences, Bentham kept his personality off the page, but Cornell, with whatever degree of consciousness, was constructing a public persona by projecting the same identity across fanzines and *DWM* – an unusual synergy in 1982.

When the nineteenth season began, in January 1982, the mag-azine again focused mostly on the episodes being screened. The previews of new stories were three times as long as a year earlier, however, and struck a quite different tone. Readers awaiting trans-mission of 'Kinda' were told, in issue 62 (March, 1982, p. 24), to expect a story 'combining the world of physical sensation with visual interpretations of thought and thought processes – with the domains of dreams and mental experience.' If that sounded ambitious, readers were reassured that Peter Grimwade was once more in the director's chair, and Bentham cited his previous sto-ries as 'proof of his ability to convey drama with visual imagery'. Reviews were similarly extended, giving Bentham room to expand on his favoured theme: that all the different techniques of televi-sion should be used for formal effect. In this respect, there never was a show so perfectly matched to him as Nathan-Turner's visually excessive version of *Doctor Who*. If the gap between seasons had found him expanding general principles, the reviews of season 19 were a course in practical criticism. In reviewing 'Castrovalva', he applauded a scene set in the TARDIS' Zero Room as

> an example of narrative style at its televisual best – a means to tell a story using the powerful tools of the television industry. For that short scene alone we had Davison's commanding voice dipped with stirring reverberation courtesy of the sound technicians, the unusual sight of the Doctor apparently levitating via the use of CSO (I still maintain his coat tails should have hung down towards the vertical, though), very mood-evoking lighting and the considerable enhancing effect of the Radiophonic incidental music.[18]

Bentham's analysis of the programme's aesthetic was rooted in authorship, with every effect and nuance understood to be rooted in the work of a BBC employee somewhere off-screen. The reviews were complemented by interviews with every technician, performer, designer or title-sequence creator Bentham could find, and they explained how they came to work for the BBC, and what their job entailed. Since Nathan-Turner made available to the publication far more photographs than his predecessor, these articles were amply illustrated with examples of the craft under discussion. A partial list of the areas of television production which Bentham discussed, applauded or otherwise alluded to in the course of 1982 includes lighting, pacing, the use of off-screen sound to suggest a vast spaceship, biblical references, the question of whether an anti-imperialist subtext in 'Kinda' was really necessary, the blessings and imitations of CSO, the standard of performances, and the different qualities of images recorded on film and videotape. This last would become something of a touchstone for *Who* fandom in the 1980s. Knowing at a glance whether a sequence was shot on film or video was a talisman of fan viewing, something which differentiated it from general television watching.

In the days before widespread video ownership few *DWM* readers could follow Bentham down this route. When a May issue reviewed episodes screened in January, he was writing about details which much of the readership had possibly never actually noticed the first time, couldn't remember now, and had no way of checking up on. Readers understood the aesthetic principles, however, and this informed their subsequent viewing. From 1981 their views were also solicited for the first of many annual season polls dedicated to nominating the best stories, monsters and individual episodes. Throughout the 1980s the categories would expand and be reordered with a greater emphasis on production skills than on content such as 'best monster'. Many of Bentham's concerns weren't new if you were a DWAS member, but membership of that organization was only a thousand. The majority of the magazine's readers never joined the DWAS or active fandom, but anyone who paid money to read this sort of prose month after month was imbibing the fan take on the programme. When DWAS membership tripled in 1983/84, the newbies were already up to speed. In 1984, the magazine would change its name to *The Official Doctor Who Magazine* (later just *Doctor Who Magazine*), and a decade after that it would go to a four-weekly release, producing 13 issues a year. However, to a generation of fans raised on Bentham's guide to television production it remains 'the monthly'.

Simultaneously with this new style of reviewing, the letters page was reinvented as a community of interpreters. Sporadically at first, then permanently, it moved to two pages, and printed longer letters. The October 1982 issue features a letter that takes up over a page and a half – unthinkable at any other point in the magazine's history – whilst more generally, readers began to respond to each other's points. The magazine was marked by a number of regular letter-writers who apparently wrote in – but were not necessarily printed – on a monthly basis. Chief amongst these was Graeme Bassett, a fantasy/comics fan from Grimsby who enjoyed a strange short-lived fame as the magazine's most notorious correspondent. His letters printed in issues 59, 63, 64, 70 and 71 made concise points about the programme and the magazine, but also called forth considerable response from other correspondents who replied in strikingly personal terms ('I could not help reading Graeme Bassett's letter (could anyone?) ... why go to the trouble of buying the mag. Does he get some form of sadistic pleasure out of criticizing it to such an extent?' – Howard Leatherbarrow, *DWM* 74, March 1983) and he responded back. By 1984 this format was curtailed. The general principles of debate remained – letters would be written in response to one another – but the experiment with personalities and recurrent correspondents was abandoned.

This shift away from the comic part of the comic/magazine format was reflected also in the demise of the backup strip. These stories, featuring monsters from the series, were dropped. Notable writers towards the end of the run were John Peel (the DWAS' most aggressive anti-Williams columnist, but also the editor of the society's fiction collections), and soon-to-be-comics-legend Alan Moore. Moore contributed, amongst other stories, some tales featuring the Time Lords fighting forces from the future, during which he became the first to use the word which, over two decades later, would resonate so strongly across Christopher Eccleston's year in the role: *timewar*.[19]

Having recreated the magazine so completely, Bentham ceased regular contributions at the end of 1982. It is testament to his influence that when his immediate successor, Richard Landen, wrote about things other than television production (the history of the police box or the cars which had appeared in the programme) there was dissent, and subsequent contributors reverted to the Bentham model. Bentham himself returned for the 1983 *Winter Special,* his magnum opus. This issue interviewed all nine of the show's producers, carving up the programme's aesthetic development in terms of their tenures.[20] Despite 25 years of subsequent research and elaboration, this is still UK fandom's default understanding of the programme's history. In just a few short years, the comic which had launched itself with free transfers of Tom Baker's Doctor fleeing dinosaurs had morphed into a *Who* version of *Cahiers du Cinéma*, complete with a pantheon of the acclaimed.

That an issue I've described as Bentham's 'magnum opus' should concern producers is apt enough because the producer loomed large in fan consciousness at the time. However many different technicians or creators Bentham could find, and however aware he was of the BBC itself as an enabling entity with its own traditions and professional values, one creative signature stood out above all, filtered through coverage in *DWM* and elsewhere: the man *Weekly* readers had first glimpsed on Brighton beach, John Nathan-Turner.

'JN-T'

If *Doctor Who Weekly*'s piece on John Nathan-Turner had been short on details, readers of another Marvel magazine, *Starburst*, were given rather more. Nathan-Turner was interviewed in May 1980, and the interview published in September/October, as the new season was running its – and his – earliest episodes. Across four pages, Nathan-Turner discussed practical matters (negotiations with BBC hierarchy about season length) and laid out his aesthetic ideas publically in a way no producer had ever done before. Six-part stories dragged, he said, and he had done away with them; the Doctor had a less 'casual' look; the balance of comedy and drama had been amended; continuity and using new writers were important; companions served functions regarding audience identification, so he'd introduced a male one and brought the age down; incidental music was an 'essential' part of the programme. He discussed the practicalities of storytelling, and how it determined production decisions: 'if you split up the Doctor and a companion, they've got no one to talk to. If you've got K9, the Doctor, a boy and a girl, you can split them into two groups and still have dialogue within the group.'[21]

We now take it for granted that a new *Doctor Who* producer will explain his aesthetic preferences in glossy magazines which can be found in W.H. Smiths and on television interview programmes. That we do so – and our 1970s forebears did not – shows just how thoroughly the plates were shifting. *Doctor Who Monthly* soon followed where *Starburst* had led. Issue 51 (April 81) found Bentham in the production office itself, recording the first of what became Nathan-Turner's annual interviews for the magazine, reflecting on the season gone by. Bentham approved of the new producer ('In selecting the man to replace former producer Graham Williams the BBC had made a good choice in John Nathan-Turner'[22]) before introducing him as someone fans could warm to: 'John Nathan-Turner has also brought ... an appreciation of the fans' point of view, a legacy from his own youth as a devout filmgoer when he would write copiously to movie companies in the United States'. This concern with the fans' view turned mainly on the area of continuity, season 18 having seen a wealth of references both visual (old costumes hanging on the TARDIS coat stand) and in the dialogue. Gallifrey's coordinates, mentioned in the story 'Full Circle' are the same as those given five years earlier in 'Pyramids of Mars'. (Nathan-Turner constructed an image for himself as a man familiar with the programme's continuity, but it was actually provided by a fan, Ian Levine, behind the scenes.)

Nathan-Turner's four-and-a-half page interview was illustrated with 11 photos – six of the producer himself, and five from the episodes he'd made. That might seem usual practice now, but it was new then, and it can be contrasted with the low profile adopted by the programme's script editors in the same decade. Neither Chris Bidmead nor Andrew Cartmel were interviewed by *DWM* whilst working on the programme, and the interview with Eric Saward in issue 69 is illustrated only by stills from the television episodes, not by a picture of the man himself. In addition to his yearly interview, Nathan-Turner was frequently quoted on the news pages, pleading that anyone hoarding old episodes return them to the archives, or trying to persuade the higher echelons of the BBC to sanction old repeats. To the readership, he must have seemed a tireless worker in the cause of *Who* (which many of his colleagues attest he was). By the start of the nineteenth season, this streak of apparently bottomless energy had a nickname, 'JN-T', which was used in the news pages of the DWAS newsletter *Celestial Toyroom*, though *Doctor Who Magazine* retained the more formal use of his full name.

With this high visibility, Nathan-Turner was using the magazine to develop a public image and a relationship with fans. He was likewise present at most British (and American, see next chapter) conventions and, at least at first, regularly gave interviews to even the smallest of fanzines. As the marketing of the programme hit new levels in the early 1980s, Nathan-Turner was available to all interested publications, and he would use them to add to the thriving market for interpretation, revealing layers of personal meaning which were surely invisible if you only had the text itself to work with. He would gloss 'Warriors' Gate' thus:

> Most of it was set on board a decrepit spaceship that was on its last legs with a crew of people who really have no interest whatsoever in the job that they were doing on board the ship … And, talking to the writer while he was working on the script and while we were briefing him … I suddenly realized, because he was working at Granada television, that this whole set-up – the spaceship with people who were just there to earn a living – was actually his appreciation of Granada Television.[23]

Moments like this were less interpretation (who could possibly deduce this from the text as screened?) than initiation, whereby a secret meaning was passed to the reader. Within such an environment, fans were becoming increasingly capable of generating their own complex readings of the show.

Fandom and Interpretation

Through *DWM*, Jeremy Bentham was teaching fans the arts of analysis, arts which seemed all the more relevant as the programme increasingly presented itself as a text requiring interpretation. However, it was not only on-screen that fans were meeting a new variety of discourse. At Target books, the system whereby Terrance Dicks would adapt all the episodes in a uniform style was breaking down. Increasingly, the programme's script-writers would prefer to novelize their own work. Of the seven writers on Nathan-Turner's first season, five (one of whom was Dicks himself) would adapt their own work. The next year it would be four out of seven, then four out of six in 1983, and the ratio would continue to fall throughout the 1980s to the point where Dicks would write only one Colin Baker novelization, and no Sylvester McCoys.

The different writers who novelized season 18 produced work in a variety of styles. A year earlier, writer David Fisher had taken up the option to novelize his 1979 story, 'The Creature From the Pit', but the end result was normal enough for the Target line, its only stylistic eccentricity being its use of footnotes to outline the fauna, flora and astrological houses of the planet Chloris. His subsequent book, 'Doctor Who and the Leisure Hive', however, took greater liberties with the television text, and amply demonstrates the spirit of aesthetic free play which would dominate the Target line in the 1980s.[24]

The plotline is the same as that of the television serial. A race called the Argolin have been rendered sterile by a nuclear war with a reptile race, the Foamasi, which devastated their planet in 20 minutes ('As long as that?' asks the Doctor, surprised by the apocalyptic war's lengthy duration). Within their radiation-proof dome, the Argolin have built a holiday camp – the Hive of the title – where play and simulation preach a message of peaceful coexistence. Unable to breed, since radioactive fallout from the war has rendered them sterile, the Argolin face extinction, though expensive experiments in replication and time manipulation offer them a hope of racial survival. The Hive, however, is failing financially, and they may have to sell the whole planet to the one race which can survive in the irradiated wasteland it has become, the reptilian Foamasi.

Devoid of Lovett Bickford's attention-grabbing direction, 'The Leisure Hive' still packs a stylistic punch in book form. Scenes are rearranged or deleted in the manner of Malcolm Hulke's work seven or eight years earlier. The Doctor, for instance, is given a new scene with Pangol, a scene which generates mystery when it becomes apparent that the scientist is evading his questions about the workings of the mysterious tachyon generator, the meritorious highpoint of Argolin science. The history of the Argolin race is retraced at humorous length ('warfare came as naturally as breathing to the Argolin – and about as early in their history' – p. 11), culminating in the tale of two gladiators who, for reasons of personal honour, chop all their own limbs off, dying of shock and blood loss without laying a finger on each other (p. 13). Minor new characters, with quixotic views and obsessions of their own, are created, and some of the action is relayed to the reader through them. Much of the Brighton beach sequence, for instance, is told through the eyes of a deck-chair attendant who blames comprehensive education and free school milk for the way a blue police box could mysteriously vanish off the seafront. More mystery is generated by the thoughts of a couple of marginal news reporters who watch the Earth scientist Hardin with Argolin board-member Mena and wonder why the aliens need an expert in tachyonics given their own proficiency in the discipline. The effect of all this new material is that the conclusion of the first televised episode isn't reached until p. 57 (of a 127-page book), whilst part three is whisked through in 20 pages. As regards the humorous history of the Argolin, the clear influence is ex-script editor Douglas Adams, whose science-fiction comedy *The Hitchhiker's Guide to the Galaxy* had become a massive radio success in 1978.

Other writers of the period were similarly happy to take liberties with their television scripts and expand the parameters of the *Who* novelization. John Lydecker's novel of 'Warriors' Gate' has no chapters, it is just one long run of text. 'Full Circle' uses dialogue as chapter headings, has a prologue set untold generations before the main action, and adds a couple of new characters. A children's rhyme quoted in the story is written in full as a prologue. Writer Andrew Smith spends more time than other authors in the minds of the characters, and significant action is related not in the voice of a neutral narrator but through the sensations of the characters. Thus, the marsh spider's assault is reported thus: 'Romana felt its eight legs gripping her face, felt its mossy-soft body pressed against her cheek, felt the bite before her hand could swipe the repellent creature away.'[25] Chris Bidmead's *Logopolis*, by contrast, gains atmosphere and poetry from taking the wider, philosophical view: 'Events cast shadows before them,' the novel begins, 'but the huger shadows creep over us unseen. When some great circumstance, hovering somewhere in the future, is a catastrophe of incalculable consequence, you may not see the signs in the small happenings that go before. The Doctor did, however – vaguely.'[26] Whilst Terrance Dicks had developed stock descriptions of the recurrent characters and actions, these new writers found fresh ways to describe the protagonists. Their diverse styles meant that fans would find lots to compare and contrast in the early-1980s novelizations, and the process only escalated as the decade continued.

The shift represented by these books was moral as well as aesthetic. Whilst *Doctor Who* had always dealt in global threats of domination and invasion, it kept well away from smaller human vices (aside from some of Robert Holmes' more lurid moments, and 1979's anti-drug story 'Nightmare of Eden'). When Fisher had his deckchair attendant reflect that it was weather for 'pubs' rather than the seafront, he was evoking an English institution which hadn't actually been seen in the programme since the Doctor ordered ginger pop in The Fleur-de-Lys during 'The Android Invasion' (December, 1975 – though wine had been drunk [and invariably drugged] in private homes sporadically since that time). The book also tells at length about how Earth has become a tax haven and details the rise of Foamasi gambling syndicates. Then there's the matter, which we must discuss tactfully – not least because the TV show does – of cross-species romance.

The affair in question occurs before the narrative actually begins. As the story starts, Mena, the female deputy-chairman of the Argolin returns from Earth where she has been financing and overseeing experiments in time reversal by an Earth scientist named Hardin. Though Hardin is noticeably younger than her ('For all your genius, you're young,' she says of his foibles), some sort of affair has taken place. On screen that affair is acknowledged only in their unease at being on Argolis, in a single line of dialogue ('My new position will put some distance between us') and in Hardin's determination to save Mena from death at the story's conclusion. Mena is second in the Argolin hierarchy to a male, Morix, and she ascends to leadership upon his demise. Their relationship is never clarified beyond their joint leadership of the Argolin and their shared parental responsibility for Pangol. If one takes this to mean they're married, then her affair with Hardin is extramarital, but that is a leap given that Pangol's birth is revealed to be the product of genetic experimentation. What we do have is an unusual evocation of the flames of passion, and the book fans them strongly to life. The youthful scientist is truly smitten; 'once Hardin had met the beautiful and elegant Mena he had been ready to agree to anything – even Stimson's suggestion that they fake an experiment – in order to keep her beside him' (p. 68). Mena, frequently referred to ambiguously as Morix's 'consort', is keen to end things: 'anything to distance herself from those few mad days she had spent on Terra with this man' (p. 60).

These are small touches, but they bring the relationship vividly to life, moving in emotional waters normally beyond the programme and its adaptations. The full blooming of such material was still some years away, but in Ian Marter's novelization of 'Earthshock' even parts of the female anatomy – Professor Kyle's 'ample bosom' – could now be named.[27] The books had followed *Doctor Who Monthly*, and retooled themselves away from a pre-teen audience and towards the fans desire for a more sophisticated text. Even the programme's new titling strategy led to a rethink at Target, forcing them to stick more literally to the titles as transmitted and discard their policy of inserting 'and the' onto the novelizations. 'Doctor Who and the State of Decay' was odd enough. 'Doctor Who and the Four to Doomsday' would have been meaningless. 'Doctor Who – Four to Doomsday' became the new norm, a practice approved by both the production office and the fans who demanded greatly textual fidelity in spin-off products.

Fans' analytic zeal was not confined to events off-screen. The proliferation of home video saw tapes recorded in Australia (where repeats, particularly of colour episodes, were frequent) and the US crossing the world to the UK where they were taped and taped again so that third, fourth, fifth or more generation copies circulated within fandom. Fanzine production skyrocketed, with reviews of old stories a common feature – they could fill up half or more of a 'zine. In later years such endless reviewing would be seen as padding, but at the time they were exciting exercises in exegesis and constituted the recovery of a history thought to have been unattainable. Such reviews shared the pages with articles boasting such titles as 'Kinda and Conrad', 'Historical Accuracy in the King's Demons', 'Gallifrey or Galilee: Religion in *Doctor Who*', 'Meanings of *Morbius*'. I mention these four but there were hundreds of others. Humour 'zines enjoyed a lower profile. Those advertising 'adult' content for sale to over-18s were a brief presence. By 1983, a fan body once dependent upon the BBC to duplicate its newsletters had spun way beyond the Corporation's ability to regulate, or even predict. BBC Enterprises (now BBC Worldwide, the corporation's merchandising/foreign sales arm) issued official guidance notes for fanzines – pointing out such things as copyright laws – but they were as fruitless as later attempts to police the internet.

What did an early-1980s *Doctor Who* fanzine article look like? How did it shape its arguments? What did it think worthy of note? David Richardson's 1982 article on 'The Leisure Hive' begins by placing the story's importance not in the context of the programme's visual style, but against a wider political landscape.

> If the moral aspect was missing from Doctor Who in the late 70s then it emerged with a vengeance with *The Leisure Hive* in 1980. In a year that had seen the soviet invasion of Afghanistan and the holding of American hostages in Iran, a mood of fear of nuclear weapons became evidenced in the country, and it was pleasing to see the subject treated so seriously within the framework of the series.[28]

Richardson interprets 'Hive' by mapping its themes onto recent political events, pointing out how the theme of prejudice is worked through in the differing positions taken by the various characters, and by his noting how the helmet of the ancient warrior Theron, displayed prominently in the Argolin boardroom is interpreted in diverse ways; pacific characters find it a 'symbol of shame', whilst the aggressive Pangol finds in it a 'call for revenge'. Mena's closeness to Hardin is noted as an instance of cross-cultural sympathy, an attitude again contrasted with Pangol's xenophobia. Returning to the political themes of the opening, the piece concluded in pea-cenik mode: 'Let us hope that we can all realize the symbol of our shame *before* such a thing could happen here'. If this sounds like undergraduate writing, then that represents exactly who was making the critical running at this point. Arts-based students wrote many of the pieces, forging a style which a wealth of A-level students, following behind, sought to emulate. The piece quotes 28 lines of dialogue, whilst making no reference to the direction, the production design or to the fact that it was John Nathan-Turner's first story.

The increase in fanzine production would eventually reduce the influence of the DWAS, but in the early 1980s, UK *Who* fandom was heavily centralised and operated an informal, accessible, but definitely existent, hierarchy, and a vocabulary existed to refer to it. 'Big name fans' were those known throughout fandom for their achievements (as article writers or artists) or in organising events for the Appreciation Society. A 'career' in fandom was one meta-phor used to describe the process whereby one could move up the totem pole. The existence of the 'career' metaphor could be inter-preted as suggesting that fans sought consolation here for failures in their professional lives, but that would be untrue. Members of the DWAS' executive committee held down a wide range of jobs, and it was often their professional skills which made them fit for office in the Society. DWAS positions, when vacant, were advertised in the Society newsletter, and the members of the executive chose from the candidates who applied. The rewards of these arrange-ments were the respect of a small peer group, the thrill of one's name in print, the possibility of shaping the course of fandom, and, at the very apex, small contact with the programme itself. The exec dined out once a year with the cast and production team, and as convention organisers, they had access to the hospitality suites where guests relaxed away from the attendees. These arrangements were not, for the most part, resented, though some private pas-sion burned. Academic readers of this volume will need no introduc-tion to the unlikely levels of ambition and resentment which can be generated by even the smallest of rewards in a tight-knit com-munity. There were some amongst fandom who felt that the life of the DWAS executive was more glamorous than it really was, and a small but vocal local authority felt that the Society's officers should be democratically elected.

A fan 'career' would normally be built up in the pages of the fanzines. *Who* fanzines of the period ran from 20 to 40 pages of A5 paper, with text usually reduced from A4. They were frequently black and white, and litho-printed from masters produced at home on the editor's typewriter. The crucial editorial tool of the period was a bottle of Tippex. A pile of fanzines from the period is a monument to a moment, gone now, when even small British towns supported a number of high street printshops which serviced a wealth of commercial and amateur enterprises. Many 'zines only lasted for a few issues, but a number of committed editors had kept up their labours for years. *Shada, Frontier Worlds, Cygnus Alpha, Skaro* and others produced a dozen or more issues, and built up committed readerships based on their distinct personalities and article mixes. Since a fanzine's production quality tended to increase with each issue as the editor gained experience and confidence, these relatively long-running (i.e.: four or five years) titles were marked by noticeable production superiority such as card covers, occasional use of colour, higher quality paper, photographic content, sophisticated printing techniques, justified text and a wider range of typefaces. By the time of Davison's departure from the series, these were rivalling the production standards of the Society's own publications. The progress of someone's fan 'career' would normally be marked from humble beginnings in the smaller 'zines, up through to the major ones. The society held an annual 'Best Fanzine' poll, so the gradations between the major publications could be measured (though whether this was ever more than an exercise whereby a limited number of people voted for their best friends' work is perhaps open to question). Shortcuts up the fan ladder were starting your own fanzine and joining the Executive.

But what of 'The Leisure Hive' itself? How did the episode which heralded Nathan-Turner's arrival fare interpretatively as fandom became more confident and the producer himself more controversial? As Nathan-Turner remained producer for year after year, so the story came to be read primarily for its importance in the history of the show itself. In 2006, for instance, James Chapman began his discussion of the story on strong thematic terrain ('David

Fisher's script is an examination of the political economy of the leisure industries'), then summarized the plot and concluded that 'What is most remarkable about 'The Leisure Hive', however, is its extraordinary visual elegance', contextualizing the story's importance within debates about Nathan-Turner's new, improved production values.[29] By contrast, interpretations which favour the story's strong moral and social themes mostly emerge on those few occasions when it is viewed by non-fans for whom the producer is an irrelevant question. One brave American fan showed the story to his junior high school class in the late 1980s, a context where not only Nathan-Turner, but even Tom Baker, failed to register as the centre of attention.

> I was surprised how many people talked about the Argolins, and not the Doctor or the monsters. I guess, not knowing a thing about WHO, they picked up on their story and saw it as being about a demoralized, devastated race. One guy said the Argolins were an analogy for the way Native Americans are all starting casinos these days – something that never would have occurred to me!! (Even if that obviously wasn't David Fisher's intention, it still works!) More than one person thought the Argolins built the Hive out of a bomb shelter.[30]

Intriguing stuff, but it is not where *Who* fandom was heading in the early 1980s. It was more concerned with the programme's own aesthetic history, a reading encouraged by the eighteenth season's plethora of references to the programme's past, and the return of the Cybermen in 1982 after a seven-year absence. The impact of the latter was such that similar experiments with other monsters would follow, with diminishing returns. Looming over all of this was the programme's twentieth anniversary in 1983.

This self-consciousness about the programme's history had not been primarily generated by fans, who were not yet in positions of authority sufficient to initiate such things. However, they were starting to enter the programme's orbit. Steve Cambden, a DWAS member who had wrangled a position as K9's assistant operator was one of several fans acquiring low-profile technical positions at the BBC in this period, and their influence would be felt in the years to come. More spectacularly, *Doctor Who Weekly*'s first ever correspondent Matthew Waterhouse was cast as the Doctor's new companion, Adric. It is often suggested, with little elaboration, that companions represent the viewers (e.g.: they ask the same questions the viewers do), but Adric, an adolescent boy blessed with more intellectual skills than social ones, was the first attempt to render a more specific picture of what the audience – or, at least, one highly visible component of it – looked like. Brendan, a computer-literate public school boy in the Christmas 1981 spin-off *K9 and Company* was another. With parts for young males proliferating, it is no surprise that fans seemed to be congregating in the corridors of the casting department. Waterhouse won the part of Adric ahead of another fan, Bernard Padden, who was subsequently given another role in 'Full Circle' (on the DVD of that story, he recalls creeping off with Waterhouse to watch the summer 1980 repeat of 'Destiny of the Daleks'). Another DWAS member, Gary Russell, reached the final three in the casting of Brendan.

As regards fandom's behaviour, perhaps the most influential DWAS member to contribute was Andrew Smith, an 18-year-old fan from Scotland who had contributed sketches to the BBC's satirical series *Not the Nine O'clock News* and other comedy shows. He began submitting stories to the *Who* production office, having learnt the correct layout from the script extracts reprinted in *The Making of Doctor Who*. When one of his stories was made – 'Full Circle' – it was massively publicized in magazines like *Radio Times*, and seemed to prove to a generation of fans that it was possible to come out of nowhere and write for the programme. This became a major ambition for many, and events over the following decades would put them in a position to do just that.

* * *

That ends the main argument of the chapter, but something remains to be said about the new title sequence which Nathan-Turner introduced for the programme. Throughout transmission of season eighteen, he would tease the press and public about a campaign to save K9 (whom he had no intention of retaining) and with the possibility of a female Doctor (which he had no intention of casting). Such playfulness was reserved for publicity campaigns, however, and behind the scenes he ruthlessly dispensed with some of the imagery which seemed to define the programme in the public mind, such as Tom Baker's jelly babies and multicoloured scarf. He also replaced the programme's opening logo and titles – and these proved to be more deeply rooted in the public's relationship with the show than anyone realized at the time.

The title sequence with which Nathan-Turner dispensed had served the programme, with minor modification when Pertwee regenerated into Baker, for seven years, a television lifetime in the pre-video age – literally so in the case of the programme's younger followers. Created by Bernard Lodge, it began as two bright ribbons of colour (predominantly blue) ran from the edge of the screen back to an apparent distant point at the centre where the image of the TARDIS appears. The colours fill out, encompassing the whole screen and the TARDIS vanishes, replaced by a circular pattern with a white light at the centre. It is traditional within fandom to call this abstract pattern a 'time-tunnel', but that is a substantial interpretative leap and in 'The Deadly Assassin' (1976) it is used to signify something else entirely: the entry-point to the Doctor's mind.

However, if the outgoing sequence was one which required interpretation, Nathan-Turner's new one seemed more literal. A starscape appears, at the centre of which are some brightly coloured stars. They're predominantly white and yellow, but with touches of red, green and blue at the edges. They speed towards the camera. Viewers seem to be rushing forward through space with incredible speed, and the stars at the middle coalesce into an image of the Doctor's face. That image becomes a photo of Tom Baker which rushes forward and bleeds to the edge of the screen. We rush forward, and more stars coalesce, this time forming the programme's new logo, which apes the look of neon tubing. It flares into clarity, holds the screen momentarily, then it too bleeds outwards, and we continue rushing forwards as the story title, script-writer, and episode number are overlaid. The image then mixes into the opening shot of the new episode. At the episode's conclusion, the journey is reversed. We rush backwards as the stars zoom in from somewhere behind the camera and speedily recede. A final, bright star recedes, then rushes forward again, consuming the whole screen in a final burst of white, and the episode ends.

This is, I think, a more complex arrangement than was given credit for at the time. In 1980, those decrying the disappearance of the tunnel effect felt that the new arrangement, whilst emphasizing outer space, lacked the temporal element required

by a programme about travel in time. That seems a narrow interpretation since the rapid movement of stars may denote masses
of passing time. Indeed, if the opening starburst is the Big Bang,
and the final white climax is the end of everything, then the two
sequences together cover all of time and space, a universe expanding then contracting to nothing. This interpretation didn't circulate at the time. Fans likened it to *Star Wars* or the *Space Invaders*
arcade game, implying an excess of visual flash at the expense of
something more soulful. Writing in 1990, fan turned academic Tim
Robins would argue that the new title sequence trapped the programme within the generic reading of science fiction, something
previous, more abstract imagery had avoided. That's hindsight and
education speaking – fans at the time lacked the vocabulary to
articulate their concerns so clearly – but it well captures what fans
were groping at.[31]

Time tunnel anxiety (my phrase) would subsequently haunt the
programme. In 1984, with the starfield sequence reworked for Colin
Baker's Doctor, Nathan-Turner would add what he felt was a tunnel
effect, a series of colourful lines shimmering out from the centre of
the screen. The 1996 television film projects its credits as we move
down a tunnel, and the 2005 reboot is the most literal version yet
as the TARDIS travels down red and blue-tinged corridors, coded
within the programme itself as routes to the past and future. A time
tunnel effect similarly opens the animated menus which grace the
classic series DVDs, and even *The Sarah Jane Adventures* (the 2007
spin-off, which rarely travels through time, and never down a tunnel
of any sort) has one. None of these bears any relation to the strange
effect – the opening credits of the Baker years – from which they
notionally descend. Announcing the 1984 version at a convention
in London, Nathan-Turner received applause. He seemed to genuinely believe he was giving fans what they wanted – a tunnel – and
they seemed to think so too. The end result, however, pleased no
one. Perhaps what people wanted wasn't a 'tunnel' as such, but the
abstraction of the earlier title sequence.[32] In later years, when fans
became disillusioned with John Nathan-Turner, they would castigate
him for losing the abstract soul of the series, and replacing it with
high production values and flashy effects. The new title sequence
would be cited as evidence of this. Such complaints began to register as the Davison era continued through the early 1980s.

This, then, was Doctor Who, circa 1982. Shifted from the Saturday evening slot it had held for 18 years, and shot with an artful self-consciousness unparalleled elsewhere in pre-watershed UK TV drama of the time, it was unafraid to make even the most recondite allusions and had a growing body of fans set to interpret it ambitiously. *Doctor Who* had become something it hadn't been only two years earlier. No one understood the implications of all this at the time, but they would play themselves out over the next five years.

AMERICAN EXPRESS

The Fifth Doctor – Peter Davison
Season Twenty (03/01/83 – 16/03/83)

Arc of Infinity (4 episodes)
Snakedance (4 episodes)
Mawdryn Undead (4 episodes)
Terminus (4 episodes)
Enlightenment (4 episodes)
The King's Demons (2 episodes)

Season was to have concluded with the story which became **Resurrection of the Daleks,** but this was abandoned due to industrial action at the BBC.

20th Anniversary Special (25/11/83)
(premiere transmission was in US 23/11/83)
The Five Doctors (1 X 90 minutes)

Season Twenty-One (05/01/84 – 30/03/84)

Warriors of the Deep (4 episodes)
The Awakening (2 episodes)
Frontios (4 episodes)

Resurrection of the Daleks (2 x 50 minute episodes – unusual format caused by disruption of regular schedule by coverage of the Winter Olympics)
Planet of Fire (4 episodes)
The Caves of Androzani (4 episodes)

Season concluded with the first story featuring the Sixth Doctor, **The Twin Dilemma.**

All produced by John Nathan-Turner and script-edited by Eric Saward.

For 1983 and 1984, *Doctor Who* retained its twice-weekly transmission pattern. Ratings slipped to around seven million. The 1983 season featured a surfeit of old enemies, including some whom no one but fans could be expected to remember (the renegade Time Lord Omega returns after a ten-year absence). A Dalek story, intended to end the season on a high-note, had to be abandoned due to a strike at the BBC, leaving the season to fizzle out unconvincingly. The number of companions in the TARDIS was trimmed back to the point where, when Davison left, he was down to one – the 1970s format had reasserted itself. These series were less well received by fandom, and by the time of Davison's departure there was notable discontent in some corners. This disillusion was slow to form given the long lead times of fanzine production. The 1983 season ended in March, but might not be reviewed in a 'zine until the summer, whereupon responses to reviews could be printed as late in the year as Christmas, as the next series approached. A BBC-organized convention held at Longleat in Wiltshire over the Easter 1983 weekend seemed to reaffirm the programme's popularity, as attendance was double the expectations, roads around the venue became gridlocked and the corporation was forced to use all of its news channels to ask people NOT to attend unless they had pre-booked tickets. This juxtaposition of a declining general audience and a smaller, but sizeable, devoted following became all too apparent in the following years.

Events conspired in the early 1980s to push *Doctor Who* towards self-consciousness about its own past. The departure of Tom Baker after seven years was followed swiftly by a repeat season of 'old Doctors' on BBC2 and the programme's 20th anniversary. Davison was the first Doctor to talk, in early media interviews, about his childhood memories of the programme. This wasn't just a matter of age (he was the first Doctor young enough to have such memories), but also a symptom of the facts that the production team wanted to present the show this way (as the site of significant personal and national nostalgia) and that there was now known to be an audience for such reflections. This self-consciousness, along with his own creative inclinations and merchandising instincts, led Nathan-Turner to formalize one version of the programme's history and vocabulary. The idea that Davison was the Fifth Doctor (i.e.: a definite assertion that there were none before William Hartnell) was formalized in 'Mawdryn Undead', though previous episodes had implied the opposite. The central character was still credited as 'Doctor Who' in the end credits, until Nathan-Turner switched it from 'Castrovalva' onwards to simply 'The Doctor'. This standardization extended into the storylines themselves where all the major monsters now had the same knowledge of the Doctor that the audience did. The Cyberleader in 'Earthshock' discourses on the Doctor's continual flouting of Gallifreyan laws on non-interference, whilst the Silurian leader in 'Warriors of the Deep' requires no explanation of the Doctor's claim to have 'regenerated' since their last meeting. It had never been established before that these creatures knew so much about the Doctor's origins.[1] Similarly, whilst previous producers had – on those rare occasions when the TARDIS interior was viewed – given it a look as varied and eclectic as the contents of the Fourth Doctor's pockets, Nathan-Turner imposed a uniform design based on the inset roundels familiar from the console room. This was no small point, since this period saw increased use of the TARDIS not just as a device for landing the crew in dangerous environments, but as a site of action itself. The ship was threatened with decimation at least once a year during Davison's reign ('Castrovalva', 'Terminus', 'Frontios'), the companions' living quarters would be seen – often decorated with props from recent stories – and the ship's winding corridors became the site of regular anxious interaction between companions. As continuity references edged closer to the spine of the narrative, fans would become ambiguous. When Tom Baker recited the coordinates of Gallifrey in season 18, knowing or not knowing that they were the same as in 'Pyramids of

Mars' five years earlier made no difference to plot comprehension. When, in 'Arc of Infinity' (1983) the Fifth Doctor requires entrance to the Gallifreyan computer room and punches in the presidential entry code by, as he puts it, 'pure luck', fans agonized. It's actually a neat moment if you know that five years earlier in 'The Invasion of Time', the Doctor had himself served as President, only to have all memory of it wiped from his conscious mind – but how many viewers could be expected to remember that? *Doctor Who*, the programme which began with almost no back-story, had developed a huge continuity within which viewers could immerse themselves.

Fans could hold that whole story in their heads, of course – and they were suddenly visible. When Davison's first episode was screened, most UK viewers were unaware of the existence of *Doctor Who* fans. By the time he left, a little over two years later, they were common currency in the UK media. Indeed, fans in costume joined Davison and Colin Baker on the chat show *Harty* in March 1984 to discuss/publicize the regeneration. In short, these were the years when the DWAS went public. The organizing executive handed out recruitment leaflets at the Longleat event (attended by 56,000 people with many others unable to get in), had its contact details given in a huge-selling anniversary volume, *Doctor Who – A Celebration*, and then advertised itself in *DWM*. Regional-based local groups gained significant coverage in the local press. Membership tripled to 3,000 in the period, and for many of the newcomers, 1983 to 1984 was a short golden period of new information, shared excitement and new friendships before the serious arguments of the mid-1980s. It was a period when *Who* fandom became so large it was starting to leave behind the science fiction fandom with which it was still affiliated. Fans had traditionally assembled once a month with followers of literary SF at the One Tun pub in Saffron Hill, London, but now they left for specifically-*Who* gatherings at The Fitzroy Tavern, a West End pub with bohemian history and literary pretensions. Similarly, a *Doctor Who* regular making a convention appearance in the late 70s or very early 80s would be as likely to be appearing at a wide-ranging science fiction event as a DWAS one. From 1982 they'd be more likely to be at a *Who*-only event – and not just on this side of the Atlantic. America had discovered *Doctor Who*.

The emergence of an American fandom coincided with the development in Britain, of a distinct logic which opposed (and privileged) *Doctor Who*'s traditional values with those of American entertainment. This had been true since the release of *Star Wars*. Whilst American productions had the money for special effects, *Doctor Who* could be cheered for different reasons. For fans, this meant emphasizing writing and characterization (felt to be underappreciated arts within formulaic American television), the high values of BBC drama, a perceived English superiority in the area of acting and whatever allegories, parallels or otherwise symbolic meanings could be found/read into the programme. The wider public and media were more likely to champion wit and Heath-Robinson improvisation as its outstanding features. In 1980 the opposition between the USA and UK had been fought out on screen as ITV cut deeply into *Who*'s viewing figures with an American import *Buck Rogers in the Twenty-Fifth Century*, a series which oozed *Star Wars* whilst *Doctor Who* was evoking Antonioni.

Buck Rogers didn't last. Its first series had been transmitted a year earlier in the USA, but its second was held up by a writers strike, and wouldn't return until January 1981 when it would last only another 13 episodes. The short-lived import, however, did prove that an action series networked right across the ITV region, promoted in the press, and with toys and books in the shops could damage *Who*. Upon assuming the producer-ship, Nathan-Turner had talked of 'bringing the show into the 1980s', but the 1980s had more completely come up against it in the form of a consciously created franchise operation. This would lock *Who* into an opposition with 'American' values which would dominate media and fan debate about the future and style of the show for decades to come. These included violence (when *Doctor Who* was facing the US adventure series *The A-Team*), or sexuality (Buck's flight-leader Wilma Deering [played by actress Erin Gray] was regarded as sexier than the average *Who* companion by the tabloid press, and even offered by some newspapers in 1980 as a reason for casting a female Doctor). Fans were wary of perceived-American values, and sometimes openly hostile. The UK press were less damning, but understood the oppositions. As American production became a possibility later in the decade – first as a film, then as a replacement for the cancelled TV series – the press would report Steven Spielberg's involvement or David *Knight Rider* Hasslehoff's potential casting, perfectly aware that it was juxtaposing two different types of television hero, two contrasting types of science-fiction.

For UK fans, these questions became more pertinent once the programme found a cult following in the United States. A selection of Jon Pertwee tales sold to American stations in the early 1970s had failed to find an audience. A package of Tom Baker stories (his first four seasons, 98 episodes in all), however, had found success in syndication by the decade's end. In 1982, an American convention was attended by 6,500 fans. American conventions made the BBC news bulletins in the UK, as much for the colourful pageant they presented as the novelty of a UK media success in the USA. British viewers of such broadcasts could be forgiven for thinking that *Doctor Who* was sweeping America as a prime-time hit. The truth, of course, was more mundane. It was a programming niche, often shown late at night on PBS channels, and the majority of Americans had never heard of it. UK fans understood that, but still got caught up in the hype. It was a common boast within fandom at the time that the foreign sales of *Doctor Who* made the show more money than it cost to produce, and that for this reason alone the BBC would never cancel it. The second part of this boast, of course, turned out not be true, and even the first part now appears to have been an exaggeration (the programme *was* sold widely, but often at very low rates).

TV coverage of scarf-bedecked American fans on television was, for many UK viewers, the first they had heard of the programme having fans. For the British, watching *Doctor Who* was a mainstream cultural activity. Even for those past the obvious age of watching it, it could be seen as something acceptably normal (nostalgia, habit, watching with younger family members, the male bias towards SF or just waiting for the next scheduled programme). The public appearance of fans trailing long, multicoloured scarves or even wearing full costume, however, undercut such presumptions towards the cultural centre. It suggested, instead, that watching the show denoted not a mainstream activity but a distinct identity – not a good message to send at a time of concern about falling ratings.

Fandoms Across the Water

American fandom emerged out of US 'media fandom', a wider community with an interest in a wealth of shows, often SF in content (*Star Trek*, *Battlestar Galactica*), but also including witty cult shows like the detective series *Remington Steele*. This is the slash fiction-writing, female-dominated community which has so fascinated Cultural Studies for over two decades now, and it influenced the development of *Who* fan practices in the USA. UK *Who* fandom grew up in no such context. If it acknowledged any other fandoms as a peer group or close relation it would have been the male-dominated worlds of literary SF fandom or comics fandom. Whatever else they personally chose to watch, *Who* fans acknowledged few other shows as the legitimate focus of fan activity. *Blakes Seven* and, more marginally, the sci-fi comedy *The Hitchhiker's Guide to the Galaxy* were more or less the only texts worthy of acknowledgement in *Who* zines, this based mainly on generic similarities, and their shared 'authorship' as BBC productions (with the consequent overlap of creative and technical personnel). *Fawlty Towers*, as we have seen, was definitely out.

Despite these differences, UK *Who* fans became used to living in the shadow of their US counterparts. This is as true of the academic work of later decades as it is of mid-80s tabloids. When, in 1992, Henry Jenkins published *Textual Poachers*, the book which brought the study of fandoms to the centre of Cultural Studies, UK fans appreciated its acknowledgement of the creativity and seriousness of fan culture, but actually found much of it alien to their own experience. If you'd told the average DWAS member about 'slash' (American media fandom's sexually charged fiction) in 1982, then, whatever other responses it might have generated in the heart of the average DWAS member, they'd certainly have felt it an inappropriate public response to *Doctor Who*.[2] And if the Society had been told about filk-singing (American SF fandom's tradition of making up songs about their favourite programmes and performing them together at conventions), the only ones who wouldn't have been rolling on the floor laughing at American daftness would have been the ones who didn't believe it.

Story writing, which would fill whole fanzines in America, had its champions in the UK, but was a marginal enterprise on this side of the Atlantic. Fiction-zine *Cosmic Masque* was the least regular of the Appreciation Society's publications, and the least supported. Somewhat surprisingly in the light of events in the 1990s, the tradition within *Star Trek* fandom of publishing novel-length fiction barely happened. You could count on the fingers of one hand the number of people who tried it, and none of them made any impact.

Many UK *Who* fanzines printed no fiction at all. Studying the letters pages of those which did suggests that this was the part of the 'zine generating least response, and was often written off by some readers as filler.

Similar differences were apparent in the use of art. This was an end in itself to American fans, and thus produced in a variety of materials and formats. In the UK, by contrast, artwork was mostly used as illustrations in fanzines. Thus, even if an accompanying article hadn't dictated the content of the pictures, it was frequently limited in size and form to that required by black-and-white A5 fanzines. Artwork by American artist Gail Bennett was on sale in the merchandise tent during the Longleat convention of Easter 1983 (posters, postcards, badges) and was an eye-opening introduction for UK fans to another world. Produced to a high level on quality card and heavy paper, this was work without UK equivalent. Her art appeared in *Fantasy Empire*, a US magazine dedicated to English-language fantasy fiction from outside North America. For sales reasons alone the magazine was heavily invested in *Doctor Who*, and when it was imported and sold through British science-fiction bookshops it became a major channel whereby UK fans were exposed to American fan work. Bennett skilfully homed in on the programme's most potentially emotive moments. Sarah Jane Smith remembering her time in the TARDIS and wishing, sometimes with tears, that it would restart, was a prominent theme. *Fantasy Empire* issue six finds Bennett's striking portrait of the Davison-era companion Nyssa reflecting, as she never did on screen past her opening episodes, about the multiple losses and rewards of her adventures with the Doctor; 'all I have known .... All I have loved and cherished ... is gone. I am a princess ... of nothing'.[3]

By contrast with this emotionally charged artistry, UK fandom had an analytical base which was richer than that of any other fandom (and remains so), and its grasp of both the programme's own production processes and the social/cultural place of the BBC in British life continued to grow rapidly. Home video allowed for lengthier and more complex analysis of episodes, and fan thinking was developing fast. In time, UK fandom would adopt some of the American practices, usually recontextualised within their own concern (artwork for the sake of it has never been so prominent a product in UK fandom, though it now exists), but the differences between the two fandoms caused significant concern with UK fans feeling that viewers watching media representations of American fandom incorrectly assumed UK fans to behave the same way. They were particularly displeased when press photographers seeking to cover UK events or local groups wanted them to conform to the US model of costume wearing. Indeed, the wearing of costumes became a touchstone issue for some fans who regarded it as an immature behaviour that brought ridicule upon a fandom desperate for adult credibility. 'It is the type of people who organise these [costume competitions], who give SF fans the lousy name they have with the rest of the media,' wrote one prominent DWAS member in a leading 'zine after attending his first *Blakes 7* convention, 'I have nothing against people modelling accurate renditions of costumes and masks from series, but people who get up in silly, unrelated bits of flashy material and paint their faces green make me ill.' The term 'modelling' is tellingly used to define skilled craftsmanship against 'dressing-up', the more commonly used disparaging term for costumery. *Who* fans, of course, were themselves the butt of cruel stereotypes, but could also hand them out in their wars of self-definition against other fandoms, this writer concluding that 'another very interesting fact is that a majority of BLAKE fans appear to be middle aged, sex deprived females.'[4] As that makes clear, some *Who* fans looked down on UK *Blakes Seven* fans. A fan club, *Link-Up*, run out of Dorset and covering both programmes in the style of US fandom, was little more than a blip on the DWAS radar, and when it organized its first *Who* convention (in Swindon in 1984, with competitions for drama, dressing up and short story-writing) the Society's executive committee and most 'big name fans' didn't attend. One Wiltshire fan, Paul Cornell, did attend, and won one of the two short story competitions.

If the attitude of *Who* fans at this point seems humourless and judgmental, the context wasn't only a need to feel intellectually justified in watching a programme routinely regarded as a children's show. It was also falling ratings, and a subsequent concern that anything which made watching the programme seem like a niche activity might put off potential viewers. Even with those heady factors in play, the differences might not have mattered very much, except that US fandom, though statistically insignificant as part of the American population, was huge compared to the DWAS, and American fans had money to spend in a way which was ... well, simply not British.

The financial differences between UK and American fandom were massive and stark. DWAS events were cheap (registration for the one-day *Interface III* in 1983, which featured an impressive roster of guests including Jon Pertwee, was six pounds), partly because the society didn't realize it should be charging VAT on tickets (when the tax bill came years later, retrospectively applied, it was huge). No such financial naivety was in evidence across the Atlantic where US conventions were run as profit-making events, attracting thousands of fans from across North America and beyond. For *The Ultimate Celebration*, a convention held on the twentieth-anniversary weekend of 26 and 27 November, 1983, organizers, *Spirit of Light*, took out full-page colour ads on the back of *Doctor Who Magazine* with contact numbers listed for both US and international callers, promising 'the greatest assemblage of DOCTOR WHO celebrities ever gathered together' and inviting readers to 'join John Nathan-Turner, your host and master of ceremonies, in salute of this prestigious event.[5]

The huge (by UK standards) fees that fans paid to attend such events gave the organizers a large budget with which to attract guests. The programme's cast, past and present, were invited onto 'the circuit', often by John Nathan-Turner. Guests were paid handsomely, but made to work hard for their fee, signing thousands of photos, and often performing cabaret acts for the benefit of those guests who'd paid a further fee to view them over an evening meal.[6] This necessarily generated resentment. UK fans who despaired of ever seeing Patrick Troughton at a DWAS event could read in DWM how he and Jon Pertwee formed a comedy double-act for the benefit of American audiences. The DWAS took the moral and organizational high ground when David Saunders (who held the position of Coordinator) reported that 'I flew to Chicago for "Doctor Who – the Ultimate Celebration" in order to "fly the flag" at a convention celebrating 20 years of what is, after all, our programme. I'm sorry to say that despite the proliferation of guests the gathering paled beside similar DWAS events. The organization was of a lower standard than the Longleat event and left much to be desired'[7]. As membership skyrocketed, however, the Society could afford to be less dismissive of large events as increased resources meant that UK conventions began to pay appearance fees, and guest lists expanded accordingly. Even then, however, American resources could still frustrate UK efforts. In

February 1984, Saunders took to the stage at a one-day DWAS event and announced that the society would stage its biggest event ever over the anniversary weekend of 23 to 25 November. 'We're going to give the Americans a run for their money,' he boomed to enthusiastic applause. The event was cancelled in the summer when it became apparent that all the anticipated guests would be at a rescheduled event in the USA.

Worse still, whilst the fans faithfully recited the binary oppositions of the UK versus the USA, there were signs that the production office favoured the Americans. When Lord Bath opened the Longleat convention he declared it the first such event in the UK, provoking murmurs from those who knew otherwise. He made the same assertion in the opening paragraph of the commemorative programme: 'I am very proud that once again Longleat has scored a first. Never before has a *Doctor Who* celebration been staged this side of the Atlantic'.[8] Nathan-Turner himself (who surely proofread Lord Bath's introduction) wore a 'Doctor Who Fan Club of America' jacket for much of the first day. Later that year, the programme's twentieth anniversary special, 'The Five Doctors', had received its first transmission in the USA. UK fans had to wait an extra two days.[9] The year 1984 brought an American companion, who made her photo call waving a stars and stripes flag, and 1985 found Nathan-Turner inserting a Gail Bennett painting of the Third Doctor into the storyline of 'Timelash'. Fandom was well aware, in early 1984, that Nathan-Turner was actively pursuing a US co-production deal with filming in New Orleans for the following year (it subsequently became Spain when the deal foundered) and these signs, along with his seeming ubiquity at American events and apparent closeness to the organizers led many fans in England to direct their bitterness towards the production office itself. Fanzine cartoons depicted Nathan-Turner reclining on a couch whilst American fans fed him grapes. Stories began to circulate that he was using his position on the programme to substantially line his own pockets with these extracurricular activities. (This is hard to square with the fact that he remained on the programme throughout the 1980s because no one else in the BBC wanted to produce the series. If the more lurid stories of riches were true, you'd have thought people would have been lining up.)

When Nathan-Turner had first become producer, the perceived shoddiness of the programme had been an issue for fans, and his ability to wring higher production values from the show's budget was a cause for celebration, but when the charge was pandering to an American market, even this could be reinterpreted as an American-style preference for glossy visuals over traditional UK values. Thus, a 1983 review of 1975's 'Planet of Evil' concluded that the episodes were 'not only a superb production (which we are used to now) but a brilliant story (which is now somewhat rarer).'[10] Reviews of the season 20 opener found the overseas filming in Amsterdam pleasant but pointless (the artistic themes of season 17's 'City of Death', the obvious comparison because of the overseas filming, meant that that story's use of Paris was seen as more thematically meaningful).[11] In the face of such attitudes, you could hardly blame the producer if he did prefer the reception he got abroad.

That American fans did not appear to share the concerns of their UK counterparts about the programme's direction was contextualised in the UK within wider stereotypes of Americans as uncritical consumers of shallow but glossy television/film products. By this point, however, the contest over the meaning of *Doctor Who* had spilled well outside the television screen.

Marketplace Struggles

The world outside fandom was understandably unaware of the controversies raging within it. For the producers of merchandise, UK and US fandoms together looked like a coherent (and sizeable) market for *Who* information and, consequently, products pitched above the age of schoolchildren began to appear. The very meaning of collecting merchandised *Who* shifted considerably. It had previously entailed searching second-hand shops and jumble sales for products which had been released before you discovered the show and were mostly aimed at children younger than the 'collector'. From this point onwards, it would mean visits to specialist stores, mail order companies and keeping up with the latest releases of products aimed at the interests of fan-consumers. The downside of this Faustian bargain was that the proliferation of books, models and toys was no longer any index of genuine public interest.

At Target, this meant a greater self-consciousness about marketing. Whilst occasional novels had been fast-tracked in the 1970s (*The*

Giant Robot, Baker's debut, and *Destiny of the Daleks* both came out within three months of their television transmission), the 1980s saw more direct tie-ins as certain novelizations became events in themselves. *An Unearthly Child*, the very first story, was novelized at a rush and released in October 1981 to coincide with a repeat screening on BBC2. *The Five Doctors*, had a release date of 26 November 1983, the day after its UK transmission. Copies arrived in shops some days earlier, and, to the annoyance of the production team, often went straight onto the shelves, offering fans a unique opportunity to read a story before its original transmission. Target also began a series of quiz books.[12] This professional interest in the show was welcomed, but some despaired of the quality. David Howe, who had replaced Jeremy Bentham as head of the Appreciation Society's Reference Department, used his column in *Celestial Toyroom* to bemoan of the first *Quiz Book* that 'as we have come to expect from the professional publications, it does have one or two mistakes in it, though not as many as the programme guide ... I really don't see why WH Allen [Target's parent company] don't ask us to check the books'.[13]

Some of Howe's objections were based less on simple mistakes than on the books' ideas of continuity and canon. Since some novelizations had added, expanded or simply changed details of the stories they constituted alternative versions to what had been shown on television. Obviously, this could be tricky for a quiz book. What qualifications had the Doctor acquired at the Time Lord Academy on Gallifrey (page 15, question 5)? If the televised version of 'The Ribos Operation' (1978) described them as 'scraping through with 51 per cent at the second attempt', but the novel had amended this to his receiving a Double Gamma, it is not surprising that a Target-published quiz book was going to treat the novels as the authentic version (more pragmatically, most of the readers would answer the questions by referring to those same novelizations). Similarly, the quiz books were prepared to acknowledge the existence of 'Shada', the story abandoned mid-production in 1979 due to industrial action, and ask questions on the subject: 'What was the true identity of Professor Chronotis whom the Doctor and Romana met at Cambridge?' 'What is Shada?'[14] Howe was having none of that, suggesting that the questions were 'both pointless as no one will ever know the answers.' (The story was never finished nor shown.)[15] Nobody knew it then, but this was an early volley in a war about canonicity which would explode in the 1990s.

Howe was arguing about the details of the programme's fictional world, but merchandise would become an arena within which fans asserted not only their preferred version of continuity, but also its values and its aesthetic, locking horns with the producers over the meanings of *Doctor Who*. As a significant part of the audience for such products, even ones notionally aimed at younger or more generalised audiences, they were in a strong position. Marvel had already attuned their product to fan requirements, and much of the rest of the next few chapters is the story of how fans won other battles. The stakes were highest, of course, when it came to the episodes themselves, and the rise of home video made this contest inevitable.

The BBC entered the home video market in 1983, a time when rental was still the dominant model for both players and tapes. Attendees at the Longleat convention that Easter could fill in a form nominating the story they most wished to see released. The oft-repeated story goes that Patrick Troughton's 'The Tomb of the Cybermen' (1967) came top and when the BBC realized that this story no longer existed in the archives they released Tom Baker's 'Revenge of the Cybermen' instead. If this is an accurate account of proceedings, it might demonstrate how far the BBC were from actually understanding the market which they had notionally consulted. They assumed that the fans had voted for a favourite monster. In fact, they'd more likely voted for aesthetic/formal reasons, choosing the story most often held up as the epitome of scary, atmospheric *Who*. Possibly, they were also voting for Troughton himself, who had vocal champions amongst the older fans who had risen to the top of the DWAS, and whose views carried weight. Of course, given high awareness of the depleted state of the BBC's archive, some fans may have voted for 'Tomb' as a wishful joke. For its part, the BBC might well have shied from launching the video line with black and white material, something they would remain wary of until the end of the decade. Many, inside and out of fandom, would have agreed with the reviewer for *Video Business*, who praised 'Revenge' and stated that 'this reviewer happens to think that Tom Baker was far and away the best Doctor Who' On the other hand, it seems unlikely that many fans would agree with the BBC Video advert which asserted that 'Revenge' was 'one of the definitive adventures in the BBC's mega saga of time travel, pneumatic assistants and long scarves'

Neither the judgement about 'Revenge' nor the language would have appealed to fandom.[16]

Fans were certainly unimpressed with the video. Aimed at the rental market, then dominated by Hollywood, the story had been edited into a movie format with all cliffhanger reprises deleted and a single set of opening and closing credits. This didn't appeal to fans who were, after Bentham had initiated them so completely into the technicalities of television production, strongly aware of the specific forms and language of television as a medium (and who were affectionate about the programme's cliff hanger tradition). They similarly objected to the packaging, for this 1970s story came wrapped in Nathan-Turner-era imagery. The *Doctor Who* logo was the neon one that was used on the latest episodes, not the popular diamond design used on 'Revenge' itself, and the images on the cover – Tom Baker in his later (1980/81) maroon costume and a 1982 Cyberman – failed to match the ones on the episodes themselves. These pictures sat amidst imagery taken from the then-current 'starfield' title sequence.

The BBC's attempt – if such it was –to contextualise this old release within the framework of the programme's then-current imagery is hardly surprising, and might be seen as an early attempt at projecting a consistent image across product lines. We recognise that strategy now – it is common in the era when series are widely marketed. In the early 1980s, however, no one knew that there even was a market for (what we now call) 'cult TV' on video, let alone what form it would take, and the packaging brushed up against the fans' sense that old episodes should be understood within their historical context, and not gobbled up by the present.

The arguments over these issues would run for a decade, with fans slowly winning. With the second release, 'The Brain of Morbius' in 1984, the diamond design of the Tom Baker era became the favoured logo. As the issuing of videos speeded up in the 1990s (at their peak the BBC released two *Who* videos every other month), so the presentation of stories in episodic format became the norm, though even then the definition of an edit would remain contested. During its first three seasons (1963–1966, the majority of William Hartnell's tenure), each episode would end with a caption giving the title of the next episode. The BBC, treating each video release as a discrete entity, deleted those captions if the episode in question was not on the video. Fans, of course, objected to any such treatment, with letters pages reflecting their anger regarding the release of the first story, 'An Unearthly Child', which claimed to be 'complete and unedited' when the final caption ('Next Episode the Dead Planet') had been deleted. There was talk of legal cases, or of reports to Trading Standards authorities.

It is an axiom of fan demands that textual fidelity be adhered too, of course. But what was at stake, at a time when access to video copies was patchy and factual books still rare, was a history of the programme. That history, it was assumed at the time, could be reconstructed without serious problems. This was far from true. Deprived of access to official BBC documentation, fans often reconstructed the history of the programme through the memories of production personnel. Those memories were necessarily patchy at times, and sometimes open to misinterpretation. When Hartnell-era producer Innes Lloyd asserted, during the late 1970s, that the figures for the season three story 'The Gunfighters' had been the lowest ever, it became an oft-repeated 'fact' that the story had hit a trough in its viewership. That Lloyd was actually referring to the 'Audience Appreciation' figures (which measured viewer satisfaction with what they've just watched) took almost another decade to come to light. It is necessary to understand that inaccurate information circulated at the time, but it takes nothing away from the researchers of the period, whose work laid the basis for our modern understanding of the programme. 'Facts', correct or otherwise, jumped from fan circles into the commercial products because they were often written by the same people. One consequence of this, and of the limited number of providers in the market for *Who* information, meant that the programme's aesthetic history became standardized remarkably quickly. This was one effect of *Doctor Who Monthly*, but possibly the biggest influence was the twentieth-anniversary volume *Doctor Who – A Celebration: Two Decades in Time and Space*.

Published by W. H. Allen in September, 1983, *Celebration*, by accident or design, hit the market at just the right moment. Impressively packaged as a smart, coffee-table book, it must have made John Nathan-Turner's heart sing when he saw it. It was everything he wanted *Who* to be: mainstream, stylish, colourful and happy to rehearse the programme's continuity as he'd so-recently codified it: 'The transformation of the Doctor from one likeness to another – his regeneration, to give the process its correct title . . .'[17] The book was written – or rather collated, for much of its word-age was prepared by others – by Peter Haining, a journalist and anthologist who knew far less about the programme than the aver-age *DWM* reader. Haining understood, however, how to smooth the edges of production and continuity information so that they could be presented not as geekery but as legitimate nostalgia for a popular series. Fans already knew every fact in the book (including the many which were subsequently found to be untrue) but were prepared to buy them all again in this smart new form. The cover was a nicely mainstream image of the TARDIS with balloons floating out of the door. The celebratory tone would have jarred just two years later, when public interest in the programme seemingly plum-meted, and fandom's own opinions of the show had polarized.

Celebration became one of W. H. Allen's most successful books, selling over a hundred thousand copies in hardback alone. Haining would write similar volumes – four more over the next five years – with rapidly diminishing returns as the requirements of fans and the general audience sharply diverged, but this first volume deftly surfed the major trends of the *Doctor Who* market. Many were sold in America, and extra income was generated through the release of a luxury limited edition, leather-bound volume and given a slipcase (neatly anticipating the later trend for expensive collectible editions aimed into the fan market).

Although Haining's name appeared on the cover, the book's largest section was *The Whoniverse*, a story-by-story guide to the show written by *Doctor Who Monthly*'s Jeremy Bentham which mixed brief plot summary with critical commentary. DWM toed a line which blunted criticism, but in *Celebration*, Bentham was freer to critique a strictly limited range of targets. The effect was to solid-ify an emerging canon of judgments which would last for almost a decade, until videos of old episodes were so common that people could form their own opinions for themselves. The mid-Troughton era comes off well. Of 'The Evil of the Daleks': 'Every so often a *Doctor Who* story comes along which is universally recognised as a classic of it's kind': on 'The Tomb of the Cybermen': 'the peak of its kind' Recent productions about which fans had complained were recuperated through generic readjustment. Thus, the December/January transmission of 'The Horns of Nimon' became the key to reading what the DWAS had largely declared to be the worst serial ever: 'Christmas time is traditionally the time for panto entertainment, and, as the festive month of December 1979 entered the Yuletide week, so *Doctor Who* unfurled its homage to generations of Widow Twankeys and Abanazers'.[18]

That was an audacious rereading which sought to redeem the story, turning its perceived dramatic failings into timely, seasonal indulgences. About Hartnell's 'The Gunfighters', however, the book is simply dismissive. The review begins with the assertion that the story had received *Who*'s lowest ratings ever, and perhaps it is that perceived failure with audiences which licensed the usually cautious Bentham to let rip with his distaste: 'What made this serial so poor is the cumulative effect of so many bad points which on their own would be forgiven in most other stories. The script was pure Talbot Rothwell, the acting was not even bad Vaudeville … it was not good. It was bad and it was ugly.'[19] As a ten-year-old viewer, watching it upon transmission, Bentham had disliked the story, linking it with *Carry on Cowboy* which he had seen a month or two earlier (an association clearly still meaningful for him given his evocation of Rothwell, the film's scriptwriter) as an example of how the British couldn't do Westerns. In the 1990s, a new generation of fan writers would reappraise the story and find it genuinely witty, though Bentham still dislikes it. At the time, he was unaware at the authority his views carried to impressionable young minds who could hear no opposing viewpoints.

Haining's book was a 'big tent' within which everyone could find a space, either revelling in new information or in seeing it repackaged in a glossy format, and with all serious criticism (i.e.: the 'Gunfighters' review) aimed so far into the past as to be irrelevant. The anniversary celebrations, however, were papering over sizeable cracks, and the moment when such an approach worked – when the diverse interests of different groups could be so easily reconciled – was a brief one.

From our post-millennial perspective, this notion of a fragmented audience does not seem odd. Nowadays, we accept the notion that a television audience, even for a programme broadcast terrestrially to an entire nation, is more frequently a collection of diverse groups who watch for different reasons. That was increasingly true of *Doctor Who* in the 1980s, but if the theory of coalition audiences is understood today, and built into the modern production/marketing process, it was less understood then. In the modern production process, fans constitute a valuable audience component because their consumption of related products constitutes a secondary revenue stream, and because fan activities can support a series and render it visible where it may get lost in the multi-channel jungle. This model didn't work for 1980s *Who*. The BBC, though happy to take the accumulated money, didn't fully explore the merchandising possibilities which the programme offered. Nathan-Turner tried to control it and attempted to integrate it into the values of the programme itself, but it was too much work for one person. With the full resources of the BBC licensing department behind him, and if more of the merchandise had been produced in-house, he might have managed it.

More than this, though, the model outlined above explains why a devoted niche audience might be useful to a programme of marginal interest seeking greater exposure. Fan activities may propel such a series to greater audiences. *Doctor Who* was coming from the opposite direction. The entirety of Britain more-or-less knew what it was about, and the appearance of a distinct niche audience only threatened to pull it towards esoterica. When the series returned in 2005, all of this was understood and built into the production model, but in the 1980s the programme was at a cutting edge nobody understood, and it would feel increasingly like a crisis as things continued. Nathan-Turner's answer to balancing the programme's diverse audiences was to up the monster content, and to cram alien creatures into the programme's more sophisticated scripts whether it needed them or not. Thus, 'Kinda' gained a giant snake, 'The Caves of Androzani' – the most powerful human drama of the Nathan-Turner years – an unnecessary Magma Beast, and 'Ghost Light' some animated husks. When other members of the production team for the serial 'Warriors of the Deep' urged that a monster, the Myrka, be removed because it looked less like a powerful and destructive sea beast and more like a pantomime horse, Nathan-Turner insisted the material be retained. This last example takes us to the Davison story most mired in Anglo-American relations. Fans make political interpretations of various episodes, and often cite them when the programme's 'adult' credentials are attacked, but if there is one 80s story within which fans and general viewers alike would recognize political themes it is surely 'Warriors'.

Warriors of the Deep

In 1984 the fanzine *Skaro* published an article entitled 'Working for the Yankee Dollar'. Three years later, another fanzine published a separate article of the same title.[20] The title alone tells you that both authors were mining a rich, pre-existing vein of anti-Americanism. The fears of *Doctor Who* fans about US influence on the series mirrored – and perhaps had their origins in – wider fears across British/European society throughout the 1980s. The Thatcher government's liberalization of the market and privatization shifted the economy towards the US model and influential elements within the cabinet thought that television should go the same way. The possibility of abolishing the BBC's licence fee has never since left the political agenda, though it waxes and wanes in prominence. UK cinema audiences were rising again, but mostly for Hollywood fare (at a time when Hollywood had apparently moved away from the complex, adult cinema of the 1970s), culminating in national debate in 1985 around the gung-ho American patriotism of the highly successful *Rambo: First Blood, Part II*. On the smaller screen, cable/satellite television was clearly only a few years ahead, leading some to fear an invasion of American pop culture ('Wall to wall *Dallas*' was a much-cited anxiety) and cheap, down-market home-grown programming. In the wider political world, the deployment of US nuclear weapons on UK soil led some to fear that British defence policy was dictated by the Pentagon, whilst the Reagan administration's Strategic Defense Initiative (the 'Star Wars' project) envisaged a shield of defensive satellites protecting the West, thus making the weaponization of space official US policy.

Transmitted in January 1984, 'Warriors of the Deep' explicitly takes up these concerns. The TARDIS materialises in earth orbit in 2084, encountering a military satellite which demands that it identify itself or be destroyed. Escaping to the surface, the Doctor and his companions land in an underwater Seabase, where the operatives oversee the 'proton missiles' of an unnamed global superpower, and await the order to launch them. The 'sync-operator' (the human link with the computer system) worries that he will not be able to go through with his role if the launch order comes. Meanwhile, two spies from the other side plan to steal the technology and return home with it. Enough story right there you might think, but the base is also attacked by the Doctor's Pertwee-era foes, the Silurians and the Sea-Devils. These are intelligent reptiles who ruled the Earth millions of years ago, but who went into hibernation to survive an imminent global catastrophe. Upon their awakening, they are unimpressed to find 'their' world overrun with overly evolved apes. Now they intend to use humanity's own weapons of mass destruction (yet another phrase nobody was using then) to destroy them. The story was highly budgeted (by *Who* standards) as befits a series opener and a story which was envisaged as a fast-paced tale of military personnel fighting monsters. However, a snap general election was called in 1983, and the BBC required studios for its political coverage, meaning that 'Warriors' was rushed into production with little rehearsal. This excuses some of the more obvious flaws (monster costumes with paint not yet dry), but the story is fundamentally conflicted across all the issues which UK fans summed up by referring to their transatlantic cousins.

'Warriors' is downbeat every step of the way, and the themes reflect European/British unease about American military technology. The date – 2084 – evokes 1984, not only the year of the story's transmission, but also George Orwell's totalitarian society which is organized around a permanent war footing. Prior to landing on Earth, the TARDIS encounters a military satellite – the first to grace the series – which declares 'You have entered a forbidden military zone.' Space, it seems, has been both weaponized and divided up between military powers, like Cold War Europe, though this strand is forgotten once the TARDIS escapes the satellite, landing underwater in a military Seabase. The Doctor quickly assesses the situation, with Earth 'still' split between two antagonistic power blocks. It is never stated which side's base the TARDIS has landed in, and multinational casting blurs the question. The two sides in the conflict appear morally equivalent.

A sequence in the second episode seems to embrace a unilateralist approach to disarmament. Seeking escape from the Seabase, the Doctor finds himself in a stand-off with the base's guards. They aim guns at him, and he raises an opportunistically appropriated rifle back at them. 'Your move,' the guards suggest, whereupon the Doctor hands over his weapon, declaring 'Perhaps its time for a little mutual trust.' Trust, however, turns out to be in short supply. It is a common conclusion in SF tales about warring national factions that once a third, alien, force shows its hand, the antagonists will bury their differences in a realization of shared humanity. 'Warriors' rejects this optimism completely. The enemy spies are still seeking escape to the other side when they meet their fate, no one suggests calling reinforcements from anywhere, and the Doctor's attempts at negotiation fail. He is forced to destroy the reptiles before they wipe out humanity, but not before they've killed all bar one of the base's crew (and Bulic's survival looks more like a production over-sight than anything meaningful or intended). Amidst the final pile of bodies, the Doctor bemoans 'There should have been another way', and, although not everyone has played this for the grand tragedy it is clearly meant to be, Peter Davison has given it his agonized all.

So far, so good, but 'Warriors' is a strange production where half the visuals are compromised by its rushed production, and the other half are extremely impressive. Whilst it is the rubbish half which became infamous in later years, at the time even the impres-sive bits were cause for concern. And there are some impressive moments. The underwater model work is excellent, and the sec-ond shot of episode one follows the Seabase's commander around a double-level set. He begins on the first floor, goes down the steps, and walks across the ground level, commencing dialogue with another character a full 20 seconds after the shot began. In the course of this, he passes 14 other performers. It is not a shot with many equivalents in *Doctor Who*, and was intended to send the message that the programme could compete with international competition without compromising its core standards. Many fans, however, took it as symptomatic of a programme which had simply discarded its traditional values in favour of a glossy American look.

These fears came to circulate around the character of the Doctor himself. Davison was young, handsome and his Doctor had a more straightforwardly heroic persona than previous incarnations. On screen, that meant the companions had to take up the slack of moral ambiguity, notably the unpredictable Turlough (who arrives in the TARDIS on a mission to kill the Doctor and never explains his alien origins). Off screen, publicity images attracted concern for the messages they sent. One from 'Earthshock', used on the front cover of the novel, apparently showed the Doctor using both hands to carefully aim a laser gun. A second, taken during a location shoot in Lanzarote, featured a dark-suited Davison pulling James Bond poses next to his bikini-clad co-star, Nicola Bryant. Fiction's most famous secret agent also seemed the model for the Doctor in 'Warriors' episode one. 'I'm so sorry,' the Doctor says with Bondian sarcasm as he knocks one of the sea base's guards over late in the first episode. A year later, Colin Baker's Doctor would utter an even darker quip. After two assailants end up in an acid bath (not the Doctor's intention, it should be added) rather than attempt a rescue, he quips 'Forgive me if I don't join you'. Some fans would never forgive him.

It is hard to imagine anything further removed from the bland, feel-good heroism which fans associated with US entertainment than *Warriors of the Deep*. However, for all its bleakness and its clear articulation of European anxieties, the story couldn't possibly allay fan disquiet about creeping Americanization because the term had come to stand for a number of discontents about a perceived drift towards superficial values of 'glossy' visual pleasures and traditional heroism. Nathan-Turner's once-acclaimed restoration of the show's production values became a cause of criticism when it was felt that poor scripts demonstrated how those values had become an end in themselves.

The dramatic misfires of Davison's time on the programme only made success sweeter when it came. His finale, 'The Caves of Androzani', features no returning foe and a single companion (Peri Brown – who was not bogged down with a complex backstory). It contains none of the lengthy scenes in the TARDIS interior which had so marked the previous three seasons. Instead, 'Androzani' is a gritty revenge drama about business partners turned mortal enemies fighting over control of a wonder drug which controls the effects of ageing. The moody slow-mixes between shots make it a stylish highlight even by the standards of Nathan-Turner's visually excessive *Who*. It was, however, Robert Holmes' script for which fans saved their highest praise. The man whom influential fans had dubbed 'The Grandmaster' had been script editor for the first half of Tom Baker's reign, and written for the programme for a year after that. Now he was back, five years after he'd left, with a story which would spend the subsequent years battling it out for the title of 'Greatest Story Ever.'

As fandom grew, activity increased (see next chapter) and video copies circulated, polls asking fans to rate every story ever – or every story they felt qualified to judge – became routine. As did the results. A DWAS poll in 1983 had split the top three places between Troughton, Pertwee and Baker. Holmes' triumphant return with 'Androzani' coincided with – and, possibly played some small part in cementing – the moment when the period which he had script-edited became acclaimed as the aesthetic cream of the programme. 'Androzani' would fight for the top spot – often winning – against mid-1970s high points, 'Genesis of the Daleks' and 'The Talons of Weng-Chiang'. Other stories from the period such as 'The Robots of Death', 'Pyramids of Mars' and 'The Deadly Assassin' (the story which had caused the first DWAS president such despair upon its original transmission) would usually find places elsewhere in the top ten. This shouldn't surprise us. The influx of fans in the early-to-mid 1980s brought with them their memories of the programme as it had been when they were seven or eight. Moreover, these episodes had seen *Who* hit a ratings peak in the UK, and been the stories which sparked initial American interest. There are good reasons why this period might become disproportionately influential. That influence wasn't limited to fan circles. Of the 13 stories released on video in the UK in the 1980s, 7 ('Revenge of the Cybermen', 'The Brain of Morbius', 'Pyramids of Mars', 'The Robots of Death', 'Terror of the Zygons', 'The Talons of Weng-Chiang' and 'The Ark in Space') would come from the three-year spell when Hinchcliffe was producer, and an eighth, 'The Deadly Assassin', would see release in the USA. In 1987, when the UK satellite broadcaster Super Channel began repeats of *Doctor Who* they elected early Tom Baker stories as the ones to show. The disproportionate influence of the same years continues across merchandise into the new millennium: the line of classic-series figures from the company Character Options contains many from the period; Morbius, a robot of death, a 'Pyramids'-style Mummy. There had always been favourite stories, but from the mid-1980s onwards many of them were taken from the same three-year period of the programme. *Doctor Who* now had what it had never had before – a semi-official golden age.

As the Davison era counted down towards its end, on Saturday 18 February 1984, the DWAS held a one-day event, *Interface III*, at a hotel in London, dedicated to Jon Pertwee's time as the Doctor. Signs of change – of the impact of American fandom on UK events – were apparent, but minimal, and well integrated into the traditional event. The fanzine room was big, with a wider range of titles available than ever before, but on top of this, DWAS exec member John McElroy had signed a private deal with the BBC to sell Corporation-sanctioned photographs from the programme, and he had a large stand. A handful of people in costume walked the halls, but this emergent 'costume department' would never be a big part of the DWAS. These new features didn't detract from traditional values, and were regarded as a healthy sign of increased diversity, only to be expected after society membership had doubled in the year since Longleat (the event was hugely over-subscribed and only fast negotiations with the hotel allowed the society to admit everyone who registered). Pertwee himself attended along with other production staff and performers connected with the period. John Nathan-Turner was also present, answering questions, and assuring attendees that as yet-unseen cast members Nicola Bryant and Colin Baker were good. He stayed into the evening, drinking with fans at the hotel bar. A month later, on 20 March, Davison and Colin Baker marked the passing of the baton with a joint appearance on the *Harty* chat show, where the host also talked with DWAS members in the audience wearing high quality replica costumes. If the *Interface* convention felt like business as usual, the chat show seemed to suggest that fans had found a respectable visibility and a part in the show's promotion. No one knew that everything was about to fall apart, that the centre wouldn't hold.

THE NEW VOCABULARIES

The Sixth Doctor – Colin Baker
Season Twenty-One
Producer: John Nathan-Turner Script Editor: Eric Saward
Final story only (22/03/84 – 30/03/84)

The Twin Dilemma (4 episodes)
Season Twenty-Two (05/01/85 – 20/03/85)
Producer: John Nathan-Turner Script Editor: Eric Saward

For this season only, the programme shifted to 45-minute episodes
(i.e.: a traditional four-parter was now two episodes). Foreign sales
were in the 25-minute format with each episode split in two.

Attack of the Cybermen (2 episodes)
Vengeance on Varos (2 episodes)
The Mark of the Rani (2 episodes)
The Two Doctors (3 episodes)
Timelash (2 episodes)
Revelation of the Daleks (2 episodes)

Doctor Who was then put on an 18-month hiatus during which the only new episodes were

Slipback (a six-part children's radio serial).

Season Twenty-Three (06/09/86 – 06/12/86)

Producer: John Nathan-Turner. Script Editors: Eric Saward (1–8), John Nathan-Turner (9–14, effectively)

Season comprises one 14-episode story, **The Trial of a Time Lord. This is conventionally broken down into its component pieces, with the following titles.**

The Mysterious Planet (4 episodes)
Mindwarp (4 episodes)
Terror of the Vervoids (4 episodes)
The Ultimate Foe (2 episodes)

The form of the above list – fragmented, with qualifications and explanations of shifting formats – shows at a glance what trouble *Doctor Who* descended into. Colin Baker had been announced to the press as the new Doctor in the summer of 1983, but his first episodes weren't screened until March of the following year. Baker's reign was brief but colourful, marred by controversies about violence and his sarcastic, shouting, aggressive interpretation of the role. Fan criticism, which had simmered, burst vocally to the surface. When the programme returned to its traditional Saturday evening slot in 1985 it began well with a rating of 8.9 million for the first episode, falling to 7.2 for the second. By mid-season the programme had lost nearly a third of the initial viewers, and the BBC took it off the air for 18 months, effectively skipping the 1985/86 season. Conspiracy theories abounded, though this now appears to have been one of several cost-cutting measures undertaken to fund the launch of *Breakfast Time*, early morning hours which the Corporation had never had to fill before. Press interest caused senior BBC officers to be openly critical of *Who* and highlight falling ratings. It was a brutal display of how those BBC officers – controller of BBC1, Head of

Drama, etc. – who had championed the series in the 1970s had all left, and their replacements held different views regarding the show. When *Doctor Who* returned to the screen, it was in a curtailed series of 14 25-minute episodes. Ratings slumped for this new series – season 23 – and Colin Baker was removed from a role he clearly relished. John Nathan-Turner, who by contrast wished to leave the show, was made to remain on the programme if he wished to continue as a BBC employee.

With Colin Baker's announcement as the new Doctor some in fandom found a new cause for discontent and aired their concerns long before he got in front of the cameras. His most famous role previously was as lawyer Paul Merrony in BBC drama *The Brothers*, a part which had originally been small but which had grown in scope as the character had become popular. Baker, like Davison, then, had a track record of connecting with audiences, but the fan press was, for obvious reasons, more concerned with his recent, bombastic performances in season 20's 'Arc of Infinity' and the *Blakes Seven* episode 'City at the Edge of the World' (1980). One writer recalled a small one-day event in Bath: 'We had a vote; "Who would approve of Colin Baker as the next Doctor?" I know my eyesight isn't exactly perfect, but I did not see one hand go up'.[1] Nor was this a throwaway article, but the editorial in the then-title-holder of the DWAS' 'favourite fanzine' poll. Similar quotes can be found in other agenda-setting locations.

Nathan-Turner's response came on screen. He had chosen to pay off the end of Peter Davison's contract and do the regeneration a story early, so that the conclusion of season 21 would see the new Doctor in action. 'The Twin Dilemma', a lightweight tale about sentient slugs who wish to explode a sun, thus ensuring that their eggs are blown across the galaxy in all directions to enable widespread colonization, wouldn't last two episodes but for the complications arising from the Doctor's extreme bout of post-regeneration instability. He consistently argues with his young companion Peri, seemingly to provoke his final assertion to her, and to fans, 'I am The Doctor – whether you like it or not'.

Nathan-Turner seemed to genuinely believe 'Dilemma' to be a great story. He told the assembled DWAS in February 1984 that it was one of his best, fast-tracked it for early video release in 1992, and went to his grave insisting it was an unrecognized classic. By the time of his death in May 2002, however, its reputation within fandom as The Worst Story Ever was apparently unassailable. It came bottom of *DWM* polls of all stories in 1998 and 2009 and numerous smaller surveys. Reviewers charged with re-evaluating it found themselves consistently stymied. It is worth remembering, however, that the judgement was not always so absolute. Fan consensus – which was slow to form in those days, and perhaps not really apparent until the summer – said that season 21 was better than season 20, and whilst much of that no doubt reflected on Davison, the DWAS and *DWM* polls of the 1984 season didn't even declare 'Dilemma' to be the worst of the year. It came sixth in both, beating 'Warriors of the Deep'. Reviewers at the time were keen to differentiate their criticism of the story itself from their liking for the new Doctor. 'The Doctor was better than the story' opined the reviewer in *Cygnus Alpha*, whilst his equivalent in *Capitol* spent a page raving about Baker before, sadly, declaring that 'having waxed lyrical about Colin for so long, I'm afraid I am now bound to say that the rest of the story left much to be desired.' Dominic May and Gary Russell, compiling the season poll results for the DWAS and *DWM* respectively, reported numerous comments in the same vein.[2] It was only later that 'Dilemma' took up an apparently unshiftable residence at the foot of the ladder. Possibly, it acts as a lightning rod for everything fans came to feel was wrong with mid-1980s *Who*. Certainly, it is stunning that it comes right after 'The Caves of Androzani', the story often crowned 'best ever'. Whilst some fans piled on the scorn – the respected Australian 'zine *Zerinza* was amongst the most vitriolic – others hesitated. In the summer of 1984, where you stood on the question of the show's immediate future largely depended on whether you chose 'Androzani' or 'Dilemma' as emblematic of the state of the programme.

There were certainly no lack of venues within which to debate the issue, and seemingly no end of fans to discuss them, as DWAS membership topped 3,000 – triple what it had been only a few years earlier. In 1984/85 the Society newsletter printed many apologies and had to return numerous cheques as offers and publications were over-subscribed. The network of 'local groups' expanded past 50, but no one knew how many were actually active. The Executive Committee was appalled when stories reached their ears of members turned away from local meetings because the local group leader or this month's host didn't personally get on with them. Beyond stern notices in the newsletter, however, the Society lacked the formal processes to do anything about such incidents The influx of members did, however, bring increased resources, and raised the page count of the society newsletter, *Celestial Toyroom*, which increased substantially. New printers, Design and Print, were contracted, resulting in improved paper with colour printing and, for the first time, decent photographic reproduction. This new, less amateurish looking newsletter was mailed to members in new *Doctor Who Appreciation Society* envelopes, and, since volunteers could no longer handle the mammoth job of stapling and posting the newsletter, a professional mailing company was hired.

The professional look of *Celestial Toyroom* (CT) was something no one would have anticipated even a year earlier, and with which few people would complain. However, with the new professional look came a new direction away from fan activities. The Society became adept at negotiating discounts with professional merchandisers, and reviews of their wares frequently filled the pages of a newsletter increasingly given over to written materials about the show – serious or humorous – rather than society announcements and fanzine advertisements. The Target Book Club was founded, run through *CT*, to provide members with mail-order copies of the new novels at discounted rates. In every way, links between organized fandom and the merchandisers were growing. Perhaps surprisingly, it wasn't until 1985 that Target Books took a stand at the DWAS *Panopticon* event. Thus, like Marvel, Target editorial staff and creative personnel made increasing contact with fans. They became quick to provide newsletters with the copious amounts of prerelease information which fans requested, and made themselves open to interview requests from fan magazines. By the late 1980s, production materials donated from Marvel and Target – proof pages, original artwork – were a staple part of convention auctions, though they never achieved the prestige of props or scripts related to the programme itself.

When *Celestial Toyroom*'s ad rates were increased in 1984, the announcement made it clear to fanzine editors that they had been enjoying a free (or, at least, subsidized) ride, but it was over now: 'for every advert printed, the DWAS subscription fund now pays approximately half the cost where it should not be paying at all.'[3]

If the society had been subsidising wider fan activity then some would have said that was a perfectly valid use of its funds, but obviously that argument was no longer strong. At the same time, the number of sizes in which ads could be placed was reduced to four, and those were strictly enforced (switching the specified height and width dimensions with each other, previously allowed, was now forbidden). January 1985 saw the newsletter splitting into two discrete sections. *Celestial Toyroom* became a repository of news, society information, merchandise offers, reviews and letters. Fanzine ads were relegated to a second section, *The CT Advertiser*. Fanzines could still advertise in the main section, but at premium rates, and few did so. The stated reason was a change of policy which meant that the newsletter itself would be distributed in the USA (where ads for 'zines only available in the UK would be irrelevant), but fanzine editors grumbled about marginalization. Certainly the disappearance of sometimes-scrappy adverts fitted well with the glossier, more professional look of the newsletter itself. The mood of fanzine editors further soured when, in February, the Society advertised its next event, *DWASocial 5*, to be held in April, and for the first time fanzines would be charged for their table space, and the space available was said to be 'limited'. Two months later, *CT Advertiser* editor Ian Bresman announced that 'the BBC have advised us to find out precisely what is in certain fanzines before advertising them. Needless to say we shall be complying with their wishes and I am afraid all fanzine editors who wish to place an advert should send me either a list of proposed contents or a copy of the product in question for approval.'[4] These developments were less disastrous than they might have been a few years earlier. Comic stores and SF bookshops were happy to stock an expanded range of *Who* material. Selling via such shops and a mail-order American distributor, the short-lived Swindon-based fanzine *Paradise Lost* sold out both its issues (notable for the inclusion of early fiction by Paul Cornell, including an appearance by Saul the sentient church, a character he would use in professionally produced novels) and went to extensive reprinting for the American market without need of the traditional *CT* ad.

The Society had good reason to keep fanzines at arm's length, as some of them seem likely to have been an embarrassment to a club trying to maintain good relations with the BBC. Nowhere in fandom was impassioned criticism stronger than in *DWB* (originally it stood for *Doctor Who Bulletin*, then later *DreamWatch Bulletin*). Gary Levy's self-professed newszine debuted between seasons 20 and 21, but the Colin Baker years saw it becoming the most successful *Who* fanzine ever, selling 4,000 copies per issue. Roughly keeping to its monthly schedule, the magazine saw itself as a news source on par with *Celestial Toyroom* or *Doctor Who Magazine*. With its February 1985 issue, the latter renamed itself *The Official Doctor Who Magazine*, defining itself against amateur upstarts. As page count, production values and readership grew throughout the mid-80s, *DWB* printed the harshest criticism of the production office. It always denied the frequent accusations that it blurred the line between factual reportage and comment, but *DWB* readers lived on a wholly different news diet to other publications. Was John Nathan-Turner really under internal investigation at the BBC for violating copyright restrictions when he took tapes of *Doctor Who* episodes to American conventions? Was he really appalled that a poster used for American publicity depicted only Colin Baker's face, and had had his own removed? And did this move him to such anger that he stormed into the office of Head of Drama Jonathan Powell to complain about it? Was he deliberately barring previous producers from attending US conventions? Was he unreasonably inflating the costs of those same events by insisting that peripheral figures such as production secretary Sarah Lee and his own partner Gary Downie be flown across the Atlantic as guests? This was a dark inversion of the Nathan-Turner fans had read about in 1981: still hyperactive, but now feeding his own ego rather than working endlessly to procure repeats, raise production standards or get old episodes returned to the BBC archive. Under other circumstances, of course, many of those apparently most outraged would have been cheering someone who seemed to be bankrupting American events. That so much of this involved America may suggest that it was the Trans-Atlantic axe which was being ground, if not necessarily by Levy himself then by contributors to the letters page who gleefully joined in.

DWB aspired to the look and air of journalism, but it could never really penetrate the BBC's management, so it frequently read more like conspiracy literature than anything else. 'Whereas people might argue that *DWB* has done John Nathan-Turner 'a grave injustice', *DWB* has been in a position – which many of our readers haven't – and witnessed Doctor Who itself being done a grave injustice' (*DWB* 36/37, p. 7); 'Further to my last piece in *DWB* 34, a couple of interesting rumours have come my way which may be of interest to readers. These are rumours that fans should know about, but don't' (*DWB* 36/37, p. 11); 'We would stress it has been impossible to obtain a coherent explanation from authorities at the BBC and therefore we have had to make a number of assumptions and the foregoing article contains a large amount of conjecture, albeit we feel conjecture based on plausible grounds' (*DWB* Vol 4. Nos 5/6, p. 3) 'Our [headline] 'Gallifrey destroyed in Season 23 (*DWB* 27) ... was, in fact, one of the original planned exciting endings of that subsequently disastrous season ... until, we can reveal, producer John Nathan-Turnoff discovered that his little secret was out and changed the ending simply in order to discredit' *DWB* (Issue 50, p. 2).

Fandom's increased size and visibility meant not just more fanzines than ever before, but a similar increase in conventions. In 1984 the DWAS lost its near-monopoly on *Who* events. That year the fans around the country could take the opportunity, if they wished, to meet up en masse several times over the year, no small evolution in a friendship network spread across the country. A DWAS event in February was followed by March's *Convention for 84* in Southampton and an Easter charity event at Camden Lock, before June brought a *Who*-themed Comic Mart in Westminster. In July, fans could attend *AggieCon* in Ealing, and screenings of old episodes at the Bradford Playhouse. August saw conventions in Swindon and Edinburgh whilst October brought the second DWAS event of the year, and a *Who*-themed sponsored walk in aid of UK childrens' charity Dr. Barnado's. Anyone who attended all of those could easily come to regard the programme as the centre of their social life. Some of the organizers at these events had learnt the rudiments of staging events by working as DWAS assistants, and many attendees were those who attended society events. Others, however, came from outside the DWAS completely, and ran conventions along completely different lines. *Fan-Aid* convention in Bath in 1985 operated on the principle that no old episodes be shown (the first convention to assume that home video had made this redundant), and invited more of the programme's script-writers than ever before, assembling them together for a 'writers panel' devised and chaired by Paul Cornell. *The Leisure Hive* conventions in Swindon (1984–1987) had competitions for costume-making. So far, so fair, but the nastiest confrontation of the era also occurred in Swindon when the editor of *DWB* spoke strongly against the production secretary at her question-and-answer panel. Nothing like that happened at an Appreciation Society event, where a certain decorum was observed, but the DWAS now had no control over large swathes of fan activity.

In the closely linked small world of *Who*, the boom in conventions could work hand-in-hand with the escalating merchandise and the fan niche market if a bit-part player were enterprising enough. A guest who was witty and fun, or who made the effort to address the interests of fandom could find themselves doing convention appearances out of all proportion to their actual involvement with the show. David Banks was cast as the leader of the Cybermen in four stories between 1982 to 1988. Having discovered fandom via a convention invitation, he not only joined 'the circuit' but went on to become the author of two books on the Cybermen, including a massive pseudo-history of the species.

Entrepreneurship such as Banks' had long been a feature of US fandom, where art postcards or T-shirts were available for sale at conventions or by mail order. Not always approved by the BBC, the vast range of materials available by the mid-1980s constitute an archive still waiting to be recorded. British fans, being that much closer to the BBC's lawyers, had less of such a tradition, but licensed products began to appear from enterprising fans. Early manifestations during this period were model Daleks (featured on *Blue Peter*), and model Cybermats. Sometimes, astute fans could open up avenues which remained frustratingly closed to the Society itself. In late 1983, an offer for BBC copyright photographs negotiated privately was mailed out with the same issue of *CT* which announced that the head of the Society's own photographic department was resigning in frustration at her inability to reach exactly such an arrangement. The magazine *Fantasy Image* was released by Visual Imagination, a company set by ex-DWAS supremo Stephen Payne. That magazine didn't last long, but when they purchased SF magazine *Starburst* from Marvel Comics, Visual Imagination acquired a regular place on the nation's newsstands, and a base from which to expand. Until it folded in 2009, a listing of the company's officers reads like a who's who of the DWAS' executive committee of the late 1970s and early 1980s, and the magazine was written by people who'd learnt their craft and analytical skills in fanzines.

Fan publications themselves spilled off the printed page into audio 'zines, a short-lived phenomena which was a copyright nightmare because of the inclusion of clips from the television series. The same technology was put to use under the banner Audio-Visuals to produce new *Doctor Who* dramas on tape. Produced by Gary Russell and Bill Baggs, almost 30 plays were produced between 1984 and 1991. Many of those involved would go on to work on the professional line of *Doctor Who* dramas commencing in 1999, and continuing today, under the company name Big Finish. Indeed, the first Big Finish product is dedicated to 'Everyone who was involved with the AVs. We couldn't have done this without you'.[5] These dramas featured guest appearances by actors such as Michael Wisher, Peter Miles (both veterans of the series who had played several parts) and Nabil Shaban (a popular recurring villain in 'Vengeance on Varos' [1985] and 'Mindwarp' [1986]). The actors who appeared in these and later ventures tended to be the ones who were becoming semi-regulars at British conventions. As friendship and respect grew between fan producers and television professionals, so the gap between professional and amateur productions (which was a crucial distinction in the non-profit world of fan publication) was starting to blur.[6]

Projects like Audio-Visuals constituted precision marketing by fans for fans within a specialized network, but many large, commercial firms aimed at a more general readership, one which was falling away. Such literary delights as *The Doctor Who A-Z*, the make-your-own-adventure books, *The Doctor Who Cookbook* and *The Doctor Who Pattern Book* all found themselves in the remainder bins. A good number of these doomed products had direct links with the production office. The *Cookbook* was collated by Nathan-Turner's partner Gary Downie; two of the make-your-own adventure books were written by the programme's then-current script-writers; Nathan-Turner himself wrote a couple of slim volumes, *The TARDIS Inside Out* and *The Companions*. All of these forsook fan concerns – though some fans brought them anyway – to aim at the traditional, more generalized notion of the audience. This might be taken as emblematic of where the production office sought to position the programme, but it was some way off where the buyers now were.

In this shifting environment, the traditional 'big three' (novelizations, magazine and annual) met contrasting fortunes. The *Annual* couldn't adapt to the new marketplace, and it died. Marvel and Target evolved, and were rewarded with product lines which continued long after the programme itself was cancelled.

New Ways of Speaking

The upshot of increased activity and the DWAS' loss of near-monopoly was that new ways of talking about the show emerged. Products from unusual quarters brought new vocabularies and new concerns to bear on the programme. The 1980s saw the start of academia's interest in the programme. Coincidentally or otherwise, an initial flurry of activity occurred in the anniversary year of 1983, though delays – and the usual gap between academic work appearing and making any sort of impact outside the universities – meant that *Who* fandom wouldn't debate things until the Colin Baker years. Nineteen eighty-three was to have seen a double-whammy from the British Film Institute with the publication of *Doctor Who: The Unfolding Text* and the *Doctor Who: The Developing Art* event at the National Film Theatre in London, though an excess of orders for the book meant that it sold out quickly, and many fans who'd ordered through the Appreciation Society or the adverts in *DWM* had to wait for the second printing early the next year.

Academic analysis of *Who* was carried out in the new area of Cultural Studies. This then-emergent discipline sought to marry the attention to textual detail practiced in film studies and literature with ideas about cultural and historical specificity derived from the social sciences. In practice this meant that anything was analyzable as the product of a certain time and place, and from it could be deduced a wealth of information about the power structures and behavioural norms of the society within which it was created. Although they'd have been hard put to express it quite like that, this insight was familiar enough to fans. Cultural thinking wasn't pursued rigorously by fandom at the time, but some issues had presented themselves. Most fans had encountered the arguments about whether Jon Pertwee's Doctor should have worked for the military, whether it was bad that the role of the female companion was such a subordinate one, and whether a woman could ever play the title role. Fans likewise understood enough about cultural change for the dominant discourse to assert that Pertwee's dashing man of action drew on 60s ideas of fashion and the aesthetics of the James Bond films, and that the character of Sarah Jane Smith, influenced by feminism, was an attempt to move the companion role beyond the traditional limits.

Most academic discussion of *Who* in the 1980s was produced by academics working in Australia. The programme itself had been screened in that country since January 1965, and repeat screenings (at least of colour material) were common throughout the 1970s, with the programme often shown four nights a week. Many of the videos circulating round UK fandom originated from Australian transmissions. By the early 1980s, Australia had also imported a good number of English academics in the cultural studies field. One of them, John Fiske, published his article *Dr. Who, Ideology and the Reading of a Popular Narrative Text* in *The Australian Journal of Screen Theory*. The event passed fandom by, though it was located in university libraries later by those studying the media.[7] Studying 'The Creature from the Pit' (the choice of a season 17 story alone would have sent alarm bells ringing across fandom at this point), Fiske discussed the ways in which popular narratives repeated and validated the values of the status quo. 'Creature' concerns the planet Chloris where vegetation proliferates. Metal, however, is rare, and the meagre supplies are jealously guarded by the planet's tyrannical leader, Lady Adrasta. An ambassador from another planet – where metal is plentiful but vegetables are desperately needed – has been imprisoned by Adrasta as a way of retaining her monopoly. The Doctor frees the ambassador, Adrasta is killed by her own servants and a mutually beneficial trade agreement is negotiated. Fiske argues that the programme associates all positive values with the Doctor (and thus with the capitalist free trade agreement which he enables at the end) whilst associating negative values, via Adrasta, with state ownership. He argues that the episodes reproduce patriarchal values (because Romana is 'subservient' to the Doctor), and locates the origins of the programme's good/evil conflicts in Christianity, thus infusing his reading with more religious imagery than even Malcolm Hulke would have dared in his 1970s novelizations. Thus, Fiske concentrated on the conservative values of the programme and the way that the episode offered a preferred interpretation (because viewers were expected to side with the Doctor), although he did discuss the ways in which viewers hostile to the programme might interpret it in different ways, rejecting, for instance, its conflation of evil with state monopoly.

The editor of the *Journal* was another British academic, John Tulloch. He had followed *Who* since its first episode, and, upon moving to Australia, enjoyed re-watching old episodes stripped across weekday evenings, and started to use it as part of his classes at the University of New South Wales. With British academic Manuel Alvarado, he embarked on a larger project: the book *Doctor Who: The Unfolding Text*.[8] Fiske was moving towards a theory of the audience and the ways in which they might be able to bend a text towards their own values rather than simply assenting to those imposed by its own structures. Tulloch, by contrast, pursued the question of meaning through the activities of the production team: how, in a massive, and arguably formulaic, system like broadcasting, could any individual creator bring their own values to bear within television formats, either as author/creators or simply as professionals with skills they endeavoured to use to their utmost? Researching *Who* from the perspective of both its production team and its audiences brought Tulloch into the orbit of early-80s fans, whose influence was brought to bear. Finding out how much fans despised the seventeenth season and Douglas Adams' work on the series inspired him to understand the authorial signatures of script editors in addition to the producers and performers he was already thinking about.

Skilful marketing outside of the usual academic outlets, with ads and order forms in *Doctor Who Magazine,* generated sales within fandom, a whole new market for an academic publisher. It was, thus, a significant step towards the current economy of television studies (the one underpinning this book) where academics who enjoy cult television find a ready market outside the universities for work based on programmes with fan audiences. That relationship didn't exist in 1983, and *The Unfolding Text*, packed with media and literary theory, is a denser read than later cult TV books. Fans found it bemusing, but many tried to engage. Matt Hills – now a respected academic studying, amongst other things, science-fiction fans – attempted it when he was 12. For all the good it did, I had the edge on him, being 16. There were some scathing rejections of the project. 'I don't think I have ever read such a pretentious load of old rubbish than this lengthy tome,' opined the editor of *Celestial Toyroom*, calling its citations 'the most inappropriate quotes from so-called distinguished sources', and concluding 'I feel sorry for the poor students who are going to have to wade through this book at colleges.'[9] Some fans did respond to this by writing positive reviews.

For all its virtues and ambition, *The Unfolding Text* failed to generate any ongoing academic work on *Doctor Who*. As an example of analyzing a popular text as it changed over time, Tony Bennett and Janet Woollacott's *Bond and Beyond*, published as part of the same 'Communication and Culture' series in 1987, was more accessible, and more successful in every way, becoming often cited as a model for this sort of inquiry.[10] Fiske briefly quoted his own work on the programme in his hugely influential undergraduate book *Television Culture* (where he also notes that the numerous novelizations available might affect the way one viewed the television episodes[11]). Tulloch returned to the question in his book *Television Drama* (written for a series edited by Fiske). He responded to Fiske's original article as a fan would (though in academic language), arguing that the analysis of a single story ignored the programme's long history of aesthetic shifts, and suggesting that he drew general conclusions from episodes which were not typical:

> Yet a problem I have with his analysis is that the particular text he chooses to discuss ('Creature From the Pit') is from the Douglas Adams era, consciously foregrounding its own textuality via language play, parodic acting style and over-the-top stereotyping.[12]

In the 1990s, when the study of fan activity became a major issue for Cultural Studies, he would publish his wider analysis of the programme's various audiences, research which had been undertaken as part of *The Unfolding Text*, but which had been left out for reasons of space.[13]

New Ways of Reading and Writing

New ways of thinking and writing about *Who* were not limited to new players such as academia. The novelizations and the *DWM* comic strip evolved through a wealth of aesthetic styles and vocabularies in the mid-1980s.

As Tom Baker's period as the Doctor came to an end, the task of writing the comic strip had come to Steve Parkhouse, a writer and artist with a long track record in comics and who had worked on many other magazines created by Dez Skinn. The legend says that Parkhouse didn't even own a TV set when handed the job of scripting *Who*, and it is certainly true that his vision of the Doctor took few cues from what was being broadcast. He introduced the Fifth Doctor playing cricket in the town of Stockbridge where he seems a semi-permanent resident, popular around town and living in the TARDIS which is parked in the nearby woodland. His first adventure, a seven-part epic, called *The Tides of Time* took this alternative Davison across time and space via a Gallifrey rendered in panoramas of high-tech towers quite unrealizable on screen at the time. Later, in 1984, Parkhouse gave the Sixth Doctor a wisecracking penguin, Frobisher, for a companion (more accurately, an alien shape-shifter frozen as a penguin). In his farewell to the strip, Parkhouse had the Doctor pursue a mad 'time-thief', Astrolabus through a strange domain where the difference between physical and mental space has largely dissolved. With Astrolabus sporadically aware of his own fictional status, the strip shifted style, most famously adopting the look and language of Alfred Bestall's *Rupert The Bear* strips: 'The Doctor tries to keep things cheerful, Although his pal is looking tearful'.[14]

Whilst fans were taking this stylistic experimentation in, whatever remained of a house style of the Target novelizations was dissolving completely as authors increasingly took up the option to novelize their own work. Of the 11 Colin Baker stories, Terrance Dicks would novelize only one, a significant dip from the Davison years when he still wrote six of the 19. Moreover, the monthly schedule meant that by the end of the Davison era, the company had no choice but to turn increasingly to the past for unreleased stories. The Baker years saw a wealth of Hartnell and Troughton era books – *The Aztecs*, *The Highlanders*, *The Myth Makers*, *Galaxy Four*, *The Ark*, *The Savages*, *Fury From The Deep*, and many others. Fans were being exposed to a wealth of unusual *Whos*, from the purely historical tales without any fantastic elements to slow-paced science fiction of the sort which the programme hadn't dabbled in on screen for over a decade. These books were written by people with diverse styles who played cut-and-paste with their television scripts in a way that went beyond even what Malcolm Hulke had been prepared to do a decade earlier. Unbound by the limits of television, 1960s author Paul Erickson reimagined his studio-bound story 'The Ark' so that it took place amidst massive vistas of the sort that only post-millennial CGI *Who* can produce on screen.

Not since Terrance Dicks had one of the programme's script editors revisited the stories he had worked as novelizations, but mid-1980s editor Eric Saward did so, using the novels to add character touches not on screen; in *Attack of the Cybermen* Peri's familiarity with weaponry, having been 'taught to use a gun by her father' was a rare acknowledgement that her American nationality brought with it distinct cultural baggage.[15] The book also contains the most pretentious dedication ever to grace a *Who* novel: 'In dedication to the memory of Bob, the father, And the splendour of the indigenous Peoples of the Americas.' *Attack* is set on the planet Telos after the Cybermen have taken it over, and driven the native populace, the Cryons, underground. It could be said to be a story of colonization (though this reading has never been widespread), and Saward's use of the dedication is a rare example of a *Who* writer attempting to cue a certain interpretation. ('Bob' is presumably Robert Holmes.) Dedications were something which Terrance Dicks had avoided, but they became common enough in the work of other novelisers, though usually of minimal length and scant detail. Similarly, Target had also taken to crediting the producer and director, buried in amongst the printing and publishing details, so text that might be of interest to the reader had slipped forward from the actual story itself.

More controversial than these shifts was the tendency of many books to add comments or background information about Time Lords and TARDISes, drawing on information that had never been part of the series when these programmes originally aired, so that 1960s stories were rewritten in the light of 1970s information. Conversely, certain stylistic points of the earlier seasons which had been glossed over before were now sporadically apparent. During the black-and-white era, stories would run into each other. One set of episodes would set up the next by ending with the TARDIS landing at its next location, or particularly dramatic conclusions might be run like cliff-hangers across the end of one story and the beginning of the next. This was something the novelizations had traditionally avoided, preferring to keep the stories discretely packaged in single books, but in the new world of aesthetic experimentation, and with knowledge of the programme's stylistic tics now well circulated, Ian Marter could begin his adaptation of the Troughton-era Cyberman story *The Invasion* with the TARDIS reforming itself after the events of the previous story. Indeed, Marter continued to push the stylistic envelope in various ways. Even some of those who had thrilled to his descriptions in books like *Earthshock* were unsure about the fit of descriptive excess which opened *The Dominators*.

> A huge crescent of brilliant pinpoints of light sliced through the unimaginable emptiness of space near the edge of a remote spiral galaxy. Like a colossal scimitar, it flashed in a relentless sweep towards an insignificant little planet which orbited an isolated minor star. Suddenly the very tip of the nearer point of the crescent separated itself from the rest. It decelerated into a tight curving path which gradually spiralled closer and closer to the to the pale-ochre-coloured planet. Far above, the gigantic blade of lights swept on through the galaxy, leaving the meteor-like object to burn its deadly way down through the hot dry atmosphere towards the barren waste shimmering below.[16]

It continues in the same vein for three more lengthy paragraphs before characters appear and movement and dialogue begin. Is that 'total nonsense', as one reviewer in *CT* suggested? Or 'some of the best description I've ever seen in a *DW* book' as another riposted a month later.[17] Note not just the extended simile of the crescent, but also the 'pale ochre' of the planet itself. More than any other novelization, *The Dominators* describes the colour of things, making a point of something which couldn't have been apparent in the black-and-white original. As the arguments in *CT* suggest, consensus about what constituted the style and vocabulary of *Doctor Who* had broken down.

The biggest question which hung over the novelizations, however, was the growing age of their readers, and their ability to provide adult content for them. What, however, was 'adult content' in a *Doctor Who* novelization? Marter, again, was at the forefront of the battle for more explicit content, be it swear words (or, as he called them, 'the odd intelligently-used expletive'[18]) or gory violence. 'Routledge remained standing like a waxen dummy for several seconds. Then he vomited a stream of blood and pitched forward onto his face'[19] he wrote in *The Invasion*, a passage that came in for a critical mauling in the *DWM* review column: 'It's the sort of writing style teenagers adopt when writing home-grown James Bond novels – and then hopefully drop as writing skill takes over from writing hack.[20] For years, Marter had been the literary yang alternative to Terrance Dicks' meat-and-potatoes yin. Anyone wanting more than Dicks had to offer had to look to him. However, Marter came in for more sustained fan criticism once other models of sophisticated *Who* writing became available. By contrast with his full-frontal approach, others preferred inserting adult content less explicitly, be it the 'muttered obscenities' of *Attack of the Cybermen* or the moment in 'Frontios' where the character of Range is warned to keep his young daughter inside whilst the planet's desperate men riot outside.[21]

Less controversial were those who smuggled their sex and vio-lence in under the guise of humour. Donald Cotton and Eric Saward favoured this approach. Cotton was the Hartnell-era author of two humorous stories, *The Myth Makers* (where the TARDIS lands at the Trojan war) and *The Gunfighters*, the Western which had acquired so low a reputation in the early 1980s. In the novelizations, Cotton escalates the humour, and narrates them in the first person through the eyes of, respectively, Homer and Doc Holliday. Writing from such perspectives means that Cotton takes extensive liberties with the televised version, particularly once Homer is blinded, thus limit-ing the amount of information he is able to gather. Major events on television – most obviously Katarina's joining the TARDIS crew at the end of 'The Myth Makers' – are thrown away in a line or two. What replaces them is a humour with a frame of reference not seen before in *Doctor Who*. *The Myth Makers* gives the books their first refer-ence to homosexuality (not surprisingly, given its classical themes) and virginity loss, *The Gunfighters* its first jokes about prostitution. Bum's rush, cesspit, goddam, unmentionables (as a synonym for female underwear), love-nest, puke, lewdness, pert, billet-doux, satyr, 'For God's sake', and 'hoofed him in the slats' (p. 96) are all words or phrases which make their first *Doctor Who* appearance in *The Gunfighters* novelization. As for 'a-canoodlin' with your fancy piece of small-time, low-tone, high-falutin' jailbait' (p. 76) ... well, the number of adjectives alone meant that nobody got accused of that on Terrance Dicks' watch.

Since the major audience for *Who* novels was now in its teens and above, none of these words was particularly shocking, and all were rendered more-or-less innocuous by the knockabout comedy which contextualizes them. (No small point this, as a few years later author Ian Briggs would find the word 'knickers' excised from the more-conventionally narrated *Dragonfire* novelization.) Cotton's importance, however, and his comedy, wasn't limited to the amount of innuendo he could get away with. The colourful language is only part of the diverse vocabulary at work in the books. Both narrators, regardless of their supposed historical situation, speak in modern voices, cynical of authority, making jokes about the brutality of old West law keepers and the overrated nature of Greek culture. Anachronistic references abound, Homeric heroes drop in and out of blank verse, gunfighter Johnny Ringo craves conversation in Latin, and Wyatt Earp's speech is ripe in Biblical allusion (including Ezekiel, the book which closed Malcolm Hulke's *Doctor Who and the Dinosaur Invasion*, which surely makes it the only Biblical book cited twice in the novelizations and not at all on screen).

Eric Saward's books looked to mine the same vein of humour, but his work was less focused than Cotton's, less disciplined, and – if we're honest – less funny. Cotton had his own voice, even if he did filter it through Homer and Doc Holliday, but Saward struggled to escape the shadow of one of his predecessors in the script editor's office, Douglas Adams. Adams had left *Who* when his science fiction comedy *The Hitchhiker's Guide to the Galaxy* became a smash-hit and Saward's novelizations of *The Twin Dilemma* and *Slipback* are full of lengthy digression in the *Hitchhikers'* vein. The universe's most complex cooker, the most depressing planet ever, and a vain Time Lord consistently underwhelmed by his new regenerations are only three of them. When *The Twin Dilemma* revealed that cats were the most intelligent creatures on the Earth, it felt awfully like Adams' own revelations about mice and dolphins. In the same book, Professor Archie Sylvest's academic fame as the man who calculated square routes to minus numbers recalls Marvin the Paranoid Android's claim to have done the same.[22] Like Adams, this style of humour leads inevitably to cynicism, here focused on human motivations, and as with other authors (such as

David Fisher, whose *Leisure Hive* novelization discussed in Chapter Two was similarly indebted to Adams and *Hitchhikers*), such digressions were most easily inserted towards the start of the narrative, and they resulted in books where the proportional balance of the episodes – which got a near-identical amount of space in the work of Terrance Dicks – varied wildly. The early episodes got lengthy treatment and later ones were rushed through. The four-episode *Dilemma* has 138 pages, but doesn't reach the end of part one until page 55. In *Attack of the Cybermen*, the Doctor doesn't appear until page 32, after 25 pages filled mostly with crime drama.

What's most striking about Saward's novels, though, is the incredibly material universe they depict. *The Leisure Hive* had presented the relationship between Mena and Hardin as an admirable example of cross-cultural understanding, but the affair in *Twin Dilemma* gets less-idealised treatment. Indeed, every innovation of *The Leisure Hive* is escalated in Saward's novels, including the pub reference. Archie Sylvest, a minor married character on screen, seeks regular solace drinking with the similarly married Vestral Smith, 'a person of deep warmth, deep personal understanding and even deeper blue eyes' (p. 8). These arrangements go badly awry when her husband turns up. Archie's alcoholic drink of choice is Voxnic, which he consumes in large quantities to numb himself against the pains of his sad life. References to this drink litter both *Dilemma* and *Slipback*, and the latter tells us how the pursuit of fine wine is the surest way to speedy cultural development, requiring as it does the development of glass, cork and distillation technology. Nor is Sylvest the only drinker. *Dilemma* has the Doctor reminiscing about an alcoholic night on the town which ended in a fountain, whilst *Slipback* finds him drunk as he enters the story. Peri too has an eye for the bottle, for when trapped in an alien dome rigged to explode she goes off to explore and 'when she discovered the wine cellar, she also knew that she wouldn't die sober' (*Twin Dilemma*, p. 83). Escaping this exploding dome entails the Doctor working 'with all the energy and passion of a lecherous stallion,' an unusual – to say the least – description of him without parallel elsewhere in the books. He finally rigs an escape by turning a 'revitalising modulator' into a matter transporter. The original function of this booth-like device was for anyone who stepped inside to be 'gently pummelled and massaged into an oblivion of ecstasy' (p. 73). This is surely as close as the programme's ever going to get to the Orgasmatron from Woody Allen's *Sleeper*.

Breaking the Text

Cotton, Saward and other authors were certainly pushing *Doctor Who* into new forms which no one had ever expected it to take, but they weren't the only ones. With the spread of video, fan readings of the show diverged further and further from the mainstream. When fandoms became the object of academic study, researchers would often focus on the way that video allows fans 'control' of the text. With the episodes accessible, fans could re-edit them at will, making compilations of related moments which made visible recurrent themes or emphasised and escalated underplayed emotions and motifs. Remarkably little of this occurred in UK *Who* fandom, though 'tribute' compilations, often to deceased cast members, were made. Rather, fans' re-watching and/or freeze-framing of episodes threw up a catalogue of textual details which had previously remained obscured.

Outside of fandom, nothing on the following list could be regarded as remotely important, or even worth noticing, but all became the subject of mirth or analysis within it: the original title sequence, as used in the first three and half years momentarily renders the programme's title as *Doctor Oho*; off-screen sound is common in 1960s *Who*, as are the shadows cast by boom-mikes, which tend to be visible on the backs of people's heads; the initial narrative enigma of the story 'Kinda' (the disappearance of the colonist Roberts) is never resolved, but simply forgotten about; the third episode of a four-part story is where the padding is; in 'The Horns of Nimon', actor Malcolm Terris splits his trousers, and you can clearly see his underpants; the body parts of numerous technicians are momentarily visible in many stories as they work moveable scenery, or (most famously) hold in place the cushion upon which Sutekh the Destroyer sits out his eternal imprisonment. Acknowledging these moments, understanding references to them and being able to make jokes about them above the tabloid level of 'the sets wobble' would become one marker of fan identity.[23]

Above the endless examples of cameras visible in shot or the reflections of studio personnel in shiny parts of the set, the production deficiency which, more than any other, fans took to heart was strangely delivered lines. Unlikely inflections which would once have passed without being remembered were rehashed and lampooned at length. Despite the wealth of nostalgia icons in place, nearly 30 years after its transmission, 'The Five Doctors' remains most memorable to many for the Cyberleader's strangely emotive 'Excellent' and actor Paul Jerricho's bizarre delivery of the line 'No, not the mind probe' (In defence of the actors honoured by fandom in this way, some of the dialogue in *Doctor Who* would cause anyone problems.) Odd delivery was far from limited to the guest stars, and consideration of this allowed fans to recognise the strengths and limitations of actors they had previously hero-worshipped. William Hartnell, well into his fifties when he accepted the part and suffering from arteriosclerosis, would often forget the second half of his lines, leading to sentences which begin on point, but wander off into nothingness ('Billyfluffs' in fan jargon): 'I rather fancy that's settled that little bit of solution' ('The Sensorites'); 'You'll end up as a couple of cinders flying around in Spain – in space!' ('The Chase'); 'I'm not a mountain goat, and I prefer walking to any day. And I hate climbing' ('The Time Meddler').

For fans who enjoyed these moments, the semiotic thickness of the text of *Doctor Who* had expanded because they were prepared to engage with parts of it which they would previously have ignored or literally not have consciously noticed (not everyone registers boom-mic shadows, however obvious they appear to those who do). Some films – most famously, those of Hollywood B-movie director Ed Wood – have acquired cult status precisely because their lack of artistic merit (manifested in such things as bad acting, unlikely dialogue and poorly motivated character actions/plot twists) constituted an oppositional aesthetic to mainstream notions of artistic achievement. This 'it's-so-bad-it's-good' mode of appreciation was popularised during the 1980s, notably by film critic Michael Medved who, in books and on television, made bad films the recipients of his 'Golden Turkey' awards. *Who* fans were never going to go very far down this route (they judged the programme by traditional aesthetic categories, and judged it highly), but it gave them a model for how production deficiencies could become the object of affectionate jokes.[24] Moreover this visibility of production information within the episodes themselves, or circling around it in fanzines and professional magazines, made possible new readings, moments such as this extract from a late 80s review of the 1977 Tom Baker story 'The Invisible Enemy'. In the episodes – a homage/rip-off of the 1966 film *Fantastic Voyage* – the Doctor's body has been infected by a viral intelligence. To investigate this force's infiltration of his anatomy, miniaturized clones of the Time Lord and his companion, Leela, are injected into his body and search for the source of infection. The review continues

> A synaptic junction fires and a blue spark zaps slowly overhead. 'Just a passing thought' quoth he. All right, maybe it's the way he tells it. More amusing perhaps now we know what Tom's hobbies are was his diverting the phagocytes trying to digest Leela by telling his immune system that his liver was disintegrating.[25]

This reading explicitly prefers a witticism tied to Tom Baker's allegedly prolific drinking during his time on the programme over the 'passing thought' joke which the writers actually scripted. It is the product of a fan mind which has gone far beyond a consideration of the plot, the theme or any part of the manifest or symbolic content (anything in short which the BBC consciously put effort into producing) and is directed instead towards the construction of its own joke.

Across the 26 years of programme's original run – not to mention the reboot – there are endless moments, invisible to the non-initiate, to be activated and become the next round of in-jokes. It is at this point, I think, that the metaphor of *consumption*, so often used in audience studies, breaks down. The cult text is never consumed (i.e. destroyed or used up) in its reading. It is always available, complete and undiminished, bristling with new moments to be activated. Unsurprisingly perhaps, this manner of textual reading was most prominent amongst the graduate fans who emerged at the decade's end with degrees in literature and media studies, people who'd been taught to deduce much from small textual details and to read against the grain of a given text. This reading embraced a whole diversity of *Doctor Whos* – the texts that the BBC actually made, the spin-offs, and those which only existed as ideas in the subculture and magazines which circulated around it – and its inclusiveness led to a wider sense of what the programme might be. For this reason, I would argue, though it is something of a generalization, those who ascribed to the cult reading of the show kept their distance from the more vicious attacks upon Nathan-Turner. Those who criticized loudest were those with a more rigid sense of what the show should be (watch from behind the sofa, British writing vs. American gloss, 'it's not a children's show, it's produced by the drama department'…, etc.) and would thus attack the production team for not delivering it.

The New Adventures (A Pre-history)

In 1989 *Doctor Who* would be taken off-air, and Target – by then bought up by the Virgin imprint – would continue the saga in its series of original novels named *The New Adventures*. No one knew this during the mid-1980s although Target was already making approaches to the BBC about original fiction. At this point, however, the corporation preferred them to continue with novelizations whilst there were stories still to be adapted.

Nothing that happened during the reign of the Sixth Doctor was consciously done with the intention of defining the style of what would become *The New Adventures*, but it is possible in retrospect to sift through the diverse writings of the mid-1980s and see that style emerging. Saward's starkly materialistic world where the drink flowed freely and relationships were troubled would be retrospectively recognizable to *New Adventures* readers. He could surely have found employment there had he sought it.

A second strand of the tone adopted by the *New Adventures* was to use in-jokes and references as a direct address to those who would understand them. Ian Marter had, in his 1985 novelisation of 'The Invasion' renamed a Russian airbase Nykortny, punning on the name of actor Nicholas Courtney, but this form of address found its first sustained home not in an actual *Who* book, but in a spin-off, Peter Grimwade's *Robot*. Grimwade was a product of the BBC, having worked his way up through the production roles to become one of the most-acclaimed directors to work on the show in the early 1980s. That employment had ended following a falling-out with John Nathan-Turner, but Eric Saward had continued to contract him to write for the programme. In this capacity, he wrote both the introductory and final stories for the Doctor's male alien companion, Turlough, during the Davison era. On this basis, he argued that he had created the character and that Target's publication of a spin-off novel – *Turlough and the Earthlink Dilemma* – had inadvertently infringed his copyright. As a goodwill gesture, the company agreed to publish a non-*Who* science fiction novel, *Robot*.[26]

The plot concerns two opposing forces of robots whose conflict brings them to Earth, and whose final battle may well consume the planet. One robot falls into the hands of the military who have their own plans for it. One military figure, who plans to use these aliens to 'see Great Britain walk tall again' (p. 119), could have walked straight out of an old Malcolm Hulke novelization. It similarly places the story in a contemporary world of real politics, but with a harder edge because Grimwade is prepared to be more specific and name names; Ireland, Iran, Nicaragua and Margaret Thatcher are all mentioned. However, whilst Hulke's books were aimed at the widest, most general readership, Grimwade's carries coded references for the inner circle of *Who* fans. To name but three; the action takes place in a town called Turlow (commemorating the legal origins of the novel's publication); a computer expert is called Bidmead (for season 18's IT-literate script editor, Christopher H. Bidmead) and a local policeman Barnfather (for prominent fan Keith Barnfather).

With its littering of such in-jokes the book addresses *Doctor Who* fans as a target group with a large repository of knowledge. Like the fans who relate on-screen moments to off-screen drinking habits, the book recontextualises names and information for the enjoyment of those who understand the transformation which has taken place. As we shall see in the next chapter, this process rapidly escalated once fans themselves began writing original novels. But, if Target was working towards the tone that those books would take, a second question was *what sort of stories would they tell?* They would be longer than the television stories, and thus seek a wider canvas and larger themes. The books, not the comic strip, would become the most widely discussed form of *Who* fiction once the series was cancelled, but a foretaste of the future was unknowingly found within the final Colin Baker strip, *The World Shapers*.

Written by Grant Morrison – later an icon of adult comics – in 1987 after Steve Parkhouse had left, *The World Shapers* has the TARDIS land on the planet Marinus, last visited by the First Doctor, William Hartnell, in 1964. Reflecting the same spirit of bricolage which was gaining ground in fandom, the Doctor, pondering on his previous visit, recollects both the television serial and its sequel, presented in the first annual (1965). The 'World Shapers' of the title are a couple of aliens who aim to massively transform the planet by accelerating time and evolution. Their reference to Marinus as 'Planet Fourteen' triggers a memory in the Doctor, but, unable to place it, he goes to visit his Troughton-era companion, Culloden-refugee Jamie McCrimmon. Jamie is now an aged man, regarded as mad by all who know him because of his babbling about travelling in space. Whilst the Time Lords had supposedly wiped Jamie's mind of his travels in the TARDIS, it turns out that the brain-wipe didn't work, and he remembers that when they met the Cybermen (in 'The Invasion' – 1968), the Cyber Director mentioned meeting them on Planet Fourteen. Jamie travels with the Doctor to Marinus, where they find that evolution has continued at accelerated pace, so that the indigenous species whom Hartnell met, the Voord, have become the Cybermen. One of the Cybermen – who will later be the Cyber Director in 'The Invasion' – registers the 'aura' of the Doctor and Jamie, before the Scotsman gives his life to smash the world-shaper machine, thus stopping time and evolution advancing any further. The Doctor ponders whether to destroy the Cybermen now, at their very origins, before being stopped by some other Time Lords who, having viewed the future, know that, for all the destruction they will cause in the coming centuries the long-term evolution of the Cybermen is towards a non-physical existence which will lead all of sentient life to a new age of peace. All of this in just 24 pages.

Fan criticism of *The World Shapers* has been often harsh. Scott Gray's comments are representative.

> It's been observed that the Sixth Doctor's final television adventure was lumbered with an overly-complicated continuity-laden storyline. Sadly, his last comic strip tale follows suit. 'The World

Shapers' sees Grant Morrison proudly exposing his anorak with a story hopelessly tangled in the TV series' history.[27]

True enough, but the exact form those tangles take in *The World Shapers* is far removed from the television series with which Gray compares it. Much of the story's form is retrospectively familiar to anyone who read the novels produced in the 1990s. Three points would recur as ideas for future narratives.

1) An old companion is reintroduced, the effect of their travels with the Doctor is examined and they are finally killed (as will happen frequently in later novels: to Dodo in *Who Killed Kennedy*, Liz Shaw in *Eternity Weeps*, and Sarah Jane Smith in *Bullet Time*).[28]

2) Two distinct areas of the show are linked by process of historical change – here Marinus becomes Mondas, home planet of the Cybermen. *The New Adventures*, published by Virgin in the 1990s would be particularly fond of such links. Andy Lane and Jim Mortimores' novel *Lucifer Rising* would suggest that the Guild of Adjudicators ('Colony In Space', 1971) became the Grand Order of Oberon ('Revelation of the Daleks', 1985), whilst Gary Russell's book *Legacy* ties the 'Guardian of the Solar System' position from 'The Daleks' Master Plan' (1965/6) to the Galactic Federation seen in a couple of Pertwee stories ('The Curse of Peladon' [1972]/'The Monster of Peladon' [1974]). Martin Day's *The Menagerie* suggests that the Issigri Mining Company ('The Space Pirates', 1969) became the Interplanetary Mining Company ('Colony in Space', 1971), Steve Lyons' *Conundrum* asserts that the Land of Fiction ('The Mind Robber', 1968) was created by/for the Gods of Ragnarok ('The Greatest Show in the Galaxy', 1988), and Craig Hinton's *GodEngine* would establish that the Dalek invasion of Mars referred to by the Doctor in 'Genesis of the Daleks' (1975) occurred simultaneously to their invasion of Earth ('The Dalek Invasion of Earth', 1964). Other examples can be found.[29]

3) A minor, but unresolved, question of continuity (what did the Cyberleader mean in 1968 when he referred to a meeting on Planet Fourteen?) becomes a focal point of a whole story. Again, such narratives would proliferate in later years. The unlikely phrase 'silent gas dirigibles of the Hoothi,' uttered in passing in 1976's 'The Brain of Morbius' became the basis for the novel *Love and War*. The daddy of all examples may be Stephen Cole's *To the Slaughter* which was written with the express intent of explaining why the Doctor, speaking in 'Revenge of the Cybermen' (1975) got the number of moons of Jupiter wrong. The Doctor's line in that story, implying that a new moon would be the planet's thirteenth, was correct

when written, but outdated by transmission and scientists now count more than 60. Cole's book explodes dozens of them so that by the time of 'Revenge' (set in the far future) there are 12 again, and so the Doctor's astronomy is correct. Possibly, the only thing more bizarre than writing a book for this purpose is the author's willingness to publicly admit it in a note at the end.[30]

Whatever value we ascribe to these narrative manoeuvres, whether we love them or loathe them, they would become cornerstones of the 1990s storytelling format. The greater length of the novels would allow for far more subtle exposition in all areas, though some fans criticized them for exactly the same reasons that *The World Shapers* is decried.

Colin Baker's era came to an end amidst off-screen acrimony, as the discontent of fans and some production personnel alike spilled into the public arena in a way no television series has done before or since. Script editor Eric Saward left the programme, and immediately gave an interview with SF magazine *Starburst*, published in the September 1986 edition (available in August for the tail-end of the convention season) attacking Nathan-Turner's disinterest in storytelling and accusing him of spending too much time attending American conventions and overseeing merchandise. On ITV, writer/director Peter Grimwade, alienated by Nathan-Turner some years earlier, made *The Comeuppance of Captain Katt*, a one-off play about the behind-the-scenes shenanigans on a cheap SF show. Even the BBC hosted significant criticism, for whilst the Davison era had ended with Russell Harty, Colin Baker's concluded with *Open Air*. The *Harty* party had found cast and costumed fans smiling and confident about the future, and Russell Harty himself, whatever he really thought, was happy to appear keen on the programme and to discuss its apparent American success. On *Open Air*, overly earnest, bespectacled male fans from Merseyside (there were women sitting with them, possibly fans, but they were never invited to talk) faced writers Pip and Jane Baker in an item structured towards confrontation, and presenter Pattie Coldwell made no effort to hide her indifference: 'I have to say though, I've never got it. It's never struck me.'

Coldwell's opening gambit ('Do you have a favourite Doctor? ... Peter Davison, why?') struck a mainstream note, but conversation then turned around the incomprehensibility of the conclusion to the just-finished season-length story 'The Trial of a Time Lord'. The notion of comprehending the plot hobbled all further discussion about making a 'demanding' (Pip Baker's word) or 'challenging' (fan Chris Chibnall) programme, as if the only issue implied by such terms were following the story. Chibnall, as befits someone who would later write for the revived series and for *Torchwood*, made articulate points about 'Terror of the Vervoids': 'the story has been done in different ways ... a whodunit on board a starliner, very traditional sort of thing.' Familiarity with fan discourse – for those of us who have it – blinds us to the number of concepts in such a sentence: that *Who* repeats very specific formulas, that a whodunnit set on a starliner is one of them and that 'traditional' is a term with many, sometimes opposing connotations. None of these was taken up by the Bakers ('But I thought a lot of you *Doctor Who* fans liked traditional stories'; 'I'm glad not all *Doctor Who* fans come from Liverpool') or Coldwell, and how could anyone seriously expect them to? Twenty years later Chibnall would regret the antagonistic tone and recall 'I was struggling for words',[31] but what vocabulary could possibly bridge the conceptual gaps evident here?

Although the *Open Air* team probably weren't aware of exactly what they were doing, it is not purely coincidence that it was the programme's writers who took the brunt of public criticism, any more than it was coincidence that a writer was what Chibnall went on to become. Writing was what many fans aspired to do, and was the skill they most valued. Saward's *Starburst* interview set the agenda for criticism of Nathan-Turner for years afterwards not just because it as the most spectacularly public falling-out in the programme's history, but because it spoke to the same concerns. Whatever anyone thought of Saward's own writing, or the quality of the scripting under his editorship, his complaints were those of a writer who felt writing was being wrongly marginalized by other priorities. Fans had thrilled, through the 1980s, to comic strips more abstract, complex and experimental than anything on screen. It was to these fans that Target was responding in reshaping its novelizations towards greater length, more adult vocabularies and more individualistic styles. This was somewhere Nathan-Turner couldn't go. He lacked the background in writing and script-editing which some of his predecessors had brought to the producer's chair. The skills he had brought – getting the best visual look possible out of a

BBC budget – had been acclaimed in 1980/81 when fans' biggest concern was the allegedly 'shoddy' look of production values under Graham Williams, but for those who craved parity with the most prestigious of BBC dramas, a failure of narrative understanding was something which Nathan-Turner could never make up. When many thought that the programme had returned to form in 1988 the credit was given to the new script editor, Andrew Cartmel, who was widely credited with having a 'master plan' to renew the show.

THE NEXT GENERATION

The Seventh Doctor (Sylvester McCoy)

Season Twenty-Four (07/09/87 – 07/12/87)
Time and the Rani (4 episodes)
Paradise Towers (4 episodes)
Delta and the Bannermen (3 episodes)
Dragonfire (3 episodes)

Season Twenty-Five (05/10/88 – 04/01/89)
Remembrance of the Daleks (4 episodes)
The Happiness Patrol (3 episodes)
Silver Nemesis (3 episodes)
The Greatest Show in the Galaxy (4 episodes)

Season Twenty-Six (06/09/89 – 06/12/89)
Battlefield (4 episodes)
Ghost Light (3 episodes)
The Curse of Fenric (4 episodes)
Survival (3 episodes)

All produced by John Nathan-Turner and script edited by Andrew Cartmel (though Cartmel consistently distances himself from the opening story, which is certainly nothing like the ones he himself commissioned.)

Dimensions in Time
(3-D charity skit produced by John Nathan-Turner in which numerous Doctors, companions and monsters crossover into *EastEnders*. Broadcast as part of the *Children In Need* telethon and *Noel's House Party*).

Sylvester McCoy became the Seventh Doctor while the press continued to record the programme's ratings decline and fan discontent. The media were also continually reporting rumours that a new version – either on television or the big screen – would be made in America, possibly with Steven Spielberg's involvement. A binary opposition between the programme as it was being screened and some hypothetical glossy Hollywood version refused to go away, even though the beginnings of computer-generated graphics and the adoption of video for all location work (which had previously been done on film) created a new look for the programme. New script editor Andrew Cartmel hired young writers to reinvigorate the show. Many in fandom felt he had succeeded, and celebrated a vibrant return to form. It was not, however, enough to stop ratings decline and the axe finally fell on the programme in 1989. The BBC never publicly declared the demise of *Doctor Who*. By making statements about a new series sometime soon they denied fans and the press a moment of outright cancellation to rally round. Behind the scenes, the real concern appears to have been with American co-production deals, and this would finally bear fruit in 1996. In the absence of a programme itself, niche-marketed merchandise, often written and edited by fans for fans, proliferated, notably *The New Adventures*, a series of novels which presented itself as the official continuation of the deceased programme. This was the period when the professionals looked like fans and the fans turned professional. The historian's pen hovers before jumping in: *when everything's this connected, where to begin?*

What, we might ask, was it actually like watching *Doctor Who* as it staggered towards cancellation? There are as many answers to that as there are viewers, but it certainly became possible to answer the question in ways unthinkable a decade before. Jonathan Coe – who in the 1990s would become one of the nation's leading writers with acclaimed books such as *What A Carve Up* and *The Rotters Club* – cites the programme in his second novel, *The Dwarves of Death*. The narrator has dropped out of university after a year to pursue a career in music, and reflects

> For some reason I never took to student life – all those sad men cooking up Pot Noodles for themselves in shabby communal kitchens, taking them back to their rooms and eating them in front of *Dr Who* on a portable black and white TV.[1]

Had the experience of watching *Who* ever been described in such bleak terms before? References to the programme's Saturday slot would always evoke family, cosiness and 'tea-time'. Now it is seen as the preserve of 'sad' men in 'shabby' kitchens, who forego communality to watch, isolated, in their own rooms, on small, black-and-white televisions, a programme they should have outgrown over half a decade earlier. The 'tea-time' of *Who* mythology might cover a lot of things, but it surely meant a better meal than Pot Noodle. The novel being set in late 1988, Coe is probably talking about Season 24 (McCoy's debut) screened early in the last academic year (though I doubt he was thinking that exactly; nothing marks him as an outsider to fandom more than his use of *Dr* as the programme's title, a distinct rarity amongst anyone writing about the show by this time). But Coe's vision, though familiar enough to many at the time I'm sure, doesn't talk about the excitement which fans found in the programme's final two seasons.

The Masterplan

Why does the nature of *Doctor Who* merchandise change? In the first half of the 1980s, I have argued, John Nathan-Turner's visually aggressive version of the series coincided with the emergence of a fandom keen to discuss the style and techniques of television. This created a distinct market for products – one which led publishers to switch targets from a generalized notion of a mass, largely school-aged audience towards fans conceived of as consumers. In 1987, *Doctor Who* got a new script editor, Andrew Cartmel. His shake-up would change the relationship between the series and its major product lines for years to come.

Whilst outgoing script editor Eric Saward had increasingly looked to writers of significant television experience, Cartmel, still in his late twenties and with a background of working with the BBC Script Unit, looked to develop new writing talent. He cared less for experience than he did for a 'feel' (his recurrent word) for science fiction. Pip and Jane Baker, the Saward-era leftovers who kick off the McCoy era and then promptly vanish, probably had more on their CV than the rest of the late-1980s writers put together. With the programme marked as failing within the BBC, and some personnel consequently reluctant to work on it, this may have been inevitable, but there is nothing in Cartmel's recollections or interviews to suggest that this was anything other than his preference. He recruited from the BBC's writing workshops, and attempted to place new talent onto internal courses. He replied at length and encouragingly to submissions he felt showed promise. With few writing slots to fill, he suggested that budding writers create something of their own and directed them towards his own old stomping ground, the BBC Script Unit. This encouragement fed the ambitions of many in fandom who aspired to be authors, and who would become professionals in the 1990s. He commissioned the script 'Ghost Light' from Marc Platt. Platt was a contributor to fanzines, and a familiar face around fandom, who had been submitting stories since Philip Hinchcliffe's day. He had fallen foul of Nathan-Turner's mid-1980s policy of not hiring fans to write for the programme (when Platt and Jeremy Bentham had impressed Eric Saward with a story concerning the Sontarans set during the blitz, only to see it shelved at Nathan-Turner's insistence). The DWAS could number another *Who* writer amongst its number.[2]

Central to Cartmel's new direction was a drive to make the Doctor more proactive. Thus, the traditional format, whereby the TARDIS landed somewhere at random and its crew were drawn into local conflicts, came to share screen time with a new style of narrative. In these stories, as evil forces gathered strength, the Doctor's arrival would be revealed as far from accidental. He had come precisely to bring about a final conflict with some ancient enemy on his own terms. Some of these old enemies were the traditional favourites (Daleks, Cybermen), but some were previously unknown. The Seventh Doctor would keep his plans to himself until the precipitous moment late in the story. This, combined with a style of storytelling which often forewent the traditional scenes which sharply defined good from evil, produced a jigsaw style of storytelling which wasn't always easy to follow without a video recording to re-watch earlier episodes in the light of later ones (not even then in the case of the notoriously oblique 'Ghost Light'). Ratings unsurprisingly plummeted as the programme became something apparently designed for an analytical community used to producing and reading critical commentary in its spin-off products.

This need for interpretive work was escalated by other factors at work which compromised Cartmel's vision before it reached the screen, and meant it had to be deduced from what clues remained. The Colin Baker years had seen *Doctor Who* terribly disconnected from contemporary popular culture. Cartmel restored the link, but some of the connections he forged were with aspects of culture which were niche or oblique. Comics were primary amongst these influences, a medium itself undergoing a transformation at that time. Alan Moore's *2000AD* strip *The Ballard of Halo Jones* was recommended reading for all writers on *Who* in this period and Dr. Manhattan, a nuclear-powered superhero who viewed all of time simultaneously in the same author's *Watchmen*, came to influence Cartmel's take on the Doctor himself. He attempted to hire Moore as a writer, but it couldn't be done.

Many of the comics which enthused Cartmel weren't available in newsagents or supermarkets, but could only be purchased in specialist comics/SF stores. The readership reached in this way was older and more sophisticated. This allowed the writers and artists to play with the form of comics, privileging storytelling form over plot and engaging with sexual and political themes. Like most modernist art, the difficulty of reading some of these comics – of, in some cases, simply following the plot from one panel to another – enhanced the aura of complexity that circulated around these works. In seeking to adopt the themes of 'graphic novels', however, Cartmel's writing team faced resistance. Although the show was being transmitted at a later time than ever before (7:35

p.m. – opposite the iconic ITV soap opera *Coronation Street*) writer Ian Briggs knew that his wish to write about code-breaker Alan Turing's homosexuality in his wartime story 'The Curse of Fenric' was a non-starter, 'so instead of making him [the character of Judson] crippled by his sexual orientation we made him literally a cripple ... he's a physical cripple in the same way that Alan Turing must have felt in his life'.[3] *Doctor Who* was no stranger to allegory and symbolism, but the metaphorical jump from Judson's wheelchair to Turing's homosexuality was a big one.

Other ideas developed by Cartmel and his writers were resisted by John Nathan-Turner. One involved the idea that the Doctor was the third person of a legendary Gallifreyan trinity who had founded Time Lord society. Cartmel remembers that

> The notion of Doctor Who as God didn't sit too well with John. He felt there might be religious repercussions ... he's a Godlike being to the Gallifreyans, but John just heard the word 'God' and he was going like this [puts hands over ears], 'This is going to get us all into terrible trouble' ... so I just cut off that line of enquiry.[4]

Kevin Clarke, author of 'Silver Nemesis', recalls things differently.

> John Nathan-Turner and Andrew looked at me expectantly, I said 'The question we have all been asking ourselves for 25 years is Doctor Who? Who is the Doctor?' They both leaned forward and said 'Well, who is he?' ... I came out with 'It's obvious. He came among us, mucked things up because he is so forgetful, but has sort of worked it out in the end. He is God.' John and Andrew both looked terrified. John eventually said 'You can do that as long as you don't say it.'[5]

Quotes like this swiftly entered fandom because by the late 1980s *DWM* and *DWB* both interviewed the programme's writers as soon as they possibly could. The magazines relayed to the readers some of the material which never made it to the screen, and highlighted some of the inexplicit meanings, thus justifying the search for many more. Whichever version of Nathan-Turner's reaction to the 'Doctor as God' we accept – as a line of enquiry he had cut off completely, or as something he authorized providing it wasn't done explicitly – interpretation of the McCoy years necessarily became a search for some aborted level or hidden meaning. This process was escalated when Cartmel's instructions to write scripts as long as necessary, and not to worry about running time, led to stories coming in massively over the required length and requiring severe cutting down in the editing suite.

All of this necessarily changed the relationship between the programme and its major merchandising. The McCoy stories were all novelized by their own authors (save 'Battlefield', which was done by 'Ghost Light' author Marc Platt) with many of the excised scenes reinstated and the themes expanded. Moreover, since the show's writers had been encouraged to share ideas at large meetings, the themes of the individual stories started to bleed into each other in their novelized form. Ace's Asian friend Manisha, mentioned only in 'Ghost Light' on screen, gets several references in the novelization of 'Remembrance of the Daleks'. That same book's immersion in memories of World War Two (though it is set in 1963) means that it often covers the same thematic ground as 'The Curse of Fenric'; Alan Turing is mentioned, one character's father was 'lost at sea', as is the husband of a young woman in 'Fenric'.

For these reasons, the books began to look like the definitive versions of these stories whilst the television shows looked like précis. The search was on for a less compromised version of what became known by fans – but not the production office – as 'The Cartmel Masterplan'. When novelizations didn't quite reveal it, there were videos, and later DVDs, with excised footage returned to its proper positions, or included as extras. The DVD of 'Battlefield', released in 2008, re-edits the story, replaces some cut material and adds a small amount of new CGI shots, becoming in the process a substantial improvement upon the transmitted version. DVDs like this, or 'Ghost Light' and 'The Curse of Fenric', came loaded with authorial interviews and interpretive extras, revealing the obscured intentions more than a decade after their original transmissions. 'Millington and Judson are gay. Well, if I ever thought that then I've long since forgotten it', declared *DWM*'s reviewer, Vanessa Bishop, upon watching the extras on 'Fenric'.[6] When original novels were produced from 1991 onwards, they provided more clues, and Cartmel wrote several comic strips for DWM. All took their readers closer to the mythic master plan, but none ever quite delivered.

As the example of Judson's sexuality suggests, fans were searching not only for a narrative meaning, but also a political one, in Cartmel's *Who*. That was something which could be rendered more completely in niche-marketed novelizations than in prime-time television where the BBC would face accusations of ideological bias. Most producers and script editors had been content to keep the programme's liberal/soft-left biases as vague as possible, often blurring political edges.[7] By contrast, Cartmel's *Who* entered the culture wars with a whole load of attitude which could not be explicitly stated in a children's programme. Again, attitudes viewed fragmentarily on screen were to be found fully developed in the novels. During the final season, when a nineteenth-century churchman was devolved into an ape to show him the folly of his anti-evolutionary arguments ('Ghost Light'), and a wartime parson loses his faith ('The Curse of Fenric'), many detected anti-Christian arguments. Briggs' novelization of the latter characteristically eschews the coyness of the television episodes and lets rip full-blast, calling Christianity a 'two-thousand-year-old lie'.[8] It is hard to imagine Malcolm Hulke writing that.

I call this bluntness 'characteristic' because, whilst the novelizations had been changing fast, getting longer and more sophisticated throughout the 1980s, 'Fenric' is where all the barriers come down. Two years earlier, Briggs had complained in *DWM* about editorial changes made to his novelization of 'Dragonfire', including the substitution of the word 'underwear' for his original 'knickers'. That taboo was apparently lifted by the time he wrote 'Fenric', because there it is on p. 52: 'Come on, get your knickers on' (it is surely also the first *Who* novelization with the word 'whorehouse' used – p. 184). But even whilst 'knickers' had been pulled from the earlier book, more subtle descriptions had been allowed, or sneaked, through. Entering the service of the villain Kane is described in frankly sexual terms as Ace ponders it ('Why *shouldn't* she give herself to Kane? Even if he was evil – at least he wanted her. No one else had ever cared about her' – p. 46) and the Doctor provokes Belazs in similar terms ('How much did you sell yourself for? Was it worth it? Were *you* worth it?' – p. 66).[9]

If the novels could not actually lay out the hypothetical master-plan, these more adult themes and greater literary ambition could at least provide suitable reading for fans who were now in their twenties or older. Many of the techniques on display weren't new, and whilst some fans raved about these books, others claimed they still weren't as sophisticated as 1970s titles such as 'The Doomsday Weapon'. What was new was a formal and generic playfulness. Some books told the story not just through reported third person action, but via a range of documents and perspectives. Outside of the McCoy stories, only the novelizations of Donald Cotton (see last chapter) used such techniques, but 'The Curse of Fenric' characteristically took it to an extreme, beginning with a page long act of narration, calling the very story into being: 'Every story must have a beginning, a middle, and an end ... I'm just a grumpy old man and you want me to shut up and get on with the story.' Few novelizations were so overtly self-conscious, but it became a significant practice to begin with some present-tense philosophizing before cutting to past-tense narrative. Thus, 'Terror of the Vervoids' begins 'At the apex of the cosmic evolutionary scale is the ultimate refinement of creation – a society composed of Time Lords', 'Silver Nemesis' commences 'The closer one travels towards it from the cold silent darkness of infinite space, the more the planet Earth appears as a backcloth to some small theatrical performance taking place on a limited budget,' and 'The Ultimate Evil' opens with the observation that 'There is no total darkness in the universe'.[10]

This new self-consciousness about storytelling had its root in the programme itself. Cartmel and his writers were aware of both the programme's place in television history and its copious spin-off texts, incorporating elements of both into their scripts. In 'Ghost Light' the Doctor cites *The Hitchhikers' Guide to the Galaxy*, the best-selling radio show/novel/TV programme/towel by ex-*Who* scriptwriter Douglas Adams, whilst 'Dragonfire', in which supporting characters are named for film theorists such as Bazin and Arnheim, directly quotes the academic textbook *The Unfolding Text* when a philosophically inclined guard asks the Doctor what he thinks of the 'assertion that the semiotic thickness of a performed text varies according to the redundancy of auxiliary production codes'.[11] Boastful title aside, 'The Greatest Show in the Galaxy' concerned a circus where acts must perform for entertainment-starved aliens disguised as a nuclear family (mother, father and daughter). Once the acts cease to amuse, they are destroyed, a poignant allegory at a time when the programme's own fate was so delicately balanced. Notoriously, one of the characters was a caricature fan: an earnest and socially unskilled adolescent male who claimed to follow the circus and its history – and who was happy to tell the current acts that he knew they weren't as good as previous ones he'd only ever heard of. 'Remembrance of the Daleks' deployed a wealth of metafictional games: Daleks in the school playground, just like they were in a thousand childhood games; companion Ace hiding behind a sofa; a Dalek Emperor, like that in the 1960s comic strip; the Doctor flees upstairs from a Dalek, confident it can't follow, only for the creature to levitate after him; Ace switching off the television as it announces 'This is BBC Television. The time is a quarter past five and Saturday viewing continues with an adventure in the new science-fiction series, Do-'. This, rather than endless returns of old, half-forgotten monsters, was how to play with the programme's primal imagery. It was nothing less than the cult reading incorporated into the programme itself. For those fans who embraced that reading, the final two series constituted a remarkable return to form. For those who never took to it, the McCoy era was the final nail in the coffin. As the cult reading spread in the 1990s, some people would revise their opinion of these stories.

Again, this would all be escalated in the novelizations. 'Remembrance', the novel, vividly reimagined motifs from across the programme's history. It began with a prologue retelling part of the show's very first episode, flashed back to the development of time travel by superstitious Gallifreyans (who make 'the ward sign against evil' – p. 93), cited invented history books about the programme's icons ('The Zen Military – A History of UNIT'; 'The Children of Davros: A Short History of the Dalek Race'), quoted bits of the Dalek language, and threw in *another* Timewar ('*Pa Jass-Vortan* – the time campaign, the war to end all wars' – p. 129). The book made a sentence-long attempt to reconcile the programme's two conflicting versions of the Daleks' origins (p. 29), and contained several accounts of Dalek thoughts/consciousness, complete with descriptions of how the organic being interfaces with the technological components. As a sign of its literary self-confidence, the book prefaced itself with a quote from Shakespeare's 'Richard III' (only the second *Who* novelization, after *Mawdryn Undead*, to have a prefacing quotation). 'The Curse of Fenric' evoked the same collage effect, including a hand-drawn map of Europe; a 12-year-old's school essay; a fake Icelandic saga complete with footnotes and a translation credit; a letter from Bram Stoker (implying that this story's blood-sucking monsters were the inspiration for *Dracula*); an ancient Arabian tale about how El Dok-Tar defeated an evil genie and a flash-forward to Ace's life after she'd left the Doctor.[12]

The writers could play these narrative games and intersections precisely because they were as enmeshed in pop culture as the fans were. When they attended conventions they were revealed to be young men in jeans and T-shirts, media-hip and wielding smart-alec senses of humour. Fans could look at them, and – unlike previous generations of pipe-smoking BBC stalwarts such as Robert Holmes – see themselves in a few years time. Looking at Ian Briggs, it didn't take much to imagine yourself a *Doctor Who* writer. Many would get their chance when the programme's cancellation transformed the marketplace for *Who* products.

Legacy

The programme died in 1989, but fandom continued. As the 1983/4 membership bulge entered the job market, or eyed it nervously from near-completed degree courses, they had more disposable income than ever before. Cancellation meant the end of the programme as a mass-merchandising phenomenon, but those companies which understood the niche market prospered. Virgin, who had brought out Target, would publish original novels. They began on a bimonthly schedule, moved to monthly, and were finally published twice a month, sometimes with a non-fiction publication on top. In the years immediately after the cancellation, *Doctor Who Magazine* produced annual-type *Yearbooks*, went to 13 issues a year (a four-weekly schedule, though everyone still called it 'the monthly') and garnered a sister publication, *Doctor Who Classic Comics* which reprinted old comic strips from the 1960s and 1970s. In 1995, an exhibition of props and costumes opened in Llangollen, Wales, next to the site of the Dapol toy factory, the producers of *Who* play figures. The market for all these products was small but incredibly stable. Virgin editor Peter Darvill-Evans would later explain that 'We would print 25,000 copies – but we sold virtually every one ... no returns, no wastage, predictable sales'. John Freeman, editor of the *Monthly* during this period would later report 'one issue sold 92 per cent of its print run, where most magazines expect only

50 per cent to remain profitable (that kind of efficiency impresses accountants)'.[13] *Doctor Who* was no longer broadcast – it was niche-marketed with precision. Fans, enjoying products aimed at no one but themselves, had won the interpretation wars, but the cost was not only their beloved show's cultural centrality, but its actual existence. In 1993, Gareth Roberts, later a writer on the revived programme, reflected that *Who* 'sits on a shelf in Woolies marked 'T.V. Sci-Fi' when it used to occupy the hearts of the nation's children. You can buy magazines and books containing long lists of extras' names when there used to be 'TV Comic' and Target Books.'[14]

Roberts was writing in *Skaro*, a prominent fanzine of the period. As the programme and its novels grew ever more sophisticated so did the commentary surrounding them. From November 1991, *DWM* began its Archive features, scrupulous accounts of the production of every *Who* story ever made which took advantage of the more substantial access to BBC paperwork which researchers could now enjoy. In the amateur world, fanzines had shifted to A4 paper size, a necessity because fandom had outgrown A5. It didn't show photographs to their best advantage, lacked the flexibility now open to 'zines using sophisticated printing techniques, and its small word count per page (relative to A4) was insufficient now that more detailed arguments required longer articles and interviews. Away from the excesses of its JNT-bashing editorial and letters-pages, *DWB* matured into a mixture of news, opinion, review/analysis and historical research, making available to its readers in this period the first comprehensive – and correct – list of ratings. This new information buried some myths which had circulated for a decade or more (e.g.: that 'The Gunfighters' had the worst ever ratings). The *Bulletin* inspired a host of zines, such as *Private Who*, which, despite the title, soon dropped its satirical edge and became full of location reports and merchandise reviews, and *The Frame* which covered production issues and merchandise history in previously undreamt of detail. This latter boasted production values greater than *DWM*, and was printed on paper so thick and glossy that its editorial team had to suffer jokey comparisons with pornography. All of this was inevitable as production techniques escalated with the availability of publishing packages for household computers, but it brought forth agonized hand-wringing from fans who associated the old format with a golden period of debate earlier in the decade. A5 returned in the early 1990s as a counter movement to the new upscale production values with a rush of 'zines boasting semi-silly names not taken from the series itself (*Purple Haze*, *Alien Corn*) and mixing sarcastic humour about the programme's perceived failings with graduate-analysis.

Fandom as it is known and practiced today comes into view here. An account of the programme's production history written before 1990 will appear to modern eyes to be hopelessly basic and riddled with errors. Similarly, although there are exceptions, most fanzine content before this date would seem simplistic in its critical analysis and overly earnest in its dewy-eyed blindness to the programme's failings. Fanzine articles from before the late 1980s are short to modern eyes, focus on those areas of the show where *DWM* had taught appreciation and take an inflexible view of the programme's generic affiliations. They are earnest where later writers would be relaxed, even glib, and lack what became the norm by the early 1990s: an assumption on the part of the writers that the readers shared their total familiarity with the programme's history and plotlines.

Thus, across varied publications in the late 1980s, fans came to grips with a more substantial production history of the programme, and this is the point where distinctions between fan and professional work were totally broken. Ever since Jeremy Bentham had provided episode guides for Peter Haining and John Tulloch/Manuel Alvarado, fans had worked behind the scenes of professional publications, supplying and checking the basic series information whilst the journalists and academics brought their own skills and sensibilities to bear. In 1983 that had perhaps been necessary but with fans the only audience left, the mainstream professionals had nothing to offer. The team of David J. Howe, Mark Stammers and Stephen James Walker would write professional books on the programme's history for Virgin whilst executing *The Frame* to a similarly high level of production. Similarly, the editorial reigns of the major product lines were handed to those who knew the series well. Peter Darvill-Evans applied for the editorial job at Target/Virgin because 'I'd watched Doctor Who from the very first episode ... I'd enjoyed the show and I would have described myself as a fan' (even though he was unaware that there had been novelizations for 15 years). At *DWM*, John Freeman, who had joined the DWAS in 1979, became editor from June 1988, and all editors since have needed fan pasts as well as editorial experience on their CVs. (When *DWM* wrote their own history, this phase was prefaced 'This is how the lunatics took over the asylum ...').[15]

Cancellation also allowed fandom to widen its interests. Many fans had by now held every possible conversation about the programme, and regarded fandom primarily as a social arena. They were, after all, a community of people with similar interests in the media, who thought about culture in much the same way, and a liberal politics held sway. Beyond supporting the BBC licence fee, fandom had never really had a pervasive political mood prior to the late 1980s. In the early days, the prime movers of the DWAS had mostly kept their political convictions separate to their appreciation of the programme and 'Fan-Aid' – fandom's first major charity publications/events in aid of African famine relief in the mid-1980s – had operated under a logic of charity rather than politics. When, in 1984, the DWAS newsletter, *Celestial Toyroom*, had reproduced a picture of Margaret Thatcher as a Dalek (the image was taken from a notepad available commercially) the editor was forced to explain himself to those fans who'd felt the newsletter shouldn't make political comment of any persuasion. Andrew Cartmel, however, had spun the programme substantially to the left, and younger fans, who might not yet have formed political views, were fewer on the ground. Without new episodes to act as the overriding concern, some things not apparent before came starkly into focus. People had joked about how fandom was disproportionately male since its inception, but by 1990 it was apparent that it was disproportionately gay as well, something not really visible – perhaps not even true – five years earlier.[16]

The new liberalism came to affect interpretations of the programme. In the 1970s, it had been common to regard *Doctor Who* as concerning the battle between good and evil, but the new political agenda questioned such terms. 'Survival', the final story televised, found the Doctor in conflict with the alien 'Cheetah People' (although talk of "monsters" continued to circulate extra-textually). The novelization of 'The Curse of Fenric', as ever, saw the culmination of such thinking. Questioned by his companion Ace about whether Fenric was evil, the Doctor replies 'No, simply a part that was out of balance. Nature is a perfect balance – a harmony between good and evil, between love and hate, between heaven and hell. Evil can only exist in harmony with good.'[17] It is a philosophical reading without precedent in *Who*, and in direct contradiction of some of the Doctor's previous statements on the necessity of fighting evil. There were limits to how far such a direction could go – and how many people wanted it to – given the generic necessity of villains. When the *New Adventures* series of novels began in 1991 (see below) such outright relativity would be modified into regular earnest lectures on cultural specificity. The first *New Adventure, Timewyrm: Genesys* laid out the agenda neatly with this speech by the Doctor.

> Ace, these trips of ours are supposed to broaden your mind. Stop thinking in twentieth century terms for a while … It's not just the TARDIS that has relative dimensions, Ace, but the societies that we visit too.[18]

Many such sermons followed, though the new reading was also deployed more deftly in comments such as 'I wasn't much of a military advisor – I kept holding conflict resolution seminars'.[19] For some, the programme's primary virtue came to be its apparent belief in tolerance of others and the equivalence of different cultures.

In this new intimate atmosphere, fanzines and jokey newssheets appeared designed exclusively for circulation at the Fitzroy Tavern or other gatherings. Fan Olympiads were events where fans met in (initially) Bath, to drink, meet up and take part in jokey mostly-*Who*-themed versions of popular television game shows such as *Fifteen-to-One* and *Family Fortunes*. For these new laid-back fans, the butt of many jokes were 'fanboys', a derogatory term denoting those who'd never grown out of the early stages of fan activity (collecting autographs, caring about continuity). Fan*boys* connoted not just a failure to come to maturity, but every geeky aspect of the Y chromosome. 'Emotional, if not political Nazis'[20] was perhaps the most hyperbolic judgement passed on them, and demonstrates how, in some people's minds at least, the personal failings of fandom's unwashed became tied up with the political polarizations of the Thatcher period. The term was imported from comic fandom, where it denoted those who would not read the sophisticated products of independent publishers, but who were uncritical consumers of the product of the big companies (often expressly Marvel). In *Who* fandom, the term carried all the same connotations of slavish devotion. Fanboys, though, were a mostly mythical entity. No one ever claimed to be one, or pointed the finger expressly at anyone they actually knew. They were an off-stage mass, laughed at for doing all the things which those doing the laughing had done six or seven years earlier. More than anything else, evoking 'fanboys' was a way for twenty-something fans to disassociate their current identities from their 14-year-old selves.

Some controversies remained. *DWB* continued to rake over old issues, and dissect who was responsible for the programme's demise (though in the pages of *DWB* the answer to that question was never in doubt!). The magazine promoted a 'Day of Action' (when fans should all ring the BBC and demand the programme's return) and investigated the possibility of a legal challenge, but neither generated much support. Campaigning for the programme's reinstatement would have been … well, just too fanboy. With nearly five thousand readers *DWB* boasted a readership beyond anything the fan world had seen before, but its more excitable concerns simply weren't the centre of events anymore. Arguments about good or bad ways to make the show carried less urgency now that it wasn't being made at all. Being a *Doctor Who* fan had morphed into something less about a particular show than a given way of watching television, particularly drama, and caring about its aesthetics.

This new mood played havoc with the canon of judgments which had seen fandom through the 1980s. The Graham Williams era was rehabilitated. This was partly because the detailed production research demonstrated clearly the strict limitations he was working under, but also because fans looked at his stories in a new light. Jokes which had gone over the heads of their eleven-year-old selves (such as this exchange from 'The Horns of Nimon': 'He lives in the Power Complex', 'That fits'.) were better understood. Moreover, fans with degrees in media studies, cultural studies or literature had theories of postmodernism and self-reflexive art (reading strategies also encouraged by the McCoy era) with which to appreciate those same moments which had once been decried as 'send-up'. Season 17's 'City of Death' took up full-time residence in the top ten of any sizeable poll. Similarly, 'The Gunfighters' crawled off the absolute bottom of the opinion polls, finding some champions who would regard its humour as sophisticated, though it remains low-rated to this day.

More controversial was the critical mauling handed out to the Pertwee era. Originating in the same graduate fanzines (*Perigosto Stick*, *Spectrox*) as the Williams renaissance, this view took arms against the received wisdom which said that the Third Doctor's episodes were a series highlight, and argued instead that Jon Pertwee's stories were repetitive and formally unadventurous. This wasn't just a product of fandom's new sophistication. It was also the product of new viewing conditions. No one had recognized the repetitious nature or padding of Pertwee's stories when they were watched an episode per week in the 1970s. Viewing all six episodes of a given story in one sitting, as video allowed, rendered those repetitions obvious. In the politicized fandom of the period, some viewed the Third Doctor as a patriarchal, establishment figure. Heated exchanges took place (especially when these issues spilled onto that new invention, the internet), since criticism of the Pertwee era was often felt to be linked to an assertion of the value of something more sophisticated, be it the Williams era or the McCoy stories. Most of the critical points would work into the mainstream of fan opinion. By 1996, even *DWM* would rehearse the major arguments in a piece where regular columnist Matthew Jones traced his complex journey from love with Pertwee's Doctor to boredom and political embarrassment and back again.[21] These arguments had no impact outside fandom, of course. Video sales for the period 1984 – May 1997 showed that Pertwee's stories sold marginally better than those of any other Doctor.[22]

The early 1990s was a period when the BBC would release two *Who* videos every other month, something fans could only have dreamed of a few years earlier. Indeed, although fans nursing the wounds from their ridicule, not to mention the programme's cancellation, could be forgiven for not noticing it, most of the cultural developments in the 1980/90s went their way. As the show left British screens, courses studying popular culture were an established and rapidly expanding part of the universities, whilst the emergence of 'cult TV' as a niche marketing strategy meant an ongoing stream of material released in different forms. In the US, *Star Trek: The Next Generation* debuted in September 1987, kicking off two decades of cult fantasy series: *Twin Peaks*, *The X-Files*,

Stargate, Buffy the Vampire Slayer, Babylon 5, Battlestar Galactica and many others.

When it finally arrived in the UK, three years after its US debut, the BBC tucked the new *Star Trek* away on BBC2 at 6 p.m. a slot often given over to 'family-friendly' entertainment (if not outright children's shows) as counter-programming to the 'adult' news on BBC1. *Who* fans took this as evidence of the corporation's ongoing bias against science fiction. This attitude contrasted with that of the fledgling SKY satellite/digital channel, which understood the emerging televisual economy whereby cult viewers would be a valuable audience component. Consequently, SKY stripped the show across weekdays at 5 p.m., repeated it endlessly, and made subsequent *Trek* spin-offs important parts of their evening schedules.

This raft of new programmes and the release of old fantasy shows on video set a context for the way in which *Doctor Who* would be positioned in the 1990s. If the cancelled programme could not stand on its own two feet, its legacy and back-catalogue could be inserted into this emerging mix of SF television. Nowhere was this truer than in the offices of Visual Imagination where new titles were regularly launched: *TV Zone* (debuting in 1989), *Shivers* (1992), *Cult Times* (1995), *Xpose* (1996) and others. In 1994, *DWB* cancelled itself, then relaunched professionally as *Dreamwatch*. Fan writers, students of the televisual art for a decade now, were uniquely placed to provide the commentary around these episodes which 'needed' reviewing, and whose cast and crew 'required' interviewing. From 1995, fans could also find employment with Future Publishing which entered the market with *SFX* (which rapidly became the market leader in science-fiction magazines) and, briefly, *Cult TV*. The cost was to accept the marginalization implied by the titles themselves (*Cult TV, Cult Times, TV Zone: The Magazine of Cult Television*). Barely six or seven years earlier, *Who* fans had doggedly resented such a definition of their favourite programme. Few quibbled at this point, however. Fans had saleable skills in this new information economy, and by the time the old century became the new, even genre was no barrier, with *Who* fans producing episode guides for non-fantasy dramas such as *The West Wing*.[23]

By the 1990s, fandom had evolved into a specific way of watching television programmes. It could just as easily be a way of making them. The 1990s would see many fans in their early 20s/30s emerge as writers and production staff within the industry, bringing their fan sensibilities with them. Russell T. Davies' children's series *Dark Season*, broadcast in November/December 1991, is a prime example. Commissioned as six 25-minute episodes, Davies (already proving himself as a man with the ability to revive faded formulas) split the series into two three-part stories. In the first episode, a company promises free computers to all children at a local school. This arouses the suspicions of Marcie Hatter, an unusually acute 13-year-old given to gnomic utterances, usually made to her friends, Reet (played by a young Kate Winslet) and Thomas, who can only follow in her wake. Before Marcie can investigate, however, another schoolgirl, Olivia, is taken away by the company, notionally for publicity photos with the free computers. Instead, they take her to their factory, and enact a transformation upon her, one which is activated simply by switching on the computer and typing 'Hello' at the keyboard. The episode ends on a double-cliff-hanger as Olivia returns to school, now radiant with bright, white light, whilst Reet and Thomas switch on their own computer, potentially dooming themselves to the same fate. We needn't concern ourselves with the explicit *Doctor Who* homages within the series, but rather emphasize how familiar *Who* fans would find this style of storytelling.

Though this – and a follow-up *Century Falls* – attained good reviews, the programme attracting most attention in *Who* fandom was another children's comedy-drama. This one was on ITV, and would generate its own fandom, with many members drawn from that of *Who*. *Press Gang*, written by an ex-teacher from Paisley, Steven Moffat, debuted on 16 January 1989. The series concerned the *Junior Gazette*, a children's newspaper run out of a school. The *Gazette*'s staff were made up of academic high-fliers (who held editorial positions), and delinquent underachievers (placed on the paper to shape up), and the *will they-won't they?* romance of officious editor Lynda Day, and slacker reporter Spike Thompson crossed the class divide. In the opening episode, the sign outside the office reads *Trespassers Will Be Exterminated* – Moffat's first *Who* reference occurs five minutes into his career! The programme ran for five years, generating fanzines and conventions with *Who* connections. Virgin wouldn't let Paul Cornell write an episode guide, but Jim Sangster had better luck at Leomac Publishing. *Who* fan and entrepreneur Gary Russell named several companies after episodes of the programme: *Page One Productions, Photo Finish Productions, Rock Solid Productions, At Last, A Dragon! Productions* and *Big Finish Productions*. This last, set up with another *PG*-loving *Who* fan, Jason Haigh-Ellery, would release new adventures on CD and via download featuring Doctors Five through Eight in the new millennium.

Press Gang's fan appeal lay in its generic knowingness and formal experimentation. As both an 'opposites attract' romantic comedy and an 'investigative reporters' series, *Press Gang* twisted generic expectations, played with chronology and presented stylised fantasy/dream sequences. It had striking visuals, shifted tone suddenly (after Spike and Lynda kiss for the first time, viewers, anticipating fuller development of the romantic plotline, were suddenly given a two-part story about child abuse) and sometimes broke completely with the normative style ('At Last a Dragon' featured only three of the regulars and had no scenes set in the newsroom save for flashbacks to the first episode). The plotting was dense, with episodes like 'The Big Hello' (which I'm not even going to try and summarize – watching the episode would be quicker than any explanation) cramming a more complex investigation story into 25 minutes than most detective shows manage in an hour, and the dialogue sparkled: 'Kenny, have you any idea how humiliating it is to take your escape artist home in a box?'

Beyond all of this (isn't this enough?) *Gang*'s gift to a fandom glutted on authorial signatures was Moffat's returning constantly to favored motifs. Restaurant scenes proliferate, and no one ever wrote more jokes or set-pieces around telephones. A strange amount of characters' surnames are derived from male Christian names (Colin Matthews, Spike Thompson, Kenny Phillips, Frazz Davis, Julie Craig, Chrissie Stewart and Sarah Jackson – no wonder actress Lucy Benjamin got a part). As a fan himself, Moffat gave *Press Gang* the things which TV fans loved: season finales with big cliff-hangers, rigorous continuity and a slew of running jokes and references which repaid those who watched and rewatched the text to pull out its minutia. At the end of the second season, it is remarked that the news team having been following the Spike/Lynda romance 'since page one', and only the fans remembered – or discovered on reviewing – that 'Page One' was the title of the first episode. American sci-fi writer-producers of the 1990s (Joss Whedon, Chris Carter) would do all this to rapturous acclaim, but Moffat got there first, and he did it all in a children's TV slot. His was the first show to arrive with a British fan's sensibility to formal possibilities.

Moffat and Davies were high-fliers by anyone's standards, running their own shows early in the 1990s. A lot of fan writers found a slower, but surer, route into writing careers when Virgin ran out of old *Who* adventures to novelize and so began to publish original novels as the official continuation of the cancelled series.

The New Adventures

By the time the twentieth century had become the twenty-first, *DWM* staff would occasionally muse on why their comic strip (by then featuring the Eighth Doctor, as played by Paul McGann, in an excellent run of adventures) was never considered the true inheritor of the television series in a way that the novels were – this despite the fact that the magazine sold better! By that point, the novels were published by the BBC itself, which may have been enough to authenticate them in some peoples' eyes, but the longer story is that DWM had relinquished the initiative and Virgin had seized it keenly. Once regular artist John Ridgway left – after one story featuring Sylvester McCoy – the comic strip had no ongoing creative team. Different writers and artists came and went from story to story. You can't fault the variety, and it allowed for some emergent talent to gain experience, notably Bryan Hitch, a comics artist who would become a concept artist on the revived programme. However, it also deprived the strip of the long-term thinking which had been so key to its excellence under previous creative teams. Marvel also released a new publication, *The Incredible Hulk Presents*, aimed at younger readers with a five-page *Doctor Who* comic strip with a lighter tone and less sophisticated stories. Economies were to have been made by reprinting these strips in *DWM*, something which would have fragmented even further the aesthetic tone of that magazine's strip, but *Hulk Presents* lasted only 12 issues and only one story was reprinted. In the early 1990s, *DWM* would defer all aesthetic leadership to Virgin, adopting their new companion, Bernice Summerfield, and setting its own stories in the gaps between the novels. When this failed, it gave up completely on the Seventh Doctor and presented stories featuring past incarnations. At DWM, Doctor Who's narrative seemed to have stopped. Summer and winter specials issued in the early 90s were themed, and cover copy set a completist tone ('Who is Sarah Jane Smith? Full Biography Inside', 'The Definitive Guide to the Time Lords of Gallifrey') as if the programme was something which was over and could now be recorded in its entirety. By this point it had begun to use the mid/late-seventies blue diamond logo like any other *Who* nostalgia product.[24]

These attitudes contrasted markedly with decisions made at Virgin (where they would have argued that the Time Lords were alive and well and new information was gushing forth). With only a handful of stories from the whole 26-year run remaining to be novelized, the company negotiated, in 1989, the right to produce original novels based on the show. When cancellation hit, this made them the obvious keepers of the flame. Editor Peter Darvill-Evans resisted the pleas of some fans for the diamond logo to be used or for the books to use old Doctors and companions. The novels began where the TV series ended, and continued to use the current logo, McCoy's Doctor and his companion Ace. Darvill-Evans' rhetoric was inspiring.

> With the television series off the air, apparently for ever ... It is crucial to demonstrate that Doctor Who still has the potential and the adaptability to support new stories ... that its supporters are more than a dwindling band of trainspotter types who are content to pore over old videotape ... if we spend time looking into the past of our favourite television series, we can hardly blame the BBC for failing to look to its future.[25]

These novels could do what the fans (the only audience) had waited so long for – jump from the children's section to the bookshops' adult SF shelves. This meant upping the length (the books were over 200 pages long, often nearer 300) and dealing with themes of a more adult nature. This led to some predictable tabloid coverage when sporadic subject matter (a temple prostitute in *Timewyrm: Genesys*; drugs in *The Left-Handed Hummingbird*) generated headlines juxtaposing these themes with the innocent pleasures of traditional *Who*. Virgin, a company which thrived on an edgy, rebellious image and which was linked prominently to youth culture through its record stores, was just the right company to publish such novels. Whilst the timing of these books' launch was determined to some degree by the end of the television series and the completion of the novelization process, the *New Adventures* series was very much part of a publishing trend. As television series were merchandised as never before and fantasy shows flooded onto American screens, an increasing number of programmes were spun off into the format, and a number of *New Adventures* authors wrote for the novels of other series; John Peel on *Star Trek*, Jim Mortimore for *Babylon 5*. By the late nineties, readers of literary SF were complaining about how the shelf space of SF sections was being swamped with tie-in series, and the books which interested them were being forced out.

Through the McCoy novelizations, Darvill-Evans was in contact with the programme's final scriptwriters. Recent writers Andrew Cartmel, Marc Platt and Ben Aaronovitch all contributed early volumes, as did long-term Who novelist and Pertwee-era script-editor Terrance Dicks, thus legitimizing the series as the legitimate heir of the television show. The Cartmel Masterplan (still not really called that) was finally committed to paper in a document authored by Cartmel, Platt and Aaronovitch, and dated 9/11/1990.[26] Submission guidelines had been sent out to interested parties earlier that year. A four-book sequence was planned where the Doctor would face a cyberspace entity, the Timewyrm, across the distant past, the twentieth century, the far future and conclude in some more abstract setting. Whilst the first three books were commissioned from authors with *Who* novelizations already printed, the fourth was found from the submissions pile: *Timewyrm: Revelation* came from the pen of long-term fan, Paul Cornell.

Cornell had entered fandom as part of the post-Longleat boom, and quickly found it a focal point for his restless teenage energies. In the mid-80s he devised and spearheaded *Fan-Aid*, a series of publications and events in aid of African famine relief, which set the pattern for fan charity events ever since. The *Fan-Aid* convention was the first not to show videos of old episodes as a point of principle – atomized viewers sitting in the dark watching television simply wasn't Paul's idea of what fandom was about. Half a decade later he devised the *Fan Olympiads* – conventions stripped of videos, guests or indeed anything other than the fans themselves, there to play self-consciously daft games and socialize. He put more than a few noses out of joint in the 1980s, but no one had a vision of fandom – of what fandom could be – that was as generous and wide ranging as his. As an aspiring author, he always stuck up for the importance of fiction writing in fandom, however much a minority pastime it seemed to be. He had grown up in Wiltshire, a small walk from a white chalk horse, and the body of fan work he developed in the late 1980s used the programme – and most particularly the Fifth Doctor – as a starting point from which he could launch his own version of English pastoralism often set in the fictional Cheldon Bonniface, an English town unremarkable except that the local church was a sentient being named Saul.

Timewyrm: Revelation was a *Who* book like none before it. It followed the Cartmel-era novelizations with its superstitious Time Lords, but placed on top of that a tale of genuine human pain and experience unlike anything *Who* fiction had seen before. Beneath the SF trappings it was the story of the wounds that Ace still carries from bullying in primary school, and around this circulate other characters nursing personal damage, such as the Hutchings, a childless graduate couple. This, rather than the temple prostitute, is when the books entered adult terrain. Fifteen years later Dale Smith would describe the book as the first *Who* fiction 'that is looking back on childhood, rather than existing in a safe and exciting version of childhood',[27] capturing well how the books were reformatting themselves for an audience in their twenties and thirties. Escalating the narrative processes already at work in the novelizations such as *Fenric* and *Remembrance*, *Timewyrm: Revelation* is told from many viewpoints, packed with symbolism, and celebrates the range's entry into small-l literature with a dizzying array of literary quotations, one at the top of every chapter. Poet William Blake and Shakespeare share space with many others, some of which Cornell blatantly made up. More importantly, and what really makes it the novel where *The New Adventures* found their voice, was that Cornell filled the book with fandom. Just as Jeremy Bentham had brought state-of-the-art DWAS criticism to the Monthly a decade earlier, so Cornell brought fan attitudes squarely into the books.

The cult reading had arrived with a vengeance by 1990. Fans who had once backed John Nathan-Turner's attempts to standardize the programme's history now revelled in the joys to be found in contradictory references, muddled thinking, the compromises that a limited budget worked on authorial intentions, the unconvincing nature of certain monsters and the wonderful silliness that could be found in spin-off products which were insufficiently researched or aimed at six-year-olds. (It is no coincidence that this period also saw Marvel produce a companion to *DWM*, *Doctor Who Classic Comics* [1992 – 1994], which reprinted naive comic strips from the 1960s and 1970s.) This attitude is at work all over *Revelation* which cites various *Who* locations, whether factual (Longleat – a British stately home which had long been home to an exhibition of *Who* props and costumes) or fictional (such as Stockbridge, the fictional Gloucestershire town from DWM (not to be confused with the real one in Hampshire)). When the Fourth Doctor and a Troughton-era villain had appeared in the first two *New Adventures*, they had appeared in the literal style of 'The Five Doctors'. In *Revelation*, the Doctor's past selves live on as phantoms inside his own consciousness, and in describing them, Cornell rehashes the phrases which were repeated constantly in the novelizations; the Third Doctor has a 'shock of white hair' (p. 122), the Fourth is 'bohemian' (p. 147) and towards the book's conclusion, the TARDIS arrives with the 'wheezing, groaning sound' (p. 209) which was (overly) familiar from many novelizations. Fans had thrilled to these words in their youth, derided them as clichés in their teen years, and now held affection for them, and *Revelation* evokes all those feelings simultaneously. Similarly, the First Doctor speaks not just with the cadences of his television character, but also as William Hartnell. His line 'I believe she has radically altered the biochem ... the bi ... and she's done it to the whole garden, yes! Hmm,' (p. 91) reconstructs the style not of the dialogue as it was written, but as it was 'billyfluffed' (i.e.: the second half gets lost as Hartnell forgets it, and the production team lacked the time/resources to reshoot). Many fans are name checked (that's me on p. 114), along with such unlikely individuals as Paul Travers (the pen-name used when DWM editor John Freeman used when contributing to his own magazine). We needn't cite here the entire list of references or the novels which followed – there are lengthy websites devoted to that project – so much as to note the collapse of discrete continuities and barriers between the real and the fictional.

John Nathan-Turner, in his role as BBC liaison, ever leaned to a more mainstream version of *Who* and suggested it shouldn't be used. Darvill-Evans had stronger instincts – plus a decade's commercial information – and published it anyway. Cornell modestly declines to join those who say he invented *The New Adventures*, but he became the poster boy for the line; the first author to have a second book commissioned, the first to create a new companion (Bernice Summerfield), the writer who would be chosen to write the first *Missing Adventure* (a subsequent series featuring stories of old Doctors), the author of the fiftieth *New Adventure*, and the writer of the first Doctorless novel, when Virgin lost the contract and carried on the series with Summerfield in the adventurer's role. His first published work had been in *DWM*, but the greater prestige of the *New Adventures* and the impact of *Revelation* meant that he would always be remembered as Virgin's discovery.

As the reference game escalated, and the frame of references expanded, *Who* fandom would define books as trad(itional) or rad(ical). Trad Who fiction had the TARDIS crew turn up on an alien world, discover the existence of evil or tyranny, and fight it. Rad fiction was a multidimensional playground where different versions of *Who* intermingled and played off one another. That radicalism was limited by Virgin's own concerns that the novels be recognizably set in the same universe, one which could be referred to across the line. Even with that stipulation in place, however, the creative free play necessarily determined who would write most of the books. Who but a fan could follow, or add to, such a complex web of in-jokes and continuity points? By now, the fans had a greater grasp of the programme's history than anyone else had ever accumulated, and the early 1990s was the age of Big Ideas, often designed to tie up loose ends or continuity problems. The downbeat nature of *New Adventures* set on contemporary Earth needed reconciling with the more pristine twenty-first century presented in the programme itself (notably in the late 1960s), so 'The Big Clean-Up' was established, a worldwide effort to repair environmental damage occurring early in the century (more or less as this book is published, in fact). The programme's most powerful and abstract super beings were collected together as representatives of 'The Great Old Ones,' the Time Lords of a universe which preexisted this one who, having travelled to our reality, found themselves endowed with massive powers. The hastily executed regeneration from Sixth to Seventh Doctor, staged without Colin Baker's participation, and apparently occurring because the Time Lord hits his head on the TARDIS control console, was rewritten so that the McCoy Doctor, existing inside his predecessor's head as 'Time's

Champion' and keen to get on with his more proactive approach to defeating evil, essentially forces his former self to regenerate so he can be brought into being.

The sheer number of stories escalated as the decade continued. *The New Adventures* bred *The Missing Adventures*, stories concerning previous Doctors, and short story collections. Fans collected together anthologies for charity, and the Monthly not only had its own regular issues, but also summer and winter specials with more eclectic strips (e.g.: one where the Doctor appeared as played by Peter Cushing in the 1960s Dalek movies). Later still, there would be audio dramas. Fans-turned-professionals explored the gaps in the programme's narrative. The television series never explained where the Doctor's companion Liz Shaw went – she just vanished between seasons seven and eight – so *The Scales of Injustice* fills the gap. Some writers returned constantly to the Sixth Doctor and unpopular companion Mel (as played by Bonnie Langford) and used years of hindsight and fan debate to identify the most sympathetic and useable traits of both, seeking to redeem the lost potential. As sequels were written to even the poorest of television serials, the art of extrapolating planetary conditions and histories from old stories, a staple of 1970s *TARDIS* magazine but abolished as fandom got more sophisticated, became a valid skill once again, provided you could wrap it in an suitable story. Every fan has their favourites from the period. One of mine is *Bringer of Darkness*, a short Second Doctor comic strip which mixes and contrasts the harsher, more aggressive tone of the late 1980s with the gentler adventures of the 1960s. The tale's narrator is the Second Doctor's nineteenth century travelling companion, Victoria Waterfield. As the Doctor takes McCoy-style proactive action against a team of Daleks, she resolves to cease travelling with him once the TARDIS lands somewhere suitable. Told as an entry in her diary, the story frames Victoria's thoughts within a nineteenth-century mindset in ways that the programme itself had rarely bothered with: 'They had killed millions,' she writes of the Daleks, 'how could living souls be so lost to God?'[28]

There weren't many directions that fans couldn't stretch the format towards, though they occasionally ran up against the BBC who, inconveniently enough, continued to own the programme itself, and vetoed Virgin's plans for a regeneration into a new Doctor. The plans were made in 1993, and Virgin hoped this new Doctor would have been 'played' by David Troughton, son of Second Doctor Patrick, whose likeness would adorn covers, and who would be available for publicity shoots. His character, as pitched by Paul Cornell and Gareth Roberts would have been a strong, well-muscled man, but gentle, apparently embarrassed by his physique. Cornell's suggested regeneration involved the complete destruction of the Seventh Doctor's body, requiring the new Doctor to grow out of the ground or emerge from a cocoon.[29]

Fandom had survived the cancellation of the programme, and its creative energies thrived in the void left by the programme's absence. Many fans were beginning professional writing careers, either as novelists, television scriptwriters or science-fiction journalists. Others were in post-graduate education, preparing for university positions from which they would organize academic conferences and write articles about the show. Some remained simply fans. In December 1996 outgoing *DWM* editor Scott Gray would write that the publication 'has stopped being a magazine strictly about *Doctor Who*, and become one about the *Doctor Who* phenomenon – a celebration, not just of the television series, but of the entire subculture it's generated'.[30]

WHO WATCHES THE WATCHERS

The Eighth Doctor – Paul McGann

Doctor Who (85 min. TV Movie).

The film was retrospectively given the title **The Enemy Within** by its producer Philip Segal, and this title has its adherents, though it was never used on screen and what it might refer to is unclear.
First Transmission: 12–13/05/1996 – Selected Canadian Stations
US Transmission: 14/05/1996 – Fox Network
First UK transmission: 27/05/96 – BBC One

After a decade of speculation American *Doctor Who* became a short-lived reality: a one-off television film made by Universal for the Fox Network and BBC1. With an English leading man and an American budget, the production promised to reconcile some of the conflicting discourses and expectations which had helped destroy the programme six years earlier. Whilst the film rated well in the UK, its US screening, two weeks earlier, had not been a success and it never went to series. The BBC continued to merchandise the programme primarily around this new Doctor who became the 'current' incarnation in books and comic strips until 2005. Fans continued to debate issues, with most discussion now taking place on the internet. By the turn of the millennium, the Los Angeles-based *Outpost Gallifrey* had become the largest site and the essential news-source. New *Who* was produced in many forms, the most notable new formats being internet broadcasts by the BBC and the work of Big Finish, who produced audio adventures on CD (and later download) featuring, initially, Davison, Colin Baker and McCoy with companions old and new. McGann would later work with the company. With the Eighth Doctor's era defined on television by a single outing, the already-raging arguments about continuity and canonicity reached new heights.

With its dark shadows, Victoriana, warring Time Lords and velvet frockcoats, 'Doctor Who – The TV Movie' returned to the creative well of the early Tom Baker years, unsurprisingly given that these had been the first episodes of *Who* to attract serious audiences in the United States. Baker era icons such as jellybabies and a long multi-coloured scarf make brief appearances. For a project conceived in niche terms, this was an astute move. Two years after the TV Movie was broadcast, mid-1970s stories would again be asserted as the cream of *Who* when over 2,600 readers responded to *DWM*'s poll for the greatest stories and Hinchcliffe/Holmes productions took four of the top five places (including the top 2 – 'Genesis of the Daleks' leading 'The Talons Of Weng-Chiang'), and seven of the top 20. Third place went to Holmes' 70s-style Davison thriller, 'The Caves of Androzani'.[1] Five years after that, 2,800 readers responded via a different voting system, more or less replicating the earlier response. 'Genesis' and 'Androzani' changed places at first and third, with 'Weng-Chiang', the perpetual bridesmaid, static at number two. 'The Robots of Death' and 'Pyramids of Mars' made the top ten in both polls, whilst this second set of ratings produced six Hinchcliffe/Holmes stories in the top 20. Similar results were recorded in internet polls.[2] These preferences did not go unnoticed at BBC Worldwide. When DVD replaced video, a version of 1983's 'The Five Doctors' – without extras – was released in November 1999. When regular releases began a year later in a collectable format, 'The Robots of Death' was the first release, 'The Ark in Space' the seventh.

In 1996, the TV Movie presented the BBC with the opportunity to reposition *Doctor Who* back in the mainstream, but this ambition was thwarted in almost every way. The failure of the TV Movie in the US meant it arrived on UK screens with its future prospects already terminated. Moreover, the production office's understandable focus upon the US transmission and the diversity of UK *Who*-related publishers made it impossible to fully launch the episode in the UK as 'event TV' with reinforcing tie-ins across multiple product platforms. *Doctor Who Magazine* gave the Movie support, but it was only years later that it changed the logo on the cover from the diamond to the new image. Virgin, still producing novels tied to the old series, wasn't involved at all, though the BBC issued its own novelization of the TV film. The book cut away the literary ambition and convoluted references of the *New Adventures*. Instead, it balanced a clear written manner – perhaps owing something to the style of Terrance Dicks – appropriate to a mainstream publication. This novel, a video cassette and a book reprinting the script all bore the witty promotional slogan 'He's back … and it's about time'. If treating the programme as a multimedia franchise – and at this point it becomes hard to think of it as anything else – is a good thing, then this was the point where the BBC began to connect the dots. The *Radio Times* listings magazine gave the Movie a front cover, and inaugurated a new 'sci-fi page', half of which was given over to a comic strip featuring the new Doctor. It was an attempt to pull *Who* back into the mainstream, and yoke it together with such popular programming as *The X-Files* – not in itself a bad move considering the number of SF magazines which were using that formula.

The BBC, then, had a clear strategy for relaunching *Who*. The major problem was the episode itself. Bearing an uncanny resemblance to the popular American UFO/paranormal series *The X-Files*, the episode drew largely on adult television. The BBC's transmission slot of 8:30–9:55 p.m. straddled the watershed[3] (a rare event in those days when *The Nine O'Clock News* rigorously policed the divide, and only made possible by Bank Holiday scheduling) and even the plan to make a short-term financial killing by releasing a video to coincide with the US transmission (giving a three week window to sell to fans who couldn't wait) went awry when the shooting of schoolchildren in Dunblane, Scotland, meant the release was held up whilst the BBFC rethought its policy on including gunfire in television drama. That the programme was dragged into such a debate shows how far it had been pulled well away from the traditional definition of family entertainment.

Almost a year after the event, when Virgin's licence to publish original *Who* fiction elapsed, the BBC took control of the novels. Added to the videos, the corporation now had control of two of the main product lines. The distinction between 'new' and 'missing' adventures was abolished, all of them used the McGann logo, and the Past Doctor Adventures (as they came to be known) took on a similar look to the video releases, using swirling galaxies as a background for a picture of the Doctor. Bizarrely, whilst the BBC put head and shoulders shots of old Doctors on the relevant books, they were reluctant to give similar prominence to McGann. This strange reversal of the 1970s/80s policy (now books featured the likeness of any Doctor except the current one) failed to give the impression of a renewed series heading for the future. It seemed to emphasize the past, and in that much at least reflected the contents of the early books. Titles promised lurid B-movie pulp fiction (*The Bodysnatchers, Devil Goblins from Neptune*), or sugar rushes of old faces that would have shamed John Nathan-Turner (*The Eight Doctors, War of the Daleks*). Early non-fiction similarly misfired from a lack of focus. *The Doctor Who Book of Lists* (1997), *A Book of Monsters* (1997) and the non-BBC book Peter Haining's *The Nine Lives of Doctor Who* (1999) all ended up remaindered. They were based on a model of fan requirements that was over a decade out of date, and the pilot had failed to generate an alternative market. Many BBC Worldwide employees working on *Who* products simply failed to understand their market as demonstrated by an anecdote told to *DWM* readers by incoming editor Steve Cole about a cover he'd rejected for the video release of Season 18 story, 'Warrior's Gate': 'Originally, the picture of Tom [Baker] they'd used was from season Thirteen. "Does that matter?" someone asked.'[4] Cole – a fan since Philip Hinchcliffe's first story, 'Ark In Space', who had contributed to mid-80s fanzine *Skonnos* as well as *DWM, DWB* and *TV Zone* – well understood that it did.

However, if McGann had burned briefly, he had shone brightly for some. When, in 2000, *DWM* polled its readers as to who should be the Doctor in a Hollywood blockbuster or a new BBC series, McGann won both. His percentages don't look large – 16 per cent of the Hollywood vote, 27 per cent for the television category – but with any actor alive eligible these were landslide victories. 'I want to see more of the Eighth Doctor before I hear of the Ninth ...' wrote one correspondent. The results caused lengthy debate across the letters page, where *New Adventures* author Daniel O'Mahony, branding the TV Movie a failure which any future production team would wish to steer well clear of, declared McGann to be history. Counterarguments followed swiftly: 'If Paul McGann is not the current Doctor, then who is?' asked Terence Sands. 'There isn't one', O'Mahony replied. The debate showed the different ways in which fans could view the status of *Who*. For O'Mahony, it was dead as a TV series, and McGann's ongoing presence in books and comic strips didn't change anything, didn't constitute life in the old franchise. Those who opposed his views still regarded *Doctor Who* as active and ongoing.

Regardless of McGann's status, O'Mahony was wrong to say there was no Doctor. There were loads. The outlines of the character were well known, but with no specific incarnation active in the public mind those generalities might be fleshed out in different ways. In March 1999, Rowan Atkinson gave a credible turn for *Comic Relief* before regenerating into a host of guest-stars; the same year, Mark Gatiss provided an amiable, tea-drinking incarnation in a sketch called 'The Web of Caves' for BBC2's *Doctor Who* theme night; in 2001 Sylvester McCoy reappeared in the webcast 'Death Comes to Time' (where he dies, which is certainly one way of declaring McGann non-canonical), and McGann made a webcast of aborted Tom Baker story 'Shada' in 2003. When lost classic 'The Web of Fear' was staged in Portsmouth in 2000, lead actor Nick Scovell avoided attempting to imitate Patrick Troughton and gave his own interpretation. The BBC's thirty-fifth anniversary novel 'The Infinity Doctors' featured a new Doctor saving a Gallifrey which was familiar in its parts, but not its whole, and *DWM* staged a fake regeneration, apparently metamorphosing McGann into actor/fan Nicholas Briggs, before revealing it all as a clever ruse to smoke out an enemy. Who, as the old pun had it, is the Doctor? Even the judgements of the traditional authority – the BBC – were open to swift revision. In 2003, a new Doctor was unveiled for a Paul Cornell-scripted internet adventure, 'Scream of the Shalka'. 'Richard E. Grant is the "now" of *Doctor Who*,' producer James Goss told *DWM*. 'The Ninth Doctor, decided upon and cast by the BBC,' affirmed author Paul Cornell in the same article. Coverage of 'Shalka' was the main article of issue 336, with Grant on the cover as well. Ironically, it also contained – shoehorned in at the last minute – the news that the programme was to return to BBC1, a development that meant Richard E. Grant was consigned to the canonical margins. Grant was one of the several new Doctors who'd made his appearance in a wholly new medium/format to those in which the character had previously appeared. David Howe's publishing company Telos produced 40,000 word novellas based around the series. Big Finish Productions released monthly new stories on cassette/CD, and later download, featuring Doctors Five through Eight with the original cast, then unleashed yet more new incarnations when their 'Unbound' series featured performers new to the role such as Arabella Weir and David Warner. Fan entrepreneurs who hadn't got a license to produce *Doctor Who* could play at the edges of copyright-infringement, issuing videos with Colin Baker as 'The Stranger' or Sylvester McCoy and Sophie Aldred as 'Time Travellers'. The fact that copyrights on individual monsters were held not by the BBC but by those freelance authors who created them allowed dramas about K9, the Rani and the Zygons to be produced.

So many stories, so many Doctors: canonicity was the debate which consumed fandom in the 1990s. 'Canonicity' in these debates doesn't refer to a canon of worthy texts acclaimed for their quality (though *DW* fandom has those as well, of course), but to the assertion about which stories 'actually happened' in the *Doctor Who* universe. Whilst the TV series had been in production, these debates, insofar as there were any, had mostly concerned the status of the uncompleted story 'Shada' and whether the extra material added to books like *Doctor Who and The Doomsday Weapon* 'counted' or not. The novelizations of the McCoy era, which seemed to offer a much more substantial account of the era than the televised versions, stretched the question further. As niche-marketed *Who* proliferated, strict canonicity (already under strain in the most playful of fanzines and fictions) collapsed completely in professional products. The BBC were less concerned than Virgin with using the books to create a coherent *Who* universe which would cross reference between volumes and dropped whatever barriers between continuities remained. Frobisher the Penguin, a companion for the Sixth Doctor in mid-80s *DWM*, appeared in BBC books and Big Finish audios. Novels were set during series 6B, the fan-contrived extra season used to explain why Patrick Troughton looked so old in 'The Five Doctors'; Gary Russell's *Placebo Effect* incorporated the short-lived *Radio Times* strip into novel continuity (apparently the Doctor just popped off for an afternoon, leaving his novel companions to while away a few hours whilst he had the adventures told in the *Radio Times*); Kim Newman's novella *Time and Relative* extended the story backwards, being set several months before the events of the programme's first episode and featuring a Doctor and Susan only just arrived on Earth; Jim Mortimore's *Campaign* (notable because the BBC commissioned it, then refused to publish the final version for a variety of reasons) was set in the programme's earliest years and found the TARDIS inhabited by all versions of the earliest crew including those drawn from the Dalek films, the comic strip, the earliest novelizations, and some abandoned ideas from early production documents. In such a decentred environment, popular mid-70s companion Sarah Jane Smith could be killed off in the novel *Bullet Time*, set in 1997 (and itself a Rubicon which people would previously have shied from crossing), whilst being apparently alive in other novels set later. Little wonder that by the decade's end, the books had abandoned the original practice of clearly declaring on their back covers exactly where they fitted into continuity (e.g.: 'This adventure takes place between the TV stories ARC OF INFINITY and SNAKEDANCE') for a far vaguer formulation ('This adventure features the Fifth Doctor, Nyssa and Tegan'). Arguments about quality aside, one reason the BBC novels are less affectionately regarded than the Virgin novels which preceded them is that it's far harder to discern a house style in the mix of stories which play so consciously with the multiple histories of *Doctor Who*.

Juggling the diverse continuities could be difficult. *Doctor Who Magazine* took to using sidebars so that, when discussing a given theme, information from the novels could be present but held at one step remove from the television series. Lance Parkin has argued that with texts proliferating in this way, canonicity debates were both a practical attempt by fans to prioritize purchases (because by writing off a series of books or audio dramas as 'non-canonical' one could avoid buying them without compromising one's identity as a fan) and a thorny theoretical issue because fandom was ultimately a community built on the notion of shared texts which were common to all. Or, as one fan wrote in 1997, 'How can *The Left-Handed Hummingbird* be canonical to someone who hasn't read it?'[5]

In this malleable world the comic strip relaunched itself. No longer content to fill in the gaps between the books or to tell stories of old Doctors, the strip would now blaze its own path to the future – and the past it would take its coordinates from would not be the TV series (though that was never contradicted and Daleks and Cybermen appeared), but its own past. The Eighth Doctor began his comic strip life stepping from the TARDIS into Stockbridge, having materialized next to the same cricket pitch where his fifth incarnation began *The Tides of Time* (see Chapter 4). 'Wonder if old Mrs. Parkhouse is still baking her scones,' he ponders in his third panel, acknowledging the town's creator. When this Doctor visited Gallifrey, it was the version seen in *The Tides of Time*. Parkhouse-era Gallifreyan agent Shayde returned, as did – going even further back – Kroton the emotive Cybermen. Parkhouse's influence was also stylistic. The Eighth Doctor's first comic strip has captions written in the past tense ('Once upon a time in a sunlit meadow ... the English were at play'; 'Beneath the meadow was a valley. In the valley stood a village. And in the village ...'), an unusual practice in comic strips, and in this instance surely a deliberate allusion to Parkhouse's habit of writing the Davison comic strip that way.

Editor Gary Gillatt, reflecting as to why the *DWM* team elected to return the strip to its previous ambitious levels, pointed to how the age of the production team coincided with the magazine's own history: 'we are the first production team to grow up alongside the great Marvel strip of the eighties, as opposed to any of its often more anorexic predecessors. We grew up with the worlds of Mills and Wagner, Gibbons and Parkhouse, and from them we draw our inspiration.'[6] To further enhance the idea of a comic strip set in its own little world with distinct continuity, it became common in fan circles to regard the town/village which was attacked by the Iron Legion way back in *Doctor Who Weekly* as Stockbridge, though there's no textual evidence for this. (They do seem to have the same church tower, but a large chunk of this is blown away in *The Iron Legion*.) In the new millennium, even the magazine itself asserts this interpretation as fact; 'Long-term readers will remember that the *DWM* strip's connections to the town of Stockbridge go right back to the earliest days of *The Iron Legion* in issue 1', wrote editor Tom Spilsbury in December 2008.[7] The comic strip Eighth Doctor would find his companion, Isobel 'Izzy' Sinclair, in Stockbridge, and whilst her birthday is never referenced in the strip itself, *DWM* staff suggested extra-textually that she was 'born on the day of the Doctor's first visit there in 1979'.[8]

In an environment where the comic strip could redefine itself in this way, canonicity itself became the subject of several novels: John Peel's *War of the Daleks* contrived a complex reworking of past continuity to explain that Skaro hadn't really been destroyed during Sylvester McCoy's tenure; Lawrence Miles' *Interference* rewrote the end of the Pertwee era (though later events corrected the original timeline); Lance Parkin's *The Infinity Doctors* was set on a version of Gallifrey which drew from all representations of the planet from screen, novels, comic strips, etc., and featured an unspecified incarnation of the Doctor, not clearly recognizable as any of those familiar from the television. In his other role as critic, Parkin has noted that *War of the Daleks* is the oddball here. Apparently at the behest of Terry Nation, Peel's audacious twist (Skaro wasn't destroyed) rides roughshod over several previous stories, bending their events mercilessly to a new 'official' configuration. The events of 'Destiny of the Daleks' (1979), 'Resurrection of the Daleks' (1984), 'Revelation of the Daleks' (1985) and 'Remembrance of the Daleks' (1988) are all 'revealed' to have been stage-managed by the Daleks. The Doctor wasn't really fighting the Daleks in these stories, so the new version asserts, just jumping through the hoops of a complex plot engineered and acted out by the Daleks to ensure that the planet which he destroyed wasn't Skaro. The intention and tone here are ruthless in their undermining of previous stories and the insistence that their events be dramatically recast in accordance with a new 'official' version. The other authors are all simply gleeful about the new mix-and-match aesthetic provided by the dissolution of strict canonical boundaries.

Once *Doctor Who* had become this malleable, it was inevitable that the actual act of viewing/reading it would become a major theme, inching itself closer to the heart of stories, manifesting itself in various ways. In their final year of publication, the *New Adventures* had developed a running theme dramatising fans themselves. Upon his visits to the 1980s and 90s, the Doctor would sporadically find himself meeting his own fans, people who were trying to keep track, through press cutting and rumour mill, of his comings and goings on Earth, and publishing their findings in homemade fanzines. The holes in their knowledge led them to speculate about much the same things as fans did: in what year did the Zygon adventure occur? Could there be a female incarnation? This following developed, following much the same patterns as *Who* fandom itself had. *The Return of the Living Dad* (set in the early 1980s) showed them producing black-and-white newssheets, but by the time of *The Dying Days* (set at the century's end) their 'zines have gone glossy and the most prominent amongst their number have even given talks at American conventions.

Virgin created developing stories like this because the company was concerned to make an ongoing backdrop within which all its *Who* novels were set. That fictional environment was sufficiently solid that when the BBC withdrew the licence to publish *Who* fiction, *The New Adventures* continued for several further years as a series, featuring characters and worlds not owned by the BBC. The more decentred BBC novels had less interest in any such coherence. Thus, the act of viewing isn't tied to particular characters but appears in a diversity of ways. There are loads of examples. One – a particular favourite of mine – will suffice. It occurs in Simon Messingham's novel *Zeta Major*. The story is a sequel to the 1975 Tom Baker story 'Planet of Evil', and, to understand what is happening now the protagonists in the new story consult a ship's recording of the events of the original story.

> He flipped the box open and produced a video cassette. 'It's a copy . . . .' He pushed the playback button. On the screen: an old, old picture, scoured with lightning-style tracking lines. A rushing tunnel of colours and odd whistling sounds. The images flickered over the man in grey. 'Video feedback, he stated. 'any second now'. *Space. A planet in the distance. No stars. Zoom in on the planet. Purple. Cut to: a jungle. Oddly lit, purple and red light . . .* [9]

The rushing tunnel with odd whistling sounds is the old Tom Baker title sequence, the shotlist which follows is that of 'Planet of Evil' part one. They're watching the episode, and the tracking lines are a sure sign that this copy, like the ones fans watched in the early 1980s, was some nth generation monstrosity showing its age.

However, even whilst fans were amusing themselves with complex in-jokes about shared viewing patterns, *Doctor Who* was starting to reassert itself as a credible site of national interest.

Rehabilitation

Though the 90s might have seemed a hard decade for *Who*, a time when it was mocked and forgotten, this was not wholly the case. The programme's icons featured in advertising where they could be sure to hit the nostalgia buttons for people beyond simply the fans. We can trace a path right from 1996 to the programme's return of events and moments when its glories were revelled in, and its strengths acknowledged. Some of those who waved the flag for the series were themselves in a similar situation – traditional family favourites that were losing market share to newer, trendier options – and they saw in *Who* a popular product which spoke to their own concerns. On television, *Blue Peter* (no longer as popular as it had been, but still the BBC's primary platform for introducing children to its self-image as entertainer, educator and cultural player) ran eight items on the programme between the cancellation of the series and the announcement of the new.[10] On the High Street, W. H. Smiths had been a mainstay of the UK high street for decades, selling newspapers, popular books, stationery, and music pitched at a family audience, but by the second half of the 90s it was consistently reported to be losing out to other retailers (though it still boasted 8 million customers a day). *Doctor Who* fitted perfectly with the retailer's market position and family image, so whilst the programme's high-street visibility retreated as the decade continued, Smiths remained a supporter. Whilst other newsagents ceased to stock *Doctor Who Magazine*, most branches of Smiths could be depended upon. Videos and DVDs which disappeared almost upon release into the science-fiction sections of major music and video stores, rated mysteriously higher and stayed for longer in the W. H. Smiths chart. A number of video and DVD box sets – repackaging previously available material – were available as Smiths exclusives in the run-ups to Christmas.

The first signs of the programme's rehabilitation came in 1996 – only months after Paul McGann's TV Movie had failed to launch a new series – when the public voted on the 'Auntie' awards, bestowed by the BBC upon its most-loved programmes, and to the surprise of many, *Doctor Who* beat tabloid favourites *EastEnders* and *Casualty*. More substantial perhaps – because it could hardly be accused of being open to fans voting en masse – was the British Film Institute's survey of 1,600 television professionals in 2000. Intended to establish a list of the greatest and most influential programmes in British television history, the poll found *Who* winning the children's section and coming third overall behind *Fawlty Towers* (Ian Levine's old model for what *Doctor Who* shouldn't be) and *Cathy Come Home*, a classic television play of the 60s about homelessness. A more bizarre acknowledgement came in May, 2002, when Virgin's new Supervoyager passenger train was formally named 'Doctor Who' with a ceremony involving a Dalek and past *Doctor Who* companions. Said companions then travelled to BBC Television Centre where, with a host of other *Who* stalwarts, they watched The Heritage Foundation (the English charity which recognizes talent in sporting and entertainment, not the right-wing American think tank which so enthused Ronald Reagan) unveil blue plaques to commemorate William Hartnell, Patrick Troughton and Jon Pertwee.

By the turn of the millennium, then, *Doctor Who* was something with which the BBC were no longer embarrassed to be associated. As channels and formats multiplied, and fans within the organization now found themselves in positions to champion projects, so the Corporation began to broadcast *Who*-related material. It remained a minority taste, but television audiences were fragmenting speedily. Thus, *Who* material was found on demographic-specific channels such as BBC7 (a digital radio station dedicated to the spoken word which transmitted Big Finish's audios featuring Paul McGann, original plays, and the BBC's own backlog of audio-*Who*), BBC4 (a satellite/cable channel for documentary) and the internet. Just as it had once been used to show off the BBC's design departments, so *Who* was now yoked with the Corporation's newest technology. There was an obvious thematic link, after all, between the scientific hero and the new hard/software revolutionizing television. When Jon Pertwee stories which existed only in black and white were recolourized for video release in the early 90s, the sleeves boasted that the new technology was 'worthy of the Doctor himself'. The synergy of SF content with technological breakthrough became common thereafter. As the BBC experimented with digital technology, *Who* was at the forefront. *Death Comes to Time* allowed the Corporation to boast a record for a net-based drama. When the series returned, fans could play an interactive game and receive TARDISodes (one-minute dramatic prologues to the forthcoming episode) direct to their mobile phones. A devoted and computer-literate fanbase assured the BBC of a significant take-up if such experiments were tied to *Doctor Who*. Later, when the iPlayer service was launched, allowing people to view selected recent BBC programmes on their computers, both *Who* and its adult spin-off *Torchwood* were amongst the highest-viewed shows. This strategy of using *Who* content to generate interest in new television technology hit a new high in 2010 when the Australian Broadcasting Corporation made the episodes of Matt Smith's first series available online nearly two days before their broadcast. 'We hope the lure of *Doctor Who* will provide incentive for more viewers to discover iView,' the broadcaster announced.[11]

Unsurprisingly, some *Who*-related material of the new millennium was found in productions about the Radiophonic Workshop. In March, 2002, the multimedia 'happening' Generic Sci-fi Quarry featured a pre-recorded soundtrack from Radiophonic Alumni performed in, yes, a quarry in Oxfordshire. In December of the same year, Radio 4 transmitted a play about Delia Derbyshire, who had originally arranged *Doctor Who*'s theme music, *Blue Veils and Golden Sands*, who was also the subject matter of *Standing Wave*, a play performed in Glasgow in 2004. BBC4, the cable/satellite channel produced a documentary, *The Alchemists of Sound*, about the Workshop in May 2005. Of course, the BBC had an interest in celebrating its own history in this way. For TV/film music specialist Kevin Donnelly *Alchemists* in particular 'tends to focus on the Workshop as an avant-garde entity connected to art music practice, and perhaps this historical revisionism reflects the BBC's desire to "trade up" some of its more successful elements in an era of almost continuous questioning of the BBC's public-funded status'.[12] Not every facet of these productions necessarily served fan interests in all respects, however. A brief scene in *Blue Veils* where Derbyshire attends a *Who* convention plays to the worst stereotypes of fan ped-antry: 'And my fifth question, Delia ...' Overall, though, interest in the programme was such that in December 2003, BBC1 screened an hour-long documentary, *The Story of Doctor Who*, aimed squarely at a general audience with no fan-pleasing references to the likes of Paul McGann, the New Adventures or Big Finish. As part of an occasional series of retrospective (a previous edition had covered comedy hit *Only Fools and Horses*), it assumed the existence of a non-fan audience for a history of *Doctor Who*.

You can, if you're so inclined, follow *Doctor Who*'s same journey back to the centre of national culture not through public events but through academic criticism. When the show's position as a national favourite was secure in the late seventies/early eighties, John Fiske's analysis of 'The Creature From The Pit' had argued that the programme used its popular status to validate dominant ideology and the front cover of the UK edition of *The Unfolding Text* had underscored the programme's institutional status by juxtaposing the police box exterior of the TARDIS with Television Centre. The late nineties and the early years of the new millennium had seen work concentrating less on the broadcast episodes than on its fans, situating the series clearly in the 'cult' niche. In the new millennium Kim Newman and James Chapman reread the whole programme from end to end as a significant national narrative – and as their projects reached conclusion they found they had a whole new series to analyze. If this brief overview maps anything, of course, it's the priorities of cultural studies (from ideology the-ory, through audience analysis, to cultural history, each step build-ing on the last), but its notable that the journey ties so neatly with that taken by the show itself in British public culture.[13]

Upgraded Products

As befits a programme which had been rehabilitated in this way, *Who* in all its formats became available in a range of quality edi-tions. The sometimes-dodgy videos were replaced with DVDs which pioneered new techniques for the restoration of archive tel-evision, most notably the Vidfire process. Cassette tapes of stories which only existed as soundtracks were replaced with CDs, digitally remastered with not a second missing – not even dead air – and with narration carefully structured so as not to obscure dialogue. Panini began an ongoing programme of twice-yearly graphic novels reprinting the early Marvel strips. Replicating Dez Skinn's original strategy, the initial volumes were aimed at the comics market (where artist Dave Gibbons was now a prominent name) as much as at the *Who* fan, though later volumes, including those reprinting the Eighth Doctor strips, have also sold well.

Some of these reissues would have happened anyway simply as a result of format changes. Technology alone, however, did not determine that the BBC would make so much effort, that the DVDs, for instance, would be a benchmark for the presentation of archive television on DVD (in terms of both restoration and extras), and that old episodes of *Who* would be the raw material upon which so much research into developing restoration techniques would be tested. The presence within the BBC of talented technicians and picture/sound restorers who were themselves fans of the programme meant that the case was made for such extensive restoration work. The tele-literacy of *Who* fans meant that there was an appreciative audience for such DVDs. Such work, however, created its own issues. On the remastered discs, the shadows of boom mikes (a common interloper in sixties *Who*) and extraneous studio noise were removed. Similarly, where scene changes had been done by physical tape edits on the quad studio recordings the end result was often one- or two-frame off-locks on the film recorder at the cut point. These frames were often cut completely, decreasing each affected shot by a frame or two. On a non-technical matter, some of the contemporary pop music which was cleared for transmission in the sixties and seventies (The Fleetwood Mac track *Oh Well* in Jon Pertwee's debut, 'Spearhead From Space', for instance) was not available for use on VHS, and had to be replaced. Thus, the episodes became more polished, but were no longer true records of the limitations and conditions under which the programme – and, by extension, sixties television drama generally – were made. For many fans, that wasn't an issue, but others cared, and the technical team's website has consistently debated the question of what constitutes legitimate restoration. More substantial tampering – such as the substitution of CGI special effects for the creaky originals – was included as an extra, with the original version retained as a true record of the transmission. The stakes were aesthetic as well as historical. The inclusion of deleted scenes kept the canonicity debates running, reaching an apex with the inclusion of 'Special Editions' of certain Sylvester McCoy stories. These editions took stories which had been drastically edited to fit the parameters of 25 minute episodes, and returned to the scripts, reconstructing the original intentions with more sympathetic edits, and the reworked 'Battlefield' – released in December 2008 – was a substantial improvement upon the televised version. These processes of improvement seem never-ending, since from 2010 the BBC has re-released some of the earliest DVDs with pictures enhanced by techniques not available at the time of their original issue. This ongoing stream of updated products has meant that, for instance, Patrick Troughton's debut tale, *Power of the Daleks*, has been available as a novelization, a script book, a cassette, a CD and an MP3-CD – not bad for a serial generally described as deleted from the BBC archive. Nor was such restoration reserved for the television episodes. Reading the digitally tidied-up comic strips (reprints began in 2004) on glossy paper was a completely different tactile experience from its previous incarnation on cheap comics paper.

These new editions were, to some extent, *Who* archived for library storage and presentation (the DVD sleeves were cannily designed with no logo on the spine, so that if the logo changed the shelved discs would retain a consistent look). The programme's cancellation gave it finite limits and made it seem that a 'complete set' could be achieved. As such, the logic of 'definitiveness' which had been used by *DWM* from the early 90s onwards came to animate much turn-of-the-century activity. The *Who is Dr Who* CD collected together all the 45-rpm singles released concerning the programme during its first decade, and was intended to be followed by later volumes.[14] Those later editions didn't happen, but the BBC had more success with its own audio line *Doctor Who at the BBC* which collected old radio items (interviews, reviews, etc.). Similarly completist in scope were the reference works published as the old millennium became the new. (David) *Howe's Transcendental Toybox* took 486 pages to copiously catalogue *Doctor Who* merchandise, *The Television Companion* provided credits and information about all televised stories over 557 pages, and

Doctor Who on Location (a relatively modest read at 256 pages) researched the locations of what was filmed almost shot by shot. In the unlikely event that any other television programme generated information of this detail, let alone got it placed in mainstream booksellers, they would undoubtedly be the final word. This is *Doctor Who*, however, and work continues in all areas.[15] Later, Howe would collaborate on *The Target Book*, the definitive history of the production and cover art (but not the writing style) of the novelizations, and *DWM* would embark on a three-part history of itself during 2004 (its twenty-fifth anniversary). In this age of near-definitive works, multi-part articles were a frequent feature of the magazine. Andrew Pixley's study of the programme's scheduling was serialized across six issues in 2004. The depth of argument in the magazine by this point meant that when Douglas Adams passed away, the commemorative article in *DWM*, which covered his whole career, was surely the most substantial piece written at the time.

Works of this depth presented new analysis and research whilst also drawing from a wealth of preceding works, including fanzines which, by this point, constituted a major resource. In the early years of the new millennium, the DWAS celebrated its twenty-fifth anniversary, and a complete collection of the fan publications which had circulated during that period would number in the thousands. Such a collection would contain much that was repetitious, and some which had been supplanted by later information or more sophisticated analytical techniques. There'd also be the old 'History of Voga' articles in which fandom had simply lost interest. Beyond that, however, was a wealth of relevant information, much of it printed in magazines so basic as to be beneath the view of archivists. The period between McCoy and Eccleston saw various moves to represent some of this material in more lasting forms. *DWB* released softback collections of its major articles and its most substantial interviews, whilst Virgin released *License Denied*, an edited collection of fan writings. Later, Telos' *Talkback* series reproduced interviews with *Who* cast and crew, including much extracted from early 'zines. The *About Time* books, written by Tat Wood and Lawrence Miles, put into soft covers the cultural criticism that defined Wood's 80s/90s fanzine, *Spectrox*.[16] As I conclude the process of writing this book, a trend is apparently developing for the editors of comparatively recent 'zines to reproduce all their issues as a book.

The project of definitiveness was not without its problems. Panini publishing has yet to find a way to repackage 60s and 70s comic strips which printed panels right across the double page, a format which would obscure crucial dialogue and action if collated in book form. These strips had been created for cheap formats, and resisted being recast as a collectible. The project of historical completion, of course, was premised on the programme's death. Its return as a mammoth success changed everything. DVDs, which once appeared as archive editions for long-term fans, now look like spruced-up versions to attract new audiences, and the restored versions became the new masters available for UK transmission or purchase by foreign broadcasting organizations. Fans who had assumed that Panini would reprint the whole history of the *Doctor Who* comic suddenly found, as *Who*-related magazines multiplied during David Tennant's time, that new strips were being produced faster than the company could reprint old ones.

Of course, fans often had copies of these stories in previous formats. Those buying all of the DVDs (originally on a bi-monthly, then monthly basis) were engaged in a familiar pattern. Through the 70s and 80s, they had built up a set of novelizations, in the 90s it was videos, and now DVDs. The pleasures of anticipation (*Which story will be released next? Which Doctor will it feature?*) and delight/disappointment have been repeated across these forms and decades. A fan born in the late 60s – me, for example – who came of sufficient age to read the novelizations just as they started regular release has been collecting sets of *Doctor Who* in some format or other for literally as long as they could remember. T. S. Eliot's Prufrock counted out his life in coffee spoons – I've spent mine waiting for 'The Sun Makers' to come out.

Such purchase patterns evoke the worst stereotypes of fans as slavish consumers of any product, however similar it appears to things they already own. However, this is to misunderstand fan values. Novelizations were a substitute for the show in the 70s, and video replaced them because it was not a substitute but the show itself. DVD brought informative extras and superior picture and sound. That restoration brought previously obscured aspects to view, such as the deep-focus composition of *The Leisure Hive* (rarely-mentioned within fandom before the DVD release). It could be similarly all-revealing about the programme's production. As K9 is so badly damaged by the time winds in episode 1 of *Warriors Gate* that he starts to emit smoke, the cleaned-up, fully restored, all-singing-all-dancing DVD version clearly shows what had previously been invisible – the pipe down which the visual effects team were pumping the smoke. If it's hard to take this exactly as an 'improvement', it was more grist to the mill of fandom's grasp of production techniques, and another to add to the list of fondly held production gaffes and visibilities. Like theatregoers who watch new productions of plays they know well (or collect new editions of Shakespeare for the introductions and textual notes) fans were happy to buy products which contained a high degree of repetition because the differences could be crucial or could illuminate the story in a new way. The BBC's recent release of audio books of the novelizations is a key example. The product seems redundant in so many ways, but as different actors recite the familiar dialogue they bring out new interpretations – as actors should, of course. With the canon blown wide open, a new reading of the Time Lord's dialogue is a hint of a Doctor who never was. How many levels and small joys come packed into the audio book of 'Doctor Who and the Abominable Snowmen' when David Troughton (the Virgin Publishing Doctor who never was) reads the dialogue once spoken by his father?

By the early years of the new millennium, fans had completely taken over all official merchandise lines, vastly improving them by almost any standard you care to raise, and created successful new product lines. Non-profit products for circulation within fandom itself were, in terms of production quality, indistinguishable from professional merchandise. Fans were rising high in large media organizations, using the position to carve out a place for *Who* as a legitimate part of British nostalgia. Several fans had won BAFTAs for their original television series' which mixed a fan sensibility with mainstream genres. They had watched as the collection of television series had ceased to be the pastime of geeks, and had (with the development of the reasonably priced, stylishly slim box set) become instead a motor which drove the DVD industry. Fans watched over all these developments from senior positions within the magazines and episode guides which reviewed and debated new releases. If this book ended here – as under other circumstances it could have done – it would be the story of how fan discourse shifted out of the litho-printed A5 fanzines and into a newsagent and bookshop very near you. With their professionalization, and with the internet replacing the more consciously structured arguments of fanzines, professionally produced merchandise was where fandom did its thinking.

But surely everyone who's reading this book knows what happened next.

THE FRANCHISE OF DOOM

The Ninth, Tenth and Eleventh Doctors: Christopher Eccleston, David Tennant, Matt Smith

Series One: (26/03/05 – 18/06/05)

Rose, The End of the World, The Unquiet Dead, Aliens of London/World War Three, Dalek, The Long Game, Father's Day, The Empty Child/The Doctor Dances, Boom Town, Bad Wolf/The Parting of the Ways.
Christmas Special (25/12/05) The Christmas Invasion

Series Two (15/04/06 – 08/07/06)

New Earth, Tooth and Claw, School Reunion, The Girl in the Fireplace, Rise of the Cybermen/The Age of Steel, The Idiot's Lantern, The Impossible Planet/The Satan Pit, Love & Monsters, Fear Her, Army of Ghosts/Doomsday
Christmas Special (25/12/06) The Runaway Bride

Series Three (31/03/07 – 30/06/07)

Smith and Jones, The Shakespeare Code, Gridlock, Daleks in Manhattan/Evolution of the Daleks, The Lazarus Experiment,

42, Human Nature/The Family of Blood, Blink, Utopia/The Sound of Drums/Last of the Time Lords
Christmas Special (25/12/07) Voyage of the Damned

Series Four (05/04/08 – 05/07/08)

Partners in Crime, The Fires of Pompeii, Planet of the Ood, The Sontaran Strategem/The Poison Sky, The Doctor's Daughter, The Unicorn and the Wasp, Silence in the Library/Forest of the Dead, Midnight, Turn Left, The Stolen Earth/Journey's End.
Christmas Special (25/12/08) The Next Doctor

Specials (2009/10)

Planet of the Dead (11/04/2009)/The Waters of Mars (15/11/2009)/The End of Time (Parts 1 and 2 25/11/2009, 01/01/2010)

Series Five (03/04/10 – 26/06/10)

The Eleventh Hour, The Beast Below, Victory of the Daleks, The Time of Angels/Flesh and Stone, The Vampires of Venice, Amy's Choice, The Hungry Earth/Cold Blood, Vincent and the Doctor, The Lodger, The Pandorica Opens/The Big Bang.

Series Six (Transmitted in two blocks: 23/04/11 – 04/06/11 and 27/08/11 – 01/10/11)

The Impossible Astronaut/Day of the Moon, The Curse of the Black Spot, The Doctor's Wife, The Rebel Flesh/The Almost People, A Good Man Goes to War, Let's Kill Hitler, Night Terrors, The Girl Who Waited, The God Complex, Closing time, The Wedding of River Song

Various Producers and Script Editors. The dominant creative voice (chief writer/executive producer) until 'The End of Time' was Russell T. Davies, and since then Steven Moffat.

Does anybody really need reminding of events so recent, so celebrated and so central to current debates about television and the family demographic? Suffice to say that *Doctor Who*'s return was announced in late 2003, and its production was watched eagerly until it debuted on Easter weekend 2005, an instant hit which redefined what sort of programming could work on a Saturday early-evening. Christopher Eccleston left after a single series, and Billie Piper a year later, but the programme only became more successful. The Best Drama BAFTA for 2005 was followed by a stream of other wins for the programme and its stars in many award ceremonies, often those decided by public telephone vote. The Christmas 2007 special was the second-highest rated programme of the year (eclipsing everything on Michael Grade's ITV – revenge of a sort), and 2008 saw the programme regularly in the weekly top ten. That year's season finale was the highest-rated programme of its week. That week had seen the press speculation which had surrounded the first season's 'Bad Wolf' mystery wholly eclipsed by the even greater coverage of episode 12's *will-he-regenerate-or-not?* cliffhanger. In 2005, programmes such as *Heartbeat, Emmerdale* and *Casualty* were likely to out rate *Who*, but now it had left them behind. Whilst other programme's ratings continued to decline in a fragmented television market, *Who*'s grew to the point where it was beaten only by the nation's foremost programmes (*Coronation Street, EastEnders, The X-Factor, Britain's Got Talent, Downton Abbey Strictly Come Dancing*). Total 'reach' (the number of people who watched a given episode in the week after its transmission across all platforms: iPlayer, BBC3 repeats, digital 'Catch Up' services) meant the programme was reaching near-1970s levels of audiences, but in a vastly more competitive television market. To the episodes listed above can be added a number of charity skits (humorous but apparently canonical), 'Tardisode' prologues for season two, and a couple of animated stories, all screened as the programme expanded across the blossoming presentational platforms of the twenty-first century BBC. When David Tennant took the title role in *Hamlet* in August 2008, it was the most heavily covered art event of the summer, with gushing reviews and colour photos on the front of broadsheet newspapers.

In this book I have sought to trace the development of discourse surrounding *Doctor Who* from 1979 when Appreciation Society members Gordon Blows and, primarily, Jeremy Bentham were employed by Marvel to write articles for their weekly comic tied to the series. *Doctor Who Weekly*'s early failure to find its audience, and the economics of comic production, caused the magazine to turn monthly, seriously increasing its text content. Bentham seized the opportunity to write about the production of the series, the personnel who had worked on it, and its position within the BBC and British broadcasting. Writing such analysis of the programme was rendered easier, I have argued, by the manner in which the incoming producer remade the show. Under John Nathan-Turner, rapid-editing, lengthy pans, super-impositions and slow-motion photography would all find their place. Would Bentham's articles have been so successful – been taken so completely to heart by a generation of fans – if he had had to consider the less visually exces- sive style of the Graham Williams era? We can only speculate.

Whilst the majority of *Doctor Who Magazine*'s readers never joined active fandom, its articles and interviews projected fan read- ings and the fan interest in the programme's production to a large audience, creating a market for all sorts of commentary around television shows which have their generic roots in some fantasy scenario or which are visually stylish and critically acclaimed. In the new millennium, the generation of fans which grew up on Bentham's articles are amongst the foremost creators of that com- mentary in magazine reviews and published episode guides. The magazine also fed the already apparent desire on the part of fans to become workers on the series, a project initially thwarted when it was cancelled in 1989. By the time the new millennium rolled round, it was a truism that the BBC was riddled with fans (though the ability of the 2003 webcast 'Scream of the Shalka' to enter pro- duction without apparently being noticed and leaked might sug- gest these claims were overstated), and this was often linked to hopes that the programme would return. During the show's long period off the air, the gaps between the fans, the merchandise and *Doctor Who* itself (so to speak) completely collapsed when novels were published as the official continuation of the cancelled show, and writers emerged from fandom to author most of them.

When the programme returned in 2005, it would be inescapably tied to many of these developments, and be merchandised along multiple product lines, many of them written or created by the fans- turned-professionals who had emerged in the 1990s. If we were to ask

how did professional Doctor Who work fit within a wider writing career?
then the writing team for the 2005 season – the first of the rebooted
programme – covered almost every possible answer. Russell T. Davies
had a *New Adventure* to his credit and Steven Moffat had both a short
story for Virgin and the *The Curse of Fatal Death* comedy sketch for the
Comic Relief charity night, but both had built stellar television careers
away from *Who*. At the opposite end of the spectrum, Paul Cornell's
career was indelibly tied to the programme's offshoots, and, though
a jobbing TV writer and novelist, had never had a breakthrough
show to raise his profile significantly outside fandom. Between these
extremes, Mark Gatiss had a BAFTA as part of the comedy group *The
League of Gentlemen*, but consistently returned to *Who* projects for
Big Finish and BBC Worldwide between other engagements.

One thing which united these writers, however, was their familiarity with the wider world of *Who* spin-off projects, something
Davies lost no time in endorsing once his new job was announced.
'If you aren't into Big Finish, or the BBC books, or Scott Gray's comic
strip, then start now. They're wonderful worlds,' he told *Doctor
Who Magazine* in the first interview he gave them after the show's
return was announced.[1] Those wonderful worlds were crucial in this
connection not just because specific titles were directly adapted
or used as inspiration for specific episodes (Cornell's novel *Human
Nature* was adapted for the third season, Rob Shearman's and Marc
Platt's audios *Jubilee* and *Spare Parts* were inspiration one way or
another for 'Dalek' and 'Rise of the Cybermen'/'The Age of Steel')
nor because Davies had written a *New Adventure*, *Damaged Goods*,
about a family called Tyler living on a sinkhole housing estate,[2] but
because so many of those stories had been grappling with exactly
the same issues confronting Davies as he reshaped the show: *how
do you inject more emotional content into a Doctor Who story? How do
you make the format matter in the twenty-first century?* Paul Cornell
would recall, 'I was told, and in no uncertain terms to "use my *New
Adventures* voice" for 'Father's Day'. The new series owes so much
to those books, from small turns of phrase to entire new directions
for Doctors and companions. It is very much the *New Adventures*
by other means.'[3] Thus, by a strange twist, *Who* products which
had been precision exercises in niche-marketing in the 1990s now
constituted a massive Research and Development Division for what
became a massive mainstream hit.

There is a danger of overstating that. Those novels which were adapted needed significant adjustment,[4] but the objections from fans who disliked the development was largely the same. Whilst the keyword to dismissing the emotional content of the *New Adventures* had been 'angst' (the term is often applied to the anguished emotions of teenagers and twenty-somethings, and thus it resonated, for those who used it, with the youth of the writers), the shift to television meant that the new term of derision was 'soap opera'. You don't need to search the internet long to find comments such as this one: '*Doctor Who* was best when it was like Hammer House of Horror! Not a ruddy soap opera!'[5] This may constitute the postmillennial equivalent of the late 1970s complaint that Graham Williams had turned the programme into '*Fawlty Towers* in Space' – see Chapter One – an objection that the new genre material, however successful in its own right, was inappropriate content for *Doctor Who*. Amidst the sound and fury generated by those making such objections, it is easy to miss the more traditional influences. When Chris Chibnall was handed the job of bringing back the Silurians, chief-writer Steven Moffat advised him to start by rereading Malcolm Hulke's novelization *Doctor Who and the Cave-Monsters*.[6] Indeed, as part of the publicity for Moffat's first season, the production office released a photo of his 11-year-old self earnestly reading the very first novelization, *Doctor Who and the Daleks*.

Moffat (having withdrawn from online *Doctor Who* forums) responds to fan concerns in the pages of *Doctor Who Magazine* and on the social-networking site Twitter. It was the magazine which was Russell T. Davies' favoured venue to address the fan audience. In 1996, the magazine had been concerned that if the American pilot went to series, the publication would have little access to the production office. Geography alone would have favoured the US science-fiction magazines. With Davies in the hot seat of the new BBC production, no such problems presented themselves. Like many a fan in their 30s and 40s, his memories of growing up with the programme incorporated 'the monthly' just as much as the television broadcasts themselves and he could wax eloquently about memories of buying it as a child. *DWM* was edited and written by fans whom Davies respected and it came to influence the series in sizeable ways. When third season writer Stephen Greenhorn observed in *Doctor Who Magazine* that writing the show was different from any other because the lead character changed the world around him rather than have to undergo emotional growth himself, Davies responded by handing him a script commission – 'The Doctor's Daughter' – which would push the Time Lord emotionally further than ever before.[7] In February 2007, Davies began a 14-month email conversation with Benjamin Cook, *DWM*'s lead writer and interviewer, with the intent that the end result would become a book detailing the programme's production over the course of a year. With a candid Davies tossing out half-formed ideas more or less as they appeared in his head, the responses of an increasingly confident Cook couldn't help but be fed back into his thought processes: 'It's funny you defining the street scene as the "end of Act One" because then I thought of the next scene as the "start of Act Two" – and wrote it accordingly! This email correspondence is having a direct effect on the actual script. Is that weird?' As the correspondence continues, Cook initiates conversations which result in Davies removing the traditional end of season cliffhanger from 'Journey's End' and to the BBC rethinking the transmission dates for 'The End of Time'.[8] In the 1980s, John Nathan-Turner had granted *DWM* a level of access to the programme which was unprecedented at the time (and which other shows can only dream of *now*), but many formal barriers between the programme and its spin-off magazine were maintained. The cheery tone of postmillennial *DWM* conveyed a casualness about relationships which showed how many of those barriers had been broken down. One editorial chirped, 'David actually phoned up the *DWM* office yesterday. "Oh, I'm just editing the interview with your successor," I said, with a complete lack of tact. "Sorry, David, I didn't mean to make you feel like yesterday's man!"'[9] That tone was perhaps the major change between 1980s *DWM* and today's. The fan-produced analysis of the original run which the magazine had published during the period of cancellation fell away, replaced by interviews with cast and crew alongside reviews. Production quality and page count had both mushroomed since Jeremy Bentham first explained what a script editor did, but it was recognizably the same magazine.

This continuity at *DWM* was an example of how fan discourse was not going to die – that was never going to happen in the internet age – but certain traditional fan pastimes did became unfeasible.

Buying every spin-off product became an expense beyond the means of all but the professional collector. Collecting/scrapbooking all press coverage became similarly daunting as the cast were interviewed everywhere by a hungry media which was itself vastly expanded beyond what it had been in the days of the programme's original run. Moreover fans, no longer the only market, lost control of the major product lines. The DVD box set of the first season, a square TARDIS box, was clearly designed as an eye-catching Christmas present rather than something which could be handily stored at home, and fans disliked its size, the arrangement of the discs inside, and, later, the tendency for its cardboard construction to fall apart.[10] Nor were the discs themselves compiled with a fan's wish for every promotional interview and a complete set of trailers in mind. Instead, they were aimed at a more general – frankly, less anal – viewer. The second season box even overlooked the minute-long TARDISode prologues which were available as downloads in the week before a given episode's transmission. Similarly, the novels aimed at thirty-somethings were cancelled (along with the openness to submissions which had played such a part in their success) whilst a new series of books accessible to 10 year olds prospered. However, nothing emphasized the difference between the old dispensation – when merchandise was aimed at fans – and the new than the launch of *Doctor Who Adventures*.

First published in April 2006 to coincide with the transmission of Season Two, *Doctor Who Adventures – DWA* – was initially fortnightly, but went weekly in 2008. It was, for a while in 2008, reported to be the second best-selling comic in the country. When its style and design became the basis for a revamped *Doctor Who Annual,* that publication was similarly successful. Since 2006 saw no new *Harry Potter* novel published, the 2007 annual (released August 2006) became the best-selling children's book of the year, beating the traditional best-selling annual, *The Beano*. The comic itself seems aimed at seven year olds, and is, in every sense, an anti-collectable. Whilst *Doctor Who Magazine* is designed to be saved as a reference work for years to come (it doesn't even carry a 'remember to recycle after use' note like so many publications do, it knows it will be kept), *DWA* is full of stickers to be plastered onto walls or bedposts, posters to be similarly displayed, mini-mags to be cut out and reassembled as A5 booklets, play scenes for similar extraction with paper figures to move around and word-searches and games to be completed and written in. It has free gifts which make flat storage impossible, and sometimes comes in a plastic bag which must be cut open to access the contents. The number of pages which are intended to be read are vastly outnumbered by those which are meant to be detached. It is a product which is designed to be pulled apart and it was a long time since *Doctor Who* had generated one of those. (*DWM* itself ceased to have detachable features as a regular part of the magazine itself in the mid-90s.)

Amidst the publishing frenzy that ensued in the wake of the programme's success, themes which had been marginal to fan interest gained a public airing once more. The scientific principles underlying the show were the subject of two volumes (*The Science of Doctor Who* and *A Teaspoon and an Open Mind – The Science of Doctor Who*) as was the programme's theological content (*Back in Time: The Thinking Fan's Guide to Doctor Who* and *Behind the Sofa: A Closer Look at Doctor Who*). Neither made any impact on fan thought, but they were made for other markets. No project from the days before fandom came to dominate the agenda was so obscure that it couldn't be resurrected. Although it was obvious that there would be academic criticism, who would have thought that Matt Hills would have defined his book *Triumph of a Time Lord* so completely in terms of *Doctor Who: The Unfolding Text* even to the point of asking John Tulloch to write a foreword?[11]

The 2010 Election

With books on theology, philosophy and science proliferating, this chapter could be endless – as apparently endless as the coverage and readings which twenty-first-century *Who* generates, but perhaps nothing proved more completely how central the programme had become – and the attention given to popular culture in twenty-first-century society – than its recurrent presence in the General election of 2010. I don't mean by this the Liberal Democrat candidate for Blaenau Gwent (one Matt Smith, who came third), or even the fact that the same party's English Party chair and Federal Vice President, Brian Orrell, had appeared as a Cyberman opposite Colin Baker and Sylvester McCoy. That is just trivia. What was not trivial was the way in which, as both the 2010 election and the Eleventh Doctor's first full episode loomed, the Sylvester McCoy era suddenly entered the spotlight, generating headlines and newspaper coverage that it could only have dreamed of at the time of its first transmission.

Following comments from McCoy himself, *The Sunday Times* ran a story on its third page on 14 February detailing the left-wing bias of the show in the late 1980s (see Chapter Five).[12] Treated with the sort of seriousness which surrounds information newly released under the 30-year rule, the revelations generated further coverage in other national papers and on local radio stations the next day, culminating that evening in an item on BBC2's *Newsnight*. Terrance Dicks was interviewed earlier in the day and Andrew Cartmel appeared live in the studio alongside fan and ex-Tory MP Tim Collins. Jonathan Powell, who had been Head of Drama when *Who* went on its 1985 hiatus and Controller of BBC1 when it was finally put to rest, was interviewed in a clip about the wider issues of the time, recalling heated conversations with Norman Tebbit about alleged bias at the BBC. They made him stand next to a Dalek, but he still seemed unable to bring himself to mention *Doctor Who*.

The comments section of *The Sunday Times*'s online version had contained some right-wing fuming: 'If only the Conservatives had the guts to take a broom to the trendy BBC Lefties, all of them high on the hog on taxpayers money. The BBC staff never seem to smell the stench of hypocrisy when they preach socialism, while looting taxpayers' (posted 14 February 2010[13]). By contrast, the Conservative presence on *Newsnight* was much more relaxed. As an ex-Tory MP (he'd lost his seat in 2005), Tim Collins was something of a celebrity fan, and had been interviewed in that capacity on the DVD of the Fifth Doctor story 'Earthshock'.[14] Joining Cartmel in the studio of BBC2's late night political news show, he suggested, referring to 'The Sun Makers' (1977) and 'World War Three' (2005), that *Doctor Who* satirized governments of the day whether they were left or right, challenged the assertion that British traditions of science-fiction were uniformly left wing (citing Arthur Conan Doyle and C. S. Lewis), and recalled the relaxed view of the McCoy era taken by its Conservative fans.

> There were a whole number of us at Central Office, including peo-
> ple who then went on to become Director of Communications to
> Michael Howard, and a young David Cameron, who were watching

> *Doctor Who*, knew perfectly well what they were doing, but, partly
> because we loved the programme, and partly also because, I have
> to say, by that stage, it had the same number of viewers as the
> average.[15]

The next bit of the sentence is obscured by the interruption of presenter Gavin Esler and some general hilarity. The sentence is never
concluded, so whatever Collins was going to say after the long
subordinate clause about ratings is lost to history. The implication
seems clear though. Collins' measured response allowed him to
associate the current Tory leader with the programme whilst distancing both himself and Cameron from the heated issues of the
Thatcher administration.

On the internet, some fans speculated that now that *Who* was
such a prestigious piece of television, one which was integral to the
BBC's claims of quality and distinctiveness, that right-wing commentators would increasingly funnel their attacks on the corporation through the programme. Thus, either the *Times*' 'expose' or
Collins' more laid-back response can be seen as political manoeu-
vring. Even *DWM* took time out from its anticipation of Matt Smith's
first season to contextualize the events in terms of consistent Fleet
Street attacks on the Corporation, reminding readers that

> much of the press is clearly keen to see the BBC weakened.
> Meanwhile we have a Conservative party openly admitting that it
> will 'cut the BBC back to core broadcasting' if it gets into power.
> There is a general election in a month or two.[16]

Whilst acknowledging that 'entertainment' was a trivial issue upon
which to determine one's vote, and claiming that the editor had yet
to decide where to place his cross, the editorial left no doubt that
the programme was a serious part of debates about Public Service
Broadcasting. As part of that debate, both Russell T. Davies and
Steven Moffat let it be known that they feared for the future of the
BBC under Conservative government, and more ringing celebrity
endorsements came on 21 April when a party political broadcast by
the Labour Party began with Peter Davison addressing the camera,
and concluded with David Tennant's voice-over. Sean Pertwee, son
of Third Doctor Jon, also appeared in Tennant-voiced broadcasts
for Labour. David Cameron had to respond to journalists about

Tennant's political preferences on BBC Radio 5 ('I'm so old I'm sort of Jon Pertwee country, and a bit of Tom Baker ... that's a pity but there we are. You're never going to win over everybody. I definitely believe there's no point trying to win over everyone'[17]) and he, like all major party leaders, was later quizzed on a number of cultural choices including favourite Doctor. There had, of course, been a British election in 1979, the year that *Doctor Who Weekly* debuted, but the political parties were not quizzed then on such important policy questions as the relative merits of Pertwee or Tom Baker.

Amidst all of this, a self-referential series of images graced the front cover of the *Radio Times* for the week 17–23 April. Issued in three collectable covers, the magazine displayed Daleks in front of London landmarks during wartime. Promoting the new coloured variation to be unveiled in that week's episode ('Victory of the Daleks'), the covers featured Daleks in red, blue and yellow, the colours of Britain's major political parties. Readers could pick according to their political preference (or according to which political party they felt was most appropriately incarnated as a Dalek). The Green Party subsequently appropriated the imagery in a short video shown briefly on its YouTube page. The video divided the screen into four quarters, three of which contained the politically-coloured Daleks. The fourth contained a green rabbit. The song 'One of these things is not like the others' played atop the video until the rabbit shot all three Daleks with red eyebeams shooting from its eyes. The video's short lifespan on YouTube – it was removed within a couple of days – was probably due to the copyright infringements.

This was not the first time that an episode featuring the Doctor's arch enemies had been transmitted during an election. Five years earlier, when Christopher Eccleston was the Doctor and the new series was only six episodes old, 'Dalek' had played the weekend before the election, and *Radio Times* had conflated the two with the slogan VOTE DALEK and a memorable image of the creatures by the Houses of Parliament. The 2010 cover – again emblazoned VOTE DALEK – evoked the 2005 one, which was itself an update of an image from a widely circulated publicity still from 1964 when, in William Hartnell's 'The Dalek Invasion of Earth', the creatures had glided across Westminster bridge with Parliament in the background. The 2005 image had proven so striking that in September 2008 it was voted the most iconic magazine cover ever in a public vote held by the Periodical Publishers Association, beating other short-listed covers from iconic publications such as *Vogue* and *Time Out*. You did not need to understand all of this to enjoy the 2010 cover as a strong image in itself, but the nation's best-selling magazine was playing with the programme's imagery in a self-referential way which had previously been the hallmark of fanzines and niche-marketed products.

No less surprising was the presentation of a survey undertaken by the polling organization YouGov to establish the public response to the televised debates between party leaders (the first in the UK's history). Under a headline *'More Interesting' Than Doctor Who*, and with an accompanying picture of Matt Smith and Karen Gillan, YouGov reported '29% claimed that the leaders' debates were the most interesting programmes on TV over the past two weeks, leaving *Doctor Who* (17%) and *Britain's Got Talent* (10%) far behind.'[18]

None of these references taken individually means very much, and *Doctor Who* did not decide the course of the election. Together, however, all these references to *Who* across the election period – unthinkable a decade earlier – amply demonstrated how the new programme had become a common reference point in twenty-first century Britain. And if the *Radio Times* could play self-reflexively with the programme's history, another rubicon was crossed in 2006 when the show itself reflected at length – rather than in vicious passing as in 'The Greatest Show in the Galaxy' – upon its own, no-longer mocked fanbase.

Love & Monsters: Davies and Fandom

The children who tore *Doctor Who Adventures* to pieces in their eagerness to remove the free gift or to stick the posters up were Davies' audience, the one he enthused about when discussing book signings in his column in *DWM*. By contrast, he and his team kept organized fandom at arm's length. Unlike the 1980s, regular cast and senior staff avoided conventions. Producer Phil Collinson worked for four years on the show, but attended his first convention only after leaving. They preferred to be visible and in contact with fans through media outlets and BBC events which drew attendees from a broader range of society.

Davies would direct particular rage towards fans on the internet whose destructive criticism he could not protect his writers from.

> Now there's a new element in the room: writers wondering 'What will they say about me?' Meaning, online. More and more with every writer. It's those internet message boards. The forums. They destroy writers ... when Helen Raynor went on *Outpost Gallifrey* last month to read the reviews of her two Dalek episodes. She said that she was, literally, shaking afterwards ... Helen is ... on the verge of being really very good – and now she finds herself ruined by this wall of hostility. It makes me furious.[19]

Davies dramatized his views on the bulldozer attitude of obnoxious fans in the second season episode 'Love & Monsters'.

Because the leads were busy filming a different episode 'Love & Monsters' was an episode which would feature little of the Doctor and Rose, but would spotlight the Abzorbaloff, the winner of a monster-designing competition on *Blue Peter* which had received 43,920 entries. The story concerns a young man, Elton, who is haunted by a meeting with the Doctor when he was three or four years old. Just as the novels of the 1990s had dramatized fandom as a group of conspiracy theorists hunting down the truth about the Doctor through glimpsed encounters, rumours and shared fanzines, so Elton finds a band of kindred spirits. Their interest manifests itself in theories (one member, Colin Skinner, believes the Doctor to be less of an individual than a collection of archetypes) and creativity (one member, an artist called Bliss works on an abstract sculpture which she hopes will 'sum up the Doctor – what he means to us'). Speedily, the single-minded concern with the Doctor gives way to wider emotional support and the sharing of interests within the group. Communally engaging in music and cookery, the group members, many of whom are somewhat socially underskilled, become the group of friends that they all need.

This harmony is broken by the arrival of Victor Kennedy, the human form of the Abzorbaloff. He too seeks the Doctor, but only to absorb/consume/own him. The niceties of human interaction are beneath him. 'Don't make this personal,' he tells the group as he refixes their sights on the Doctor to the exclusion of all else. The visual metaphor for his lack of humanity is his inability to touch anyone without consuming them. Rearranging their communal space as a classroom with him dispensing 'homework', he doesn't care what the Doctor 'means to' anyone else, or their wider emotional lives, but focuses everyone on his goal, consuming nearly all of them along the way. When the Doctor arrives at the programme's conclusion he stands back from the battle. Rather than acting himself, he simply inspires – as he inspired so much of the creativity and action outlined in this book – those who have already been absorbed to act against the monster from their position inside his body/consciousness and destroy the Abzorbaloff.

It is no coincidence that at least one member of Elton's group is an aspirant author. Every DWAS local group of the 1980s had at least one, if not more. Some of them ended up working with Davies on the revamped series. On the off-chance that they read it, the parents of children whose bedrooms are bedecked with *Who* posters and toys can take some encouragement, I think, from the creativity and critical energy documented in this book. If your child lives in a TARDIS-inspired dream world and says they're going to write for *Doctor Who* – well, it is a long shot career option, but it can happen!

Will it, though? Will history repeat itself, producing a second generation of fans for whom the barrier between fan and professional became so permeable? Or will the vastly different cultural environment within which the new television series flourishes cause fandom to take a different turn? Whilst creativity has an easy outlet on the internet, it is often an unedited first-draft form, whereas the fanzine culture of the 1980s preached the virtues of precision, deftness and redrafting. We might also ask if the programme itself – now faster-paced, celebrity-packed and telling significantly shorter stories – is still capable of producing that creative spark. Literacy had always been a traditional value of the show, but is the programme, in its faster, sleeker modern form, still, as fan/comedian Toby Hadoke's argued in his one-man show *Moths Ate My* Doctor Who *Scarf*, 'a vocabulary-builder'?

We cannot, of course, know the answers yet, but the omens seem good. Whatever its speed, twenty-first-century *Who* retains its commitment to the written word. 'You want weapons?' the Doctor asks, in 'Tooth and Claw', 'We're in a library. Books! The best weapons in the world'. He puts his glasses on – always a key symbol for book-learning – and continues 'This room's the greatest arsenal we could have'. Similarly, writers feature recurrently in its list of historical guest appearances (Dickens, Shakespeare and Agatha Christie). Amidst the spin-off merchandise, books proliferate amidst the toys. *Doctor Who Adventures* is often criticised online (by those far too old to be part of its audience) for its lack of written content, but it is a comic where children's fantasy books are often advertised and/or given away as prizes. *Who* is also an annual presence in the *Quick Reads*, a series of cheap, short books designed to encourage reading. This warms the hearts of that generation of fans whose own acquisition of literacy is so tied to the early Target books (that Terrance Dicks writes some of the *Quick Reads* is the icing on this particular cake). Although *Doctor Who Magazine* has access to an unprecedented number of production crew, writers remain closest to the magazine's heart, with every scripter being interviewed under the semi-regular feature 'Script Doctors'. Atop this great mountain of literacy-encouragement sat Davies himself, and now Steven Moffat, superstars interviewed everywhere, and always a focal point of the show's most upmarket merchandise/analysis (this being *Doctor Who*, the two categories merge). Many programmes feature guest stars, but *Doctor Who* has become, under Moffat's stewardship, a show where guest star writers, famed for their work in other media, such as Richard Curtis (author of big-screen hits such as *Notting Hill*) and comics/fantasy author Neil Gaiman contribute an episode.

Paul Cornell, who has featured so recurrently in this book, has explicitly drawn the link between the past and present, the old series and the new. Writing in the book which reprinted the scripts for 2005 series, he characteristically took a long view of the place the volume held within the history of *Who*:

> One good thing Russell has done with the new Doctor Who is something Terrance [Dicks] did with the old. He's made the audience aware of the writers. I remember thumbing through Terrance's *The Making of Doctor Who* when I was a child, and finding that the only credit, for every story, was the writer, big and bold. That's a fiction, of course, in television where there's always joint authorship ... But this emphasis on writing will, hopefully, make small children again start thinking about what being a writer involves.[20]

This book, of course, has traced the process whereby Cornell and others went from reading *The Making of Doctor Who* to actually making *Doctor Who* themselves. They did it because *Doctor Who* fans, more than anything else, were children of the Word. Whatever else you want to claim for it, 1980s *Who* fandom was conservative in its aesthetic theory. It craved validation on the most traditional of terms, seeking critical parity with the BBC's authored plays and BAFTA-winning serials. Although it sought to understand every aspect of the programme's production, its critical exegesis was strongly influenced by A/degree level literature studies, and it reserved its strongest opinions and lengthiest analysis for writers and producers. That exegesis and those opinions were practiced at length in the huge fanzine market of the time where writing and editing skills were rapidly developed. By the late 1980s, the leading fanzines were produced to professional levels and those involved easily made the transition to paid employment as demand for coverage and analysis of film and television boomed in the early 1990s. At that point, few fans had developed the skills necessary to break into television production itself, but the programme's cancellation passed *Who*'s future into the hands of emergent novelists who knew the series inside out. Whilst these writers established themselves, British television looked across the Atlantic, adopting an American practice whereby a programme's leading writer – usually its creator, though that wouldn't apply in *Who*'s case – was made an executive producer with authority to oversee all aspects of the show. This further enhanced the status of writers, and was a system which would never, for instance, have placed John Nathan-Turner at the helm of the programme's creative direction. When *Doctor Who* returned, the writers of its opening season – Davies, Moffat, Cornell, Robert Shearman, Mark Gatiss – were drawn from *Who* fandom and spin-off novels. Its directors were not. This, then, was the story of one generation of UK-based *Who* fans, and those who never gained media careers could at least enjoy products and series that were tailored to their favoured styles. They could also take pride in the way that their book and magazine buying in the 1990s had nurtured the work of so many now-established professionals.

Many of those who currently enjoy Matt Smith's travels in the TARDIS, of course, were too young to be part of the story I have told. They were not born when *Skaro* was voted the DWAS' favourite fanzine, or when *DWB* was calling for the producer's head. What compensatory experiences lie ahead for today's eight-year-old viewers? What will it mean to be a fan when fan status can be worn so lightly, acquired simply by logging on and marking the new episode out of ten? They won't – unless they're extremely socially unskilled and handle it badly – be derided for collecting a television series on DVD. Nor will they know what it means for existing episodes to be as inaccessible as the Arctic and as valuable as gold dust. In the decentred world, it seems unlikely that someone could, as Jeremy Bentham did, present information which would affect the course of fandom for decades.

That is what won't happen. I don't know what will. Prediction is a dubious art in this, as in everything. No one in the August of 1979, the last summer before *Doctor Who Weekly* hit the nation's newsstands, could predict Big Finish Productions, so we can't know what this new generation's *Doctor Who* experience will be. I'd be prepared to bet, however, that one of them will, decades from now, write a book outlining how that experience developed, mixing personal memory with wider cultural mapping. And there will be a market for that book.

NOTES

Introduction

1. 'Who on Earth is ... David Tennant?' *Doctor Who Magazine* No. 400 (15 October 2008), p. 74. Davies, Russell T. 'Production Notes' *Doctor Who Magazine* No. 341 (31 March 2004), p. 50.
2. Hearn, Marcus 'Happy Times and Places? Part One 1979–1985: Comic Timing' *Doctor Who Magazine* No. 344 (23 June 2004), pp. 26–34. The article – one of a series celebrating the magazine's 25th anniversary – contains an extensive account of Skinn's acquisition of the licence to produce a magazine based on *Doctor Who*.
3. McKee, Alan 'Which is the Best Doctor Who story? A Case Study in Value Judgements Outside the Academy' *Intensities: The Journal of Cult Media* No. 1 (2001). Find it now at intensities.org/essaysMcKee.pdf
4. McKee, Alan 'Why is "City of Death" the best Doctor Who story?' in Butler, David (ed.), *Time and Relative Dissertations in Space* (Manchester, Manchester University Press, Manchester, 2007), pp. 233–245.
5. Tulloch, John and Alvarado, Manuel *Doctor Who: The Unfolding Text* (MacMillan, London, 1983), p. 328.
6. 'Hall of Mirrors' *Doctor Who Magazine* No. 119 (December 1986), pp. 40–42.

7. Fans have learnt over the years that when criticizing the Corporation they need to be careful about whom they get in bed with. Active *Who* fans overwhelmingly support the licence fee and the ambitions of public service broadcasting. Fan views on such issues are frequently aired in the forums at www. Gallifreybase.com in the 'Active Television' section. Support for the licence fee/the BBC/Public Service Broadcasting is rarely articulated simply as a matter of protecting *Doctor Who*, but the role which the programme played/plays in shaping their views on this issue would make a fascinating study for another time.

8. The most influential work of the 'poacher' paradigm was Jenkins, Henry *Textual Poachers: Television Fans and Participatory Culture* (Routledge, New York/London 1992); Hills, Matt *Fan Cultures* (Routledge, London, 2002), p. 1; Gwenllian Jones, Sarah 'Web Wars: Online Fandom and Studio Censorship' in Jancovich, Mark and Lyons, James (eds.), *Quality Popular Television* (British Film Institute, London, 2003), pp. 163–177.

9. Letters, *Skaro* No. 6 (Autumn 1992), p. 6.

10. Quoted in Howe, David J. and Walker, Stephen James *Doctor Who: The Television Companion* (London, BBC, 1998), p. 155. The book reprints fan and viewer responses of every sort and is an excellent resource.

11. A lot of the information in this and the following paragraph is taken from research by Stephen James Walker, presented originally in *Talkback: The Unofficial and Unauthorised Doctor Who Interview Book Volume One: The Sixties* (Telos, Tolworth, 2006), pp. 101–102 and *Volume Two: The Seventies* (Telos, Tolworth, 2006), pp. 216–221.

12. *The Doctor Who Annual 1975* (London, World Distributors, 1974), 'The House That Jack Built' is on pp. 6–12. I'm obliged to Keith Miller for sharing his recollections of the story's publication.

I   Blue Diamond

1. Stoppages commenced in on 6 August, with the whole ITV network down by 10 August. It returned at 5:45 p.m. on Wednesday, 24 October. During the period, it only transmitted a white-on-blue caption apologizing for the lack of programmes. The

exception was Channel Television, which, serving the Channel Islands, had different agreements with the unions. With no network programming to show, however, the company was forced to fill the entire evening with repeats of regional programming. Bizarrely, reports suggest that the white/blue caption card frequently reached audiences of a million as people sat there waiting for the network to return. Also bizarrely, *Who* hit its peak rating not during the strike itself but on the Saturday after it was over (possibly because no programming had been made during the strike and ITV's hurriedly constructed schedule wasn't a well-balanced one).

2. Collins, Andrew. *Where Did It All Go Right?* (Ebury Press, London, 2003). All page references given in the text.

3. The definitive history of the publishing, packaging and promotion – if not the literary aesthetics – of the novelizations is Howe, David J. *The Target Book* (Telos, Tolworth, 2007).

4. Marter, Ian *Doctor Who and the Ribos Operation* (Target, London, 1979); Dicks, Terrance *Doctor Who and the Pyramids of Mars* (Target, London, 1976); Dicks, Terrance *Doctor Who and the Horns of Nimon* (Target, London, 1980).

5. Cornell, Paul 'Frontier in Space' *Doctor Who Magazine Special Edition No. 2: The Complete Third Doctor* (September 2002), p. 53.

6. Hulke, Malcolm *Doctor Who and the Doomsday Weapon* (Target, London, 1974).

7. *Doctor Who and the Sea-Devils* (1974), *Doctor Who and the Green Death* (1975), *Doctor Who and the Dinosaur Invasion* (1976). All written by Hulke, all published by Target in London.

 I'd advise any fans of Hulke's *Who* work to seek out, if they don't already own it, his 1977 children's novel, *The Siege* (easily found on ebay). It is the first in a series of books in which Roger Moore puts together a group of young detectives. I won't spoil the story by explaining how the plot turns on the production of *Doctor Who* – but suffice it to say that in this fictional incarnation at least, Moore is clearly unfamiliar with the 1971 Pertwee adventure 'Terror of the Autons'. Hulke, Malcolm. *Roger Moore and the Crimefighters: The Siege* (Alpine Books, London, 1977).

8. Howe, *Target Book*, pp. 70–71 contains a list of 45 oft-repeated chapter titles.

9. On the dumbing down of the dialogue in late-seventies novelizations, giving many examples, see Henley, Dennis E. 'From Flickering Image to Printed Page' in *Fantasy Empire* No. 1 (July 1981) (New Media Publishing, Largo: Florida), pp. 36–42.

10. Gatiss, Mark *Doctor Who: Last of the Gadarene* (BBC, London, 2000). The quotation is from the Foreword (page not numbered).

11. Dicks would recall meeting Tom Baker and producer Graham Williams in the BBC bar in the late seventies and being 'completely insufferable because they asked what I was up to, and I said "well, I'm off to Paris for a few days to be on the jury of a science fiction film festival, and then I'm going over to Los Angeles". I had this mental picture of Tom and Graham sitting in the bar later saying, "It's not fair! Who's the producer? Who's the star?"' 'Third Men: (Interview with Terrance Dicks and Barry Letts)' *Doctor Who Magazine* No. 337 (10 December 2003), p. 23.

12. Parkin, Lance 'Canonicity Matters: Defining the Doctor Who Canon' in Butler, David (ed.). *Time and Relative Dissertations in Space* (Manchester University Press, Manchester, 2007), p. 249.

13. *Doctor Who Monthly* reported the issue in this manner: 'Due to the allegorical nature of this story by Robert Holmes, dealing as it does with the horrific prospects of taxation gone mad, *Target* have previously shied away from doing this adaptation for fear it might go over the heads of most readers. Terrance Dicks, however, is confident he has managed to bridge this hurdle satisfactorily, keeping all the subtle humour of tobert [sic] holmes ingenious teleplay while making it a readable Doctor Who story in its own right'. *Doctor Who Magazine* No. 71 (December 1982), p. 4.

14. Dicks, Terrance *Doctor Who and the Sunmakers* (Target, London, 1982), p. 117.

15. Hulke, Malcolm and Dicks, Terrance *The Making of Doctor Who* (Pan Books, London, 1973).

    Dicks, Terrance and Hulke, Malcolm *The Making of Doctor Who* (Target, London, 1976).

16. Hulke, Dicks, *Making*, p. 111.

17. Parkin, Lance *Time Unincorporated: The Doctor Who Fanzine Archives Volume One* (Des Moines, Mad Norwegian Press, 2009), p. 32.

18. *Doctor Who: Radio Times Special* (BBC, London, 1973), p. 24.

19. Dicks, *Making*, p. 75.

20. Lofficier, Jean-Marc *The Doctor Who Programme Guide Volume 1: The Programmes* (Target, London, 1981), p. 56.

21. Ironically, the novel of 'The Green Death' characterizes American comics in the most dismissive terms. The psychopathic security guard Hinks is a comics reader 'He had a big collection of comics, mainly American, most of them full of pictures which told stories. He preferred pictures to words because he could not read very fast, although he tried to keep this a secret. Hinks had looked through the picture story many times before, but it always fascinated him to go through it again. He was just about to turn the page that carried the first picture of the torture sequence' (pp. 54–55).

22. Another intriguing conjunction of the two occurred in 1980 when Marvel's award-winning comic *The Uncanny X-Men*, making its way at this point from fan favourite to mass sales, inadvertently ripped off a 1970s Pertwee *Who* story. In X-Men issues 141 and 142 ('Days of Future Past'), elderly X-Men in a dystopic future time jump the consciousness of one of their number back to the present day to stop the events which lead to their own grim world. 'Magically, the whole plot appeared in my head,' co-writer John Byrne would recall years later, 'and about four or five years later I was living in Chicago. *Doctor Who* was running on a local PBS and on came this episode called 'Day of the Daleks', which I had seen when I was living in London, Ontario, around 1975. It was basically 'Days of Future Past'. O dear, God! No wonder it popped into my head whole. It's the same story'. John Byrne, interviewed in DeFalco, Tom. *Comic Creators on X-Men* (Titan Books, London, 2006), p. 113.

23. *Doctor Who Weekly* No. 10 (19 December 1979).

24. For analysis of *The Star Beast*, see Barnes, Alan 'The Star Beast' in *Doctor Who Magazine Special Edition No. 6: We Love Doctor Who* (November 2003), p. 51.

25. Kroton's adventures were reprinted in *Doctor Who: The Glorious Dead* (Panini, Tunbridge Wells, 2006). Abslom Daak's were collated as the *Abslom Daak: Dalek Killer* graphic novel (Marvel, London, 1990).

26. *Doctor Who Weekly* No. 26 (9 April 1980), p. 11.

27. French, Gavin. 'Astronomy of Doctor Who: Voga' *TARDIS* Vol. 4, No. 5 (1979). Published by the Doctor Who Appreciation Society.

28. Dollin, Tim 'Teleview: City of Death' *TARDIS* Vol. 4, No. 6 (1979).

29. Vincent-Rudzki, Jan. 'The Deadly Assassin' *TARDIS,* Vol. 2, No. 1 (January/February 1977). Quoted in *Celestial Toyroom* (October 1991). Both published by the Doctor Who Appreciation Society.

30. Peel, John 'Teleview' *TARDIS* Vol. 5, No 1 (1980), p. 9.

    For more criticism in this vein (though less sarcastic), see Howe, David J. and Walker, Stephen James *Doctor Who: The Television Companion* (BBC, London, 1998). Covering every story up to its date of publication, the book collects review comments from diverse sources. Those concerning the late 70s stories contain much criticism from the period culled from fanzines.

31. Tulloch, John and Alvarado, Manuel *Doctor Who: The Unfolding Text* (Macmillan, London, 1983), p. 151. Levine's choice of *Fawlty Towers* as a reference point was perhaps influenced by John Cleese's cameo appearance as a pretentious art connoisseur in *City of Death*.

32. *Celestial Toyroom* (the DWAS newsletter), No. 2 (February 1984), p. 5.

33. 'Script Doctors: Gareth Roberts' *Doctor Who Magazine* No. 377 (3 January 2007), p. 15.

II   Jonathan and Jeremy

1. This can be contested. Lance Parkin has argued that season 17 contains better model work and jungle sets than Nathan-Turner achieved. However, this is a retrospective argument. The consensus at the time was that Nathan-Turner had markedly improved the programme's look.

    Parkin, Lance *Time Unincorporated: The Doctor Who Fanzine Archives Volume One: Lance Parkin* (Mad Norwegian Press, Des Moines, 2009), p. 37.

2. *Doctor Who: The Leisure Hive* (BBC DVD, London, 2004). BBC DVD 1351.

3. This is not to deny the existence of some striking visual moments under Graham Williams' producer-ship. Director Ken Grieve's innovative use of Steadicam on 'Destiny of the Daleks' should have earned him a place in Nathan-Turner's team of visual stylists, and the Parisian location filming for 'City of Death' produced a number of striking shots, such as the one in the first episode which begins as a close-up on a postcard in a rack, only for the card to be removed by an unseen souvenir hunter, and we see through the subsequent gap that the Doctor and Romana are walking down the road towards the camera. Taken together, however, such moments pass quickly and do less to draw attention to their own artiness than the lengthy pans and slow dissolves of the early 80s. Fan writing implicitly acknowledges this when, for example, basing claims for 'City of Death's excellence almost completely in terms of Douglas Adams' script. 'City of Death' has its own striking left-right pan. It's the opening shot of the second scene, a scene of Parisian blooms, and lasts 19 seconds. Unlike the shot in 'The Leisure Hive', our attention is drawn from the duration of the image by the witty banter of the Doctor and Romana on the soundtrack.

4. Tulloch, John and Alvarado, Manuel *Doctor Who: The Unfolding Text* (Macmillan, London, 1983), p. 249

5. Tulloch and Alvarado, *Unfolding Text*, p. 267.

6. Quoted in *In-vision: Warriors' Gate* No. 50 (1994) (Borehamwood). The production history of 'Warriors' Gate' is disputed by several of those involved. As the magazine notes, it is impossible to reconcile everyone's accounts of the writing and shooting of this story.

7. This wasn't true, but unlike the other writers of the period, author Christopher Bailey didn't make himself available for fan interviews or attend conventions, leading to fevered speculation that he was a cover name for someone more famous. Stoppard's name came into the frame when the playwright suggested in a radio interview that he'd done some work under pseudonyms for popular series' just to try different writing styles, and that one of these had concerned Buddhism.

8. Rickard, Graham *A Day With a TV Producer* (Wayland Publishers, Hove, 1980). Road, Alan *Doctor Who: The Making of a Television Series* (André Deutsch, London, 1983). Tulloch and Alvarado, *Unfolding Text*.

9. Bentham, Jeremy 'Architects of Fear', *Doctor Who Magazine* No. 48 (January 1981), pp. 16–19. The quotation is from p. 17.

10. In the 1960s, the first two Dalek serials were adapted for the big screen with Peter Cushing playing the part of 'Doctor Who'.

11. *Celestial Toyroom*, February 1982. Items featuring as actual news were the fact that Matthew Waterhouse was leaving in 'Earthshock' and the identities of the production personnel working on 'Time-Flight'.

12. *Doctor Who Magazine* No. 52 (May 1981), p. 27.

13. *Doctor Who Magazine* No. 60 (January 1982).

14. Harris, Neil 'Why DWM made me the fan I am' *Doctor Who Magazine* No. 400 (15 October 2008), p. 49.

15. Davies, Russell T. 'Production Notes' *Doctor Who Magazine* No. 346 (18 August 2004), p. 51.

16. *Doctor Who Monthly* No. 70 (November 1982), p. 6.

Cornell was by no means the only person pushing for a Sarah Sutton pin-up in the magazine. It was a running theme which some of the magazine's correspondents agreed with, but which frustrated others ('Why, why, why does Nyssa make every boy in the land head-over-heels, helplessly in love with her?' wrote Anna Hankey in issue 73's letters page). At the BBC convention held at Longleat over the Easter weekend that year, when Sarah Sutton invited questions from the audience, one teenager stuck his hand up and enquired what she was doing that night. Whatever else he thought he was doing, he was playing out a gag that was then running through the pages of *DWM*.

By the 1990s, it was a standard game at the less formal conventions to embarrass prominent fans by finding old letters they'd had printed in the magazine when much younger. Nick Pegg, for instance, by then an articulate critic of the Pertwee era, could be found in issue 55 (August 1981) declaring 'I count the Pertwee years the best', p. 4.

17. *Cygnus Alpha* No. 8 (November 1982, Published in Exeter), p. 28.

18. 'Review: Castrovalva' *Doctor Who Magazine* No. 63 (April 1982), p. 25. It may well be that Bentham's opinions were noted in the production office, for a year later, when the Doctor levitated again, his coat-tails did indeed drag downwards.

19. '4D War' script: Alan Moore, Art: David Lloyd. *Doctor Who Monthly* No. 50 (April 1981), p. 41.

20. *Doctor Who Winter Special* (December 1983).

21. Fleming, John 'The New Dr Who' in *Starburst* No. 27 (September/ October 1980). The interview covers pages 18–21. The quotation is from page 19. The title of the piece is intriguing since the Doctor remained played by Tom Baker. Did it just mean 'the new *Doctor Who* season' or did Fleming intuit that a whole-scale stylistic revolution was afoot?

22. *Doctor Who Magazine* No. 51 (April 1981). This quote and the following are from page 29.

23. Tulloch and Alvarado, *Unfolding Text*, p. 175. This was fairly scathing, since Granada's output (notably *Brideshead Revisited*, 1981) was being favourably compared to BBC productions at the time.

24. Fisher, David *Doctor Who and the Leisure Hive* (Target, London, 1982).

25. Smith, Andrew *Doctor Who – Full Circle* (Target, London, 1982), p. 70.

26. Bidmead, Christopher H. *Doctor Who – Logopolis* (Target, London, 1982), p. 52.

27. Marter, Ian *Doctor Who: Earthshock* (Target, London, 1983), p. 96.

28. Richardson, David '20 Minutes' in *Skaro* Vol. 3, No. 2 (November 1982), pp. 24–25.

29. Chapman, James *Inside The TARDIS: The Worlds of Doctor Who* (I.B.Taurus, London, 2006), p. 139.

30. http://www.gallifreyone.com/forum/showthread.php?t=5784. Accessed on 27 march 2008. This site – a wealth of fan analysis and comment – has, sadly, closed down.

31. Robins, Tim 'Who Wars' in *The Frame* (15 August 1990) (Tolworth), pp. 20–23.

32. Even within the BBC itself, replacing Lodge's titles was seen as a challenge. Sid Sutton, designer of the new titles, remembers that

replacing them was seen within the BBC as a difficult job: 'everyone was saying, "Poor old Sid! Dear, dear. Fancy having to do something after Bernard's. Rather you than me". So it was with a bit of trepidation that I actually tackled it'. Newman, Philip 'Sid Sutton Interview' *The Frame* No. 21/22 (Spring/Summer 1992) (Tolworth), p. 25.

III   American Express

1.   In a different book, with a different agenda, this could probably be substantially related to further standardizations of the programme's format in the early 1980s, a period when the previously established differences between the Doctors various foes were ignored. Since their second story, the Daleks had been consistently portrayed as a force to be reckoned with, ruling vast tracts of space, and sometimes displaying time-travel technology. The Cybermen are a significantly lesser force, seemingly stuck at much the same technological level for centuries and with their aggression permanently aimed at planet Earth. The Davison years, taking its cue not from on-screen stories but from their parity as the twin icons of the programme's history treats them as equivalent forces. 'The Five Doctors' states that both races were forbidden from the alien gladiatorial games of the Death Zone. 'Like the Daleks, they play too well,' says the Doctor of the Cybermen. In Colin Baker's first season, one guest character describes the Cybermen as 'the undisputed masters of space', which is laughable in the context of their limited ambitions and achievements as shown in previous stories. There are three *return of much-loved monster* (as opposed to 'villains') stories in Davison's tenure ('Earthshock', 'Resurrection of the Daleks' and 'Warriors of the Deep') and all three show an old foe attacking/infiltrating an isolated installation in space or beneath the sea as a staging ground for their wider assault on humanity or the Time Lords. This was standard modus operandi for the Cybermen in the 60s ('The Tenth Planet', 'The Moonbase', 'The Wheel in Space'), and in fan lexicon it's called the 'base under siege' subgenre. In the early 80s, it became the favoured tactic of all returning 'big' foes as the programme subordinated all

distinctions between them, as if, now that it was entering its third decade, the show should play to a generic folk-memory of what *Doctor Who* monsters do.

2. Sexually themed – indeed, pornographic – *Who* fanzines are extremely rare in the UK, but they do circulate within fandom. Nowadays you can read such fiction online. Before the internet it tended, rather than being openly offered for sale, to arrive unexpectedly in the post, often without anything to indicate its author or origins. Slash fiction was always going to find difficulty establishing itself within a fandom where even the more standard fiction was a low priority.

3. *Fantasy Empire* No. 6 (1982) (New Media Publishing, Tampa, Florida), p. 83.

4. *Cygnus Alpha* No. 8 (November 1982), pp. 26–27.

5. *Doctor Who Magazine* No. 82 (November 1983), p. 44 (back cover).

6. For some front-line tales from the American convention circuit see Nicholas Courtney, and Michael McManus, *Still Getting Away with It: The Life and Times of Nicholas Courtney* Published by www.scificollector.co.uk in conjunction with www.greyhoundleader.com, 2005, pp. 123–137.

7. Saunders, David 'Co-Ordinators Corner' *Celestial Toyroom* (January 1984), p. 2.

8. BBC *The Doctor Who Celebration: Twenty Years of a Time Lord* Commemorative Programme, p. 2.

9. By the time the BBC had elected to screen the programme on the twenty-fifth, international contracts had already been signed authorising foreign stations to transmit on the twenty-third, the actual anniversary. The *Doctor Who* production office always maintained that they had requested transmission on that date, but the story was held over two days for inclusion in the *Children in Need* charity broadcast. The programme – in which ex-companions and old monsters make a series of cameo appearances – doesn't look out of place. It is, obviously, inconceivable now that *Children in Need* would include an item of 90 minutes length.

10. Review of 'Planet of Evil' from *Skaro* fanzine Vol. IV, No. 1 (1983).

11. Twenty-four years later, when the story was released on DVD, writer Johnny Byrne had a metaphor to explain Amsterdam's relevance: 'It's below sea-level, and there is a hydrostatic pressure somewhere of all this water building up, and there is a sense of power here, otherwise the city would be inundated if it wasn't controlled or contained, so it's contained, and that was a nice thought and a nice image.' Whether that image of Amsterdam's power containment, let alone its metaphorical relationship to the threat of antimatter entering our universe, is clearly rendered in the finished product is something I rather doubt. Regardless, if Byrne had said this in 1983 in *DWM*, when its agenda-setting power reached right across fandom, the story's reception could have been massively different.
Doctor Who – Arc of Infinity BBC DVD 2327B, 2007.

12. *The Doctor Who Quiz Book* (December 1981), *The Doctor Who Crossword Book* (December 1982) *The Second Doctor Who Quiz Book* (December 1983), *Doctor Who: Brain Teasers and Mind Benders* (November 1984) *The Third Doctor Who Quiz Book* (October 1985) All published by Target, London. All written by Nigel Robinson, save *Brain Teasers* ... which was written by Adrian Heath, a 16-year-old fan.

13. Howe, David 'Reference Department' *Celestial Toyroom* (February 1982), p. 2.

14. Robinson, *Quiz Book*, p. 66, question 16; p. 76, question 12.

15. Howe, 'Reference Department', p. 2.

16. Both quotes from *Video Business*, review from issue dated 10 October 1983. Advert from issue dated 17 October 1983. Both quoted in Wyman, Mark 'Video Sales 1986–7' *Doctor Who Magazine* No. 278 (2 June 1999), pp. 28–9. Wyman's article contains significant information about the state of the video market in 1983 and the launch of the first BBC videos.

17. Haining, Peter, *Doctor Who – A Celebration: Two Decades Through Time and Space* (W. H. Allen, London, 1983), p. 9.

18. Haining, *Celebration,* Quotes from pages 185 ('The Evil of the Daleks'), 186 ('The Tomb of the Cybermen'), 219 ('The Horns of Nimon').

19. Haining, *Celebration* , p. 180.

20. 'Working for the Yankee Dollar' *Skaro* Vol. IV, No. 1, (October/November 1983). 'JN-T Working for the Yankee Dollar', *Doctor Who Bulletin* Summer Special (July 1986), p. 33.

IV   The New Vocabularies

1. 'No Confidence' (Editorial) *Skaro,* Vol. IV, No. 2 (December/ January 1983/84), p. 3.

2. *Cygnus Alpha* No. 12 (July 1984), p. 44; *Capitol* No. 2/3 (October 1984), p. 61; *Celestial Toyroom* No. 9 (September 1984), p. 10; *The Official Doctor Who Magazine* No. 93 (October 1984).

3. *Celestial Toyroom* (June 1984), p. 5.

4. *Celestial Toyroom* (February 1985), p. 14; *The CT Advertiser* (April 1985), p. 1.

5. *Doctor Who – The Sirens of Time* (Cassette/CD) (Big Finish Productions, Maidenhead, 1999).

6. Information on Audio Visuals is taken from Cook, Benjamin *Doctor Who: The New Audio Adventures: The Inside Story* (Big Finish Productions, Maidenhead, 2003), pp. 6–7.

7. Fiske, John 'Dr. Who, Ideology and the Reading of a Popular Narrative Text' *The Australian Journal of Screen Theory* No. 14 (1983), pp. 60–100.

8. Tulloch, John and Alvarado, Manuel *Doctor Who: The Unfolding Text* (Macmillan, London/Basingstoke, 1983).

9. 'Editorial' *Celestial Toyroom* (May 1984), p. 3.

10. Bennett, Tony and Janet Woollacott *Bond and Beyond: The Political Career of a Popular Hero* (Macmillan, London/Basingstoke, 1987).

11. Fiske, John *Television Culture* (Methuen, London/New York, 1987), pp. 10, 85.

12. Tulloch, John, *Television Drama: Agency, Audience and Myth* (Routledge, London/New York, 1990), p. 264.

13. Tulloch, John and Henry, Jenkins, *Science Fiction Audiences: Watching Doctor Who and Star Trek* (Routledge, London, 1995).

14. This story is most easily read in the 2007 Collected Comics edition. *Doctor Who: Voyager* (Panini Publishing, Tunbridge Wells, 2007). The extract quoted is on page 93 of this edition. It originally appeared in *Doctor Who Magazine* No. 98.

15. Saward, Eric *Doctor Who: Attack of the Cybermen* (Target, London, 1989), p. 50.

16. Marter, Ian *Doctor Who: The Dominators* (Target, London, 1984), p. 7.

17. *Celestial Toyroom* (September 1984), p. 6 and (October 1984), p. 10.
18. 'Ian Marter, Interview' *Paradise Lost* No. 1, (1984), p. 16.
19. Marter, Ian *Doctor Who: The Invasion* (Target, London, 1985), p. 95.
20. 'On Target' in *The Official Doctor Who Magazine* No. 96 (January 1985), p. 14.
21. Saward, *Attack*, p. 23. Bidmead, Christopher H. *Doctor Who: Frontios* (Target, London, 1984), p. 105.
22. Saward, Eric *Doctor Who: The Twin Dilemma* (Target, London, 1985).
23. This process whereby the programme's production effects are revealed is still unfolding thanks to digital restoration. The Patrick Troughton story 'The Mind Robber' takes place in a white void, and on VHS it appeared as exactly that. The cleaned-up picture on the DVD renders it obvious that the actors are performing against a white backcloth, the base of which is clearly visible as it touches the studio floor.

    The glossier series, such as *Star Trek*, to which *Doctor Who* is often compared have larger budgets and more time for retakes (many of the *Who* scenes into which boom mikes or technicians' limbs intrude might well have been reshot if time allowed). It is arguable that for this reason higher-budgeted shows do not reveal so many traces of their production as does *Doctor Who*. Someone more familiar than I with the fandoms for such shows might wish to consider how, if at all, this has affected fan interpretation.

24. In later decades, the 'so-bad-its-good' aesthetic would find more expression in *Who* fandom. How much? Gareth Roberts argued, in his 2004 DWM piece 'Strange Love' that it had become the dominant mode of appreciation of the programme within fandom, anecdotally backing this up with tales of convention hilarity: 'You see, it won't be *The Ark In Space*'s [artfully written and highly praised] 'Homo Sapiens!' speech you'll hear fanboys quoting in a convention bar at last orders, but rather *Silver Nemesis: The Extended Edition*'s 'Have you any idea how *hot* it will be?'

    I'm not at all convinced by this. As Roberts surely knows, opinions held and behaviour indulged in by the time last orders are called isn't always representative. Whatever they might jokingly perform, 'The Ark in Space', not 'Silver Nemesis', which fans actually respect. If the personal history reported in the article is accurate, Roberts adopted the practice of enjoying laughing at the programme's aesthetic failings by following the example of, and to fit in with, his brother and father who routinely derided the programme in front of him. For whatever reason – insensitivity to other peoples' opinions of the show, stronger confidence in our own aesthetic valuation, or the sheer luck of having more convivial viewing companions – not all of us had to make that accommodation. 'There must be a point,' Roberts argues, 'In the life of every fan – at least those who saw the original series on its original transmissions – when a pang of adolescent embarrassment hits you in the gullet for the first time while watching *Doctor Who*.' Call me insensitive, but though I obviously came to understand the programme's failings, I can't honestly remember any moment as visceral as the one he describes. Perhaps I was just lucky.

Roberts, Gareth 'Strange Love' *Doctor Who Magazine* No. 351 (5 January 2005), pp. 26–31. Quotes are from pages 27 and 26 respectively.

25. *Spectrox*, VIII, p. 11. The magazine would appear to have been published in 1989 or 1990.

26. Attwood, Tony *The Companions of Doctor Who – Turlough and the Earthlink Dilemma* (Target, London, 1986); Grimwade, Peter *Robot* (Star, London, 1987).

27. Gray, Scott 'The Neverending Story' *Doctor Who Magazine Special Edition: The Complete Sixth Doctor* (22 January 2003), p. 65.

28. Stevens, James and David Bishop *Doctor Who – Who Killed Kennedy* (Virgin, London, 1996); Mortimore, Jim *Doctor Who – Eternity Weeps* (Virgin, London, 1997); David A. McIntee *Doctor Who – Bullet Time* (BBC, London, 2001).

29. Lane, Andy and Jim Mortimore *Doctor Who – Lucifer Rising* (Virgin, London, 1993); Russell, Gary *Doctor Who – Legacy* (Virgin, London, 1994); Day, Martin *Doctor Who – The Menagerie* (Virgin, London, 1995); Lyons, Steve *Doctor Who – Conundrum* (Virgin, London, 1994); Hinton, Craig *Doctor Who – GodEngine* (Virgin, London, 1996).

30. Cornell, Paul *Doctor Who – Love and War* (Virgin, London, 1992); Cole, Stephen *Doctor Who – To the Slaughter* (BBC, London, 2005).
31. 'Script Doctors: Chris Chibnall' *Doctor Who Magazine* No. 381 (2 May 2007), p. 28.

V   The Next Generation

1. Coe, Jonathan *The Dwarves of Death* (Penguin, London, 1991), pp. 39–40.
2. Cartmel's longest account of his time on the show is his book *Script Doctor: The Inside Story of Doctor Who 1986–89* (Reynolds and Hearn Ltd, London, 2005). Although he largely declined to be interviewed during his time on the show, he has given a number of lengthy interviews since. One can be found in Stephen James Walker's *Talkback: The Unofficial and Unauthorised Doctor Who Interview Book Volume Three: The Eighties* (Telos, Tolworth, 2007). It was originally published in Time *Space Visualiser*, issue 40, July 1994. Some of the information about Cartmel's stylistic preferences, ambitions for the programme and his influences is taken from these sources.
3. Quoted in 'Shattering the Chains', an interview contained on the BBC DVD of *Doctor Who: The Curse of Fenric* (BBC DVD 1154, 2003).
4. Quoted in 'Endgame', a documentary on the BBC DVD of *Doctor Who: Survival* (BBC DVD 1834, 2007).
5. Interviewed by Peter Griffiths *Doctor Who Magazine* No. 244, (23 October 1996). Note the slippage between the two accounts. Cartmel insists the idea was to make the Doctor godlike to the Gallifreyans, whilst Clarke's formulation seems to suggest he's a God to humanity (presumably, the God of Judaism and Christianity).
6. Bishop, Vanessa 'Review: The Curse of Fenric' DVD, *Doctor Who Magazine* No. 336 (12 November 2003). Bishop was co-editor of an early-mid nineties fanzine, *Skaro*, which had published several articles on homosexual subtexts in another McCoy story, 'The Happiness Patrol', a debate during which nobody cited 'Fenric' as supporting evidence.
7. In the interests of balance, for instance, Tom Baker's 'The Sun Makers' would depict a 'Company' (and use left-wing language

to denounce it) exploiting the inhabitants of Pluto by means of excessive taxation (at that point, and since, a rallying call of the political right). Similarly, the conspirators in Pertwee's 'Invasion of the Dinosaurs' are simultaneously religious social conservatives and eco-extremists.

8. Briggs, Ian *Doctor Who: The Curse of Fenric* (Target, London, 1990), p. 153.

9. Briggs, Ian *Doctor Who: Dragonfire* (Target, London, 1989).

10. Briggs, Fenric Baker, Pip and Jane *Doctor Who: Terror of the Vervoids* (Target, London, 1987); Clarke, Kevin *Doctor Who: Silver Nemesis* (Target, London, 1989); Daly, Wally K. *Doctor Who: The Ultimate Evil* (Target, London, 1989).

11. 'What Elam calls the semiotic 'thickness' (multiple codes) of a performed text varies according to the 'redundancy' (high predictability) of 'auxiliary' performance codes' Tulloch, John and Alvarado, Manuel *Doctor Who: The Unfolding Text* (Macmillan, London, 1983), p. 249.

   In 'Dragonfire', the Doctor's hesitant and dubious 'Yes' might be taken as criticism of such a sentence (or perhaps he's just trying to work out how many inverted commas the man used as he spoke).

12. Aaronovitch, Ben *Doctor Who: Remembrance of the Daleks* (Target, London, 1990); Briggs, Ian *Doctor Who: The Curse of Fenric* (Target, London, 1990). The previous example of a novelization prefacing itself with a literary quotation is Peter Grimwade's *Doctor Who: Mawdryn Undead* (Target, London, 1983) which cites Richard Wagner on *The Flying Dutchman*. The spin-off novel *Turlough and the Earthlink Dilemma* by Tony Attwood (Target, London, 1986) prefaces itself with the epigram 'Philosophers merely explain the world. The thing, however, is to change it', but bizarrely doesn't make reference to the fact that this was said by Karl Marx.

13. Darvill-Evans is quoted in Smith, Dale 'Broader and Deeper: The Lineage and Impact of the Timewyrm Series' in Butler, David (ed.) *Time and Relative Dissertations in Space: Critical Perspectives on Doctor Who* (Manchester University Press, Manchester, 2007), p. 269. Freeman, John 'Back To The TARDIS' *In-Vision* No. 109 (October 2003), p. 11.

14. Roberts, Gareth '1993' *Skaro* Vol. 5, No. 8 (Autumn 1993), p. 23.

15. On Peter Darvill-Evans, see Howe, David J. and Tim Neal, *The Target Book* (Telos, Tolworth, 2007), p. 116. for *DWM* in these years see Hearn, Marcus 'Happy Times and Places: Part Two Mad Magazine' in *Doctor Who Magazine* No. 347 (15 September 2004).

16. There is one big exception to the general lack of politics around fandom in its early days. In the July/August 1978 issue of the society's magazine *TARDIS*, Gordon Blows used his editorial to talk of 'Today's Face of Evil' to expound the need for tolerance in a multiracial society, arguing that the values of those who stirred up racial tension were antithetical to those of the programme. 'I will leave it up to you to realise who The Face of Evil is in today's society. It is heartening to add, however, that on 31 April 1978, a march in London against the Face of Evil, from Trafalgar Square to Victoria Park, attracted a turnout, in support, of around 80,000 people'. The event cited was an Anti-Nazi League march at a time when Britain, and London in particular, saw a resurgence of the far right National Front party. The article was illustrated with a picture of Daleks handing out 'Dalek Front' leaflets.

    I always intended writing about this article in the relevant chapter on the late 70s, but its explicit politics makes it so atypical of the period I couldn't justify it. Great piece, though – Gordon, take a bow.

    Blows, Gordon *Editorial: Today's Face of Evil* in *TARDIS* Vol. 3, No. 4. (July/August 1978), pp. 2–4. Published by the DWAS.

17. Briggs, *Fenric*, pp. 1,897.

18. Peel, John *Doctor Who: The New Adventures – Timewyrm Genesys* (Virgin, London, 1991).

19. Orman, Kate *Doctor Who: The New Adventures – Set Piece* (Virgin, London, 1995), p. 146.

20. *Skaro* No. 5 (Spring, 1992), p. 9.

21. Jones, Matthew 'Fluid Links: The Hero That Failed' *Doctor Who Magazine* No. 249 (12 March, 1997), p. 35.

22. Pertwee's videos averaged sales of 24,740, followed by Hartnell's 21,978. Tom Baker, popularly regarded inside fandom and out as 'the best' came fourth with average sales of 21,679. Pertwee stories 'Day of the Daleks' and 'Death to the Daleks' were the only videos to have sold in excess of 50,000 copies (which, of

course, has implications in calculating averages). The average sales across the range at this point were 21,706.

Wyman, Mark 'Video Sales 1986–7' *Doctor Who Magazine* No. 278 (2 June 1999), pp. 28–9.

23. Topping, Keith *Inside Bartlett's White House: An Unauthorised and Unofficial Guide To The West Wing* (Virgin, London, 2002).

24. A more substantial account of Marvel's strategies in the late 80s/ early 90s can be found in Ainsworth, John 'Behind The Frame' *Doctor Who Classic Comics* No. 10 (18 August 1993), pp. 38– 40. In the booming comic market of the period, Marvel's UK operation was expanding rapidly, and trying out new talent in a magazine where the strip was not the centre of attention (and, thus, a failure was unlikely to sink the ship) suited the company's wider ambitions.

25. Darvill-Evans, Peter *Doctor Who: The New Adventures – Deceit* (Virgin, London, 1993), pp. 319–20. This is extracted from the afterword to the novel Darvill-Evans wrote for his own range. He had expressed these sentiments from 1990 – the first announcement of the *New Adventures* – onwards in interviews and private conversations.

26. As ever, the document itself became the subject of speculation. It finally saw public presentation, presented as possible evidence for the programme's timeline, as part of a massive chronology of the Who universe. Parkin, Lance *Doctor Who: A History of the Universe,* (London, Virgin, 1996), pp. 269–73. What was presented was 'virtually' the whole text.

27. Smith, Dale, *Broader and Deeper,* p. 273.

28. 'Bringer of Darkness' Script: Warwick Gray, Art: Martin Geraghty in *Doctor Who Magazine Summer Special* 1993.

29. Information on the regeneration which wasn't from Paul Cornell's 'The Virgin Doctor' in *Skaro* No. 9 (Summer, 1994), p. 8.

30. Gray, Scott 'Editorial', *Doctor Who Magazine* No. 246 (18 December 1996).

VI   *Who* Watches The Watchers

1. *Doctor Who Magazine* No. 265 (3 June 1998). Top Ten as follows: 'Genesis of the Daleks', 'The Talons of Weng-Chiang', 'The

Caves of Androzani', 'Pyramids of Mars', 'The Robots of Death', 'Remembrance of the Daleks', 'City of Death', 'The Tomb of The Cybermen', 'The Evil of the Daleks', 'The Web of Fear'. Holmes' 'The Deadly Assassin' came eleventh.

2. *Doctor Who Magazine 40th Anniversary special: We Love Doctor Who* November 2003. The top Ten: 'The Caves of Androzani', 'The Talons of Weng-Chiang', 'Genesis of the Daleks', 'Pyramids of Mars', 'City of Death', 'The Curse of Fenric', 'Remembrance of the Daleks', 'The Robots of Death', 'Inferno', 'The Tomb of the Cybermen'.

3. 'Watershed' is a British term denoting the point in the evening where family entertainment gives way to adult material. Traditionally in the UK this is 9:00 p.m. Aside from the TV movie, *Doctor Who* has always been screened well before this time.

4. Cole, Stephen 'Bring Me The Head Of BBC Books!' *Doctor Who Magazine* No. 259 (17 December 1997), p. 29.

5. Parkin, Lance 'Canonicity Matters: Defining the *Doctor Who* canon' in Butler, David (ed.) *Time and Relative Dissertations in Space* (Manchester University Press, Manchester, 2007), pp. 246–62.

   Laycock, Michael 'Paradigm Rift' *Skaro* No.13 (Summer 1997).

6. Gillatt, Gary 'Editorial' *Doctor Who Magazine* No. 259 (17 December 1997), p. 3.

7. Spilsbury, Tom 'Letter From The Editor' *Doctor Who Magazine* No. 403 (7 January 2008), p. 3.

8. Gary Gillatt, editor of the magazine at the time of Izzy's creation, asserts this in his review of 'The Tides of Time' in *Doctor Who Magazine 40th Anniversary Special: We Love Doctor Who* November , 2003, p. 47.

9. Messingham, Simon *Doctor Who: Zeta Major* (BBC, London, 1998), p. 134.

10. For the best analysis of the relationship between the two see *Doctor Who Magazine* No. 334 (17 September 2003). It is a *Blue Peter* special.

11. Reported on, and quoted from, www.gallifreynewsbase.com on 11 March 2010.

12. Donnelly, Kevin J. 'Between prosaic functionalism and sublime experimentation: Doctor Who and musical sound design in Butler *Relative Disserations,* p. 196.

13. Fiske, John 'Doctor Who: Ideology and the Reading of a Popular Narrative' *Australian Journal of Screen Theory* No. 14–15 (1983); Tulloch, John and Alvarado, Manuel *Doctor Who: The Unfolding Text* (Macmillan, London, 1983); Tulloch, John and Jenkins, *Henry Science Fiction Audiences: Watching 'Doctor Who' and 'Star Trek'* (Routledge, London, 1995); McKee, Alan 'Which is the Best Doctor Who Story? A Case Study in Value Judgements Outside the Academy' in *Intensities: The Journal of Cult Media* No. 1 (2001). Find it now at intensities.org/essaysMcKee.pdf.

    Chapman, James *Inside The TARDIS: The Worlds of Doctor Who* (I.B.Tauris, London, 2005); Newman, Kim *Doctor Who* (BFI, London, 2005).

14. *Who Is Dr Who* (spine reads 'Who is Doctor Who?'), released in 2000 on RPM label.

15. Howe, David J, and Arnold T Blumberg *Howe's Transcendental Toybox* (Telos/ATB Publishing, Tolworth, 2000). A second edition was released in 2003 and subsequent merchandise has been recorded in a series of supplements; Howe, David J. and Stephen James Walker *Doctor Who: the Television Companion* (BBC, London, 1998); Bignell, Richard *Doctor Who on Location* (Reynolds and Hearn, Richmond, 2001).

16. Cornell, Paul (ed.), *Licence Denied: Rumblings From The Doctor Who Underground* (Virgin, London, 1997), Walker, Stephen James (ed.) *Talkback* (Telos, Tolworth, 3 volumes, 2006–7). Wood, Tat and Lawrence, Miles, *About Time* (Des Moines, Mad Norwegian Press, 7 volumes, 2004– continuing) *Time Unincorporated* (three volumes, diverse authors/editors) (Des Moines, Mad Norwegian Press, 2009– continuing.)

VII   The Franchise of Doom

1. '*Gallifrey Guardian Extra*' *Doctor Who Magazine* No. 337 , (10 December 2003), p. 7.

2. If you can look past such (admittedly eye-catching) trivia as the name Tyler, what the book does show is the degree to which

Davies was prepared to think outside the usual generic boxes. The book concerns a weapon left over from the war which the Time Lords fought millennia ago against the Great Vampires (as recounted in the television serial 'State of Decay' [1980]) which is reactivating itself following what it takes to be vampiric presence on Earth. Shorn to the bone like this, we recognize a story format which was prominent in Tom Baker's early years, and has been part of the programme's repertoire ever since. Someone/thing believed dead has actually just been dormant, and now it is manifesting itself with the help of human serv-ants/dupes/hosts. The television series was mostly content to clothe this format in the trappings of Hammer horror films (like 'State of Decay' itself) or tales about a planet's investigation of its own historical past or mythology (1983's 'Snakedance' is the most sophisticated example). Many of the 1990s novelists were happy to retread the old generic patterns (and many readers were happy to allow them), but Davies' setting the story in a run-down estate on a northern town was one of the most strik-ing pieces of generic reimagining that the books produced – definitely rad.

3. Quoted in Simon Guerrier's *Bernice Summerfield: The Inside Story* (Big Finish Productions, Maidenhead, 2009), p. 90.

4. Consider, for instance Paul Cornell's third season scripts 'Human Nature'/'The Family of Blood'. It is recognizably the same story as the novel, but there are differences, notably in the Doctor's motivation. In the book, the Doctor undertakes his transforma-tion into a human being out of his fondness for the planet Earth and his love for/curiosity about humanity. His actions arise from a character trait that had been long discussed by fandom and which are oft-cited there as evidence of the character's com-passionate core. In the television adaptation, by contrast, the Doctor rewrites his DNA as human not because of a long-es-tablished character trait, but to escape powerful aliens who are tracking him. Thus, the threat of peril replaces character as the motor of the narrative which determines the Doctor's actions.

5. http://www.urbandictionary.com/define.php?term=Doctor%20Who

6. 'We Are Not Monsters' (Chris Chibnall Interview), *Doctor Who Magazine* No. 422 (23 June 2010), p. 23.

7. Davies, Russell T. and Benjamin Cook *Doctor Who: The Writer's Tale* (BBC, London, 2008), pp. 34–35.

8. Davies and Cook, *Writer's Tale,* p. 504.

9. Spilsbury, Tom 'Letter From the Editor' *Doctor Who Magazine* No. 405 (4 March 2009), p. 3.

10. Woody Allen's film *Annie Hall* (1977) begins with a joke about two women in a restaurant who complain amongst themselves about every aspect of their meal's taste and texture, and conclude with their final moan – the portions are so small. A variant would concern two *Who* fans complaining at length about the inadequacies of the Season One box, then moaning that the packaging for Season Two didn't match.

11. Parsons, Paul *The Science of Doctor Who* (Icon Books, London, 2007); White, Michael *A Teaspoon and an Open Mind: The Science of Doctor Who* (Penguin, London, 2006); Couch, Steve, Tony Watkins, Peter S. William *Back In Time: A Thinking Fan's Guide to Doctor Who* (DaMaris Publishing, Southampton, 2006); Thacker, Anthony *Behind the Sofa: A Closer Look at Doctor Who* (Kingsway Publications, Eastbourne, 2006); Hills, Matt *Triumph of a Time Lord: Regenerating Doctor Who in the Twenty-First Century* (I.B.Tauris, London, 2010). The description of the book as being a new series version of *The Unfolding Text* is something Hills used both in the acknowledgements and online in the months leading up to publication.

   The theological ones at least had the advantage that by considering moral and political themes within the programme they at least bore some relation to fans' normal critical practice. Indeed, theological readings were something the programme encouraged, packing itself with religious imagery to an unlikely degree (highlights from the third series include an homage to/rip-off of *The Last Temptation of Christ* in 'The Family of Blood' (when the Doctor's human form, John Smith, is granted a vision of the married life he could live if not for his necessary sacrifice) and a Messianic Doctor in 'Last of the Time Lords' who defeats the Master by forgiving him.

12. 'Doctor Who in War With Planet Maggie', *The Sunday Times,* 14 February 2010, p. 3. Accessed 6 June 2011.

13. http://entertainment.timesonline.co.uk/tol/arts_and_entertainment/tv_and_radio/article7026314.ece. Accessed 6 June 2011.

14. Fan lore, nowadays immortalised on his Wikipedia entry, has always said that Collins read the last *New Adventures* novel, aptly named *The Dying Days*, in a single sitting on the night of the 1997 General Election so that he could have read the entire series under Conservative government.
15. Collins, Tim speaking on 'Newsnight' TX: 16 February 2010 (BBC 2).
16. *Doctor Who Magazine* No. 419 (31 March 2010) (available on the high street 4 March 2010), p. 3.
17. http://newws.bbc.co.uk/1/hi/uk_politics/8452741.stm. Accessed 6 June 2011.
18. http://today.yougov.co.uk/politics/Debate-more-interesting-than-Doctor-Who. Accessed 6 June 2011.
19. Davies and Cook, *Writer's Tale*, pp. 76–77.
20. Davies, Russell T. et al. *Doctor Who: The Shooting Scripts* (BBC Books, London, 2005), p. 279.

BIBLIOGRAPHY

Doctor Who Magazine

Doctor Who Magazine – DWM – began life as a weekly comic published by the UK division of Marvel Comics in 1979. Over the years
it has had several titles: *Doctor Who Weekly*; *Doctor Who a Marvel
Monthly*; *Doctor Who Monthly*; *The Official Doctor Who Magazine*;
The Doctor Who Magazine; *Doctor Who Magazine*. This final title was
adopted in 1985 and seems to be here to stay. *DWM* appears in
this book primarily as an object of study, though – for reasons outlined in Chapter Two – all modern researchers/analysts of *Who* are
indebted to its groundbreaking coverage of the programme's production, and its ongoing content of articles and interviews provides
has provided copious information down the years. Only specific
articles/editorials cited within this study are listed here. This list also
contains bibliographic references for citations from the magazines
many 'special editions' and from its shorter-lived companion *Doctor
Who Classic Comics*.

Ainsworth, John. 'Behind The Frame' *Doctor Who Classic Comics*.
 Issue 10; 18 August 1993.
Arnopp, Jason. 'We Are Not Monsters' (Chris Chibnall Interview),
 Doctor Who Magazine. Issue 42; 23 June 2010.
Barnes, Alan. 'The Star Beast', *Doctor Who Magazine Special Edition
 No. 6: We Love Doctor Who* (Panini, Tunbridge Wells, November
 2003), p. 51.

Bentham, Jeremy. 'Architects of Fear', *Doctor Who Magazine*. Issue 48; January 1981.

—— 'Behind The Scenes Report: Script-Editing' *Doctor Who Magazine*. Issue 60; January 1982.

—— 'Castrovalva', *Doctor Who Magazine*. Issue 63; April 1982.

—— *Doctor Who Winter Special*. December 1983 (interviews all producers of the programme).

Bishop, Vanessa. 'Review: The Curse of Fenric' DVD, *Doctor Who Magazine*. Issue 336; 12 November 2003.

Cole, Stephen. 'Bring Me The Head of BBC Books!' *Doctor Who Magazine*. Issue 259; 17 December 1997.

Cornell, Paul. 'Frontier in Space' *Doctor Who Magazine Special Edition No. 2: The Complete Third Doctor*. September 2002.

Darlington, David. 'Third Men' (Interview with Terrance Dicks and Barry Letts), *Doctor Who Magazine*. Issue 337; 10 December 2003.

Davies, Russell T. 'Production Notes', *Doctor Who Magazine*. Issue 341; 31 March 2004.

—— 'Production notes', *Doctor Who Magazine*. Issue 346; 18 August 2004.

Duis, Rex. 'Script Doctors: Gareth Roberts', *Doctor Who Magazine*. Issue 377; 3 January 2007.

Gillatt, Gary. 'Editorial', *Doctor Who Magazine*. Issue 259; 17 December 1997.

—— 'The Tides of Time', *Doctor Who Magazine 40th Anniversary Special: We Love Doctor Who*. November 2003.

Gray, Scott. 'Editorial', *Doctor Who Magazine*. Issue 246; 18 December 1996.

—— 'The Neverending Story', *Doctor Who Magazine Special Edition: The Complete Sixth Doctor*. 22 January 2003, p. 65.

Griffiths, Peter. 'Doctor Who?' (Interview with Kevin Clarke), *Doctor Who Magazine*. Issue 244; 23 October 1996.

Harris, Neil. 'Why DWM Made Me The Fan I Am', *Doctor Who Magazine*. Issue 400; 15 October 2008.

Hearn, Marcus. 'Happy Times and Places? Part One 1979–1985: Comic Timing', *Doctor Who Magazine*. Issue 344; 23 June 2004.

—— 'Happy Times and Places: Part Two Mad Magazine', *Doctor Who Magazine*. Issue 347; 15 September 2004.

Pixley, Andrew. 'Who Peter', *Doctor Who Magazine*. Issue 334; 17 September 2003 (Blue Peter Special).

Russell, Gary. 'On Target', *The Official Doctor Who Magazine*. Issue 96; January 1985.

Spilsbury, Tom. 'Letter From The Editor', *Doctor Who Magazine*. Issue 403; 7 January 2008.

—— 'Letter From The Editor', *Doctor Who Magazine*. Issue 405; 4 March 2009.

—— 'Letter From The Editor', *Doctor Who Magazine*. No. 419; 31 March 2010.

Waterhouse, Matthew. 'Letter', *Doctor Who Weekly*. No. 10; 19 December 1979.

Wyman, Mark. 'Video Sales 1986–7', *Doctor Who Magazine*. Issue 278; 2 June 1999, pp. 28–29.

Not everything in *Doctor Who Magazine* is easily assigned an author. The news pages rarely carry a byline. For various reasons, the following issues, though consulted, do not fit normal bibliographic formats.

Doctor Who Weekly. Issue 26; 9 April 1980.

Doctor Who Monthly. Issue 70; November 1982.

Doctor Who Magazine. Issue 71; December 1982.

Doctor Who Magazine. Issue 82; November 1983, p. 44 (ad on back cover).

Doctor Who Magazine. Issue 265; 3 June 1998 (special issue devoted to results of massive opinion poll).

'Gallifrey Guardian Extra', *Doctor Who Magazine*. Issue 337; 10 December 2003.

'Who on Earth is … David Tennant?', *Doctor Who Magazine*. Issue 400; 15 October 2008.

Doctor Who Fiction

Aaronovitch, Ben. *Doctor Who: Remembrance of the Daleks* (Target, London, 1990).

Attwood, Tony. *Turlough and the Earthlink Dilemma* (Target, London, 1986).

Baker, Pip and Jane. *Doctor Who: Terror of the Vervoids* (Target, London, 1987).

Bidmead, Christopher H. *Doctor Who – Logopolis* (Target, London, 1982).

—— *Doctor Who: Frontios* (Target, London, 1984).

Briggs, Ian. *Doctor Who: Dragonfire* (Target, London, 1989).

—— *Doctor Who: The Curse of Fenric* (Target, London, 1990).

Clarke, Kevin. *Doctor Who: Silver Nemesis* (Target, London, 1989).

Cole, Stephen. *Doctor Who – To the Slaughter* (BBC, London, 2005).

Cornell, Paul. *Doctor Who – Love and War* (Virgin, London, 1992).

Daly, Wally K. *Doctor Who: The Ultimate Evil* (Target, London, 1989).

Darvill-Evans, Peter. *Doctor Who: The New Adventures – Deceit* (Virgin, London, 1993).

Davies, Russell T. *Doctor Who: The New Adventures – Damaged Goods* (Virgin, London, 1996).

Day, Martin. *Doctor Who – The Menagerie* (Virgin, London, 1995).

Dicks, Terrance. *Doctor Who and the Pyramids of Mars* (Target, London, 1976).

—— *Doctor Who and the Horns of Nimon* (Target, London, 1980).

—— *Doctor Who and the Sunmakers* (Target, London, 1982).

Fisher, David. *Doctor Who and the Leisure Hive* (Target, London, 1982).

Gatiss, Mark. *Doctor Who: Last of the Gadarene* (BBC, London, 2000).

Gray, Scott, et al. *Doctor Who: The Glorious Dead* (Panini, Tunbridge Wells, 2006).

—— *Doctor Who: The Flood* (Panini, Tunbridge Wells, 2007).

Grimwade, Peter. *Doctor Who: Mawdryn Undead* (Target, London, 1983).

—— *Robot* (Star, London, 1987) (not actually a *Doctor Who* book, but containing many references).

Hinton, Craig. *Doctor Who – GodEngine* (Virgin, London, 1996).

Hulke, Malcolm. *Doctor Who And The Doomsday Weapon* (Target, London, 1974).

—— *Doctor Who and Sea-Devils* (Target, London 1974).

—— *Doctor Who and the Green Death* (Target, London 1975).

—— *Doctor Who and the Dinosaur Invasion* (Target, London, 1976).

—— *Roger Moore and the Crimefighters: The Siege* (Alpine Books, London, 1977) (not actually a *Doctor Who* book, but well worth reading for fans of the programme).

Lane, Andy and Jim Mortimore. *Doctor Who – Lucifer Rising* (Virgin, London, 1993).

Lyons, Steve. *Doctor Who – Conundrum* (Virgin, London, 1994).

Marter, Ian. *Doctor Who and the Ribos Operation* (Target, London, 1979).

—— *Doctor Who: Earthshock* (Target, London, 1983).

—— *Doctor Who: The Dominators* (Target, London, 1984).

—— *Doctor Who: The Invasion* (Target, London, 1985).

McIntee, David A. *Doctor Who – Bullet Time* (BBC, London, 2001).

McKee, Alan. 'Hall of Mirrors', *Doctor Who Magazine*. Issue 119; December 1986.

Messingham, Simon. *Doctor Who: Zeta Major* (BBC, London, 1998).

Miller, Keith. 'The House That Jack Built', *The Doctor Who Annual 1975* (London, World Distributors, 1974).

Mills, Pat, John Wagner and Dave Gibbons. *Doctor Who: The Iron Legion* (Panini, Tunbridge Wells, 2004).

Moore, Alan and David Lloyd (artwork). '4D War' script: Alan Moore, Art: David Lloyd,' *Doctor Who Magazine*. Issue 50; April 1981.

Moore, Steve, et al. *Abslom Daak: Dalek Killer* (Marvel comics, London, 1990).

Mortimore, Jim. *Doctor Who – Eternity Weeps* (Virgin, London, 1997).

Parkhouse, Steve and John Ridgway (artwork). *Doctor Who: Voyager* (Panini, Tunbridge Wells, 2007).

Russell, Gary. *Doctor Who – Legacy* (Virgin, London, 1994).

Saward, Eric. *Doctor Who: The Twin Dilemma* (Target, London, 1985).

—— *Doctor Who: Attack of the Cybermen* (Target, London, 1989).

Smith, Andrew. *Doctor Who – Full Circle* (Target, London, 1982).

Stevens, James and David Bishop. *Doctor Who – Who Killed Kennedy* (Virgin, London, 1996).

Books and Articles

This listing includes both professional and fan publications. The latter do not always contain publication information in the standard form. What information is given is reproduced below. Other citations are incomplete because of a policy of granting fan writers anonymity as explained in the introduction. In these cases, the title of the fanzine is given as the author. Note that for purposes of listing its newsletters and publications, the Doctor Who Appreciation Society (DWAS) is listed here as the author, and the BBC itself as the author of two publications.

BBC. *Doctor Who: Radio Times Special* (BBC, London, 1973).

—— *The Doctor Who Celebration: Twenty Years of a Time Lord* (Commemorative Programme, 1983).

Bennett, Tony and Janet Woollacott. *Bond and Beyond: The Political Career of a Popular Hero* (Macmillan, London/Basingstoke, 1987).

Butler, David (ed). *Time and Relative Dissertations in Space* (Manchester, Manchester University Press, 2007).

Bignell, Richard. *Doctor Who on Location* (Richmond, Reynolds and Hearn, 2001).

Capitol, 2/3 October 1984. (Doctor Who fanzine).

Cartmel, Andrew. *Script Doctor: The Inside Story of Doctor Who 1986–89* (Reynolds and Hearn Ltd, London, 2005).

Chapman, James. *Inside The TARDIS: The Worlds of Doctor Who* (I.B.Tauris, London, 2006).

Coe, Jonathan. *The Dwarves of Death* (Penguin, London, 1991).

Collins, Andrew. *Where Did It All Go Right?* (Ebury Press, London, 2003).

Cook, Benjamin. *Doctor Who: The New Audio Adventures: The Inside Story* (Big Finish Productions, Maidenhead, 2003).

Cornell, Paul. 'The Virgin Doctor', *Skaro*. No. 9; Summer 1994 (published in Bath).

——(ed). *Licence Denied: Rumblings from the Doctor Who Underground* (Virgin, London, 1997).

Couch, Steve, Tony Watkins, Peter S. William. *Back in Time: A Thinking Fan's Guide to Doctor Who* (DaMaris Publishing, Southampton, 2006).

Courtney, Nicholas and Michael McManus. *Still Getting Away With It: The Life and Times of Nicholas Courtney*. Published by www.scificollector.co.uk in conjunction with www.greyhoundleader.com, 2005.

Cygnus Alpha. Issue 8, November 1982 (*Doctor Who* fanzine).

—— Issue 12, July 1984 (*Doctor Who* fanzine).

Davies, Russell T., et al. *Doctor Who: The Shooting Scripts* (BBC Books, London, 2005).

—— and Benjamin Cook. *Doctor Who: The Writer's Tale* (BBC Books, London, 2008).

DeFalco, Tom. *Comic Creators on X-Men* (Titan Books, London, 2006).

Dicks, Terrance, and Malcolm Hulke. *The Making of Doctor Who* (Target, London, 1976).

Donnelly, Kevin J. 'Between prosaic functionalism and sublime experimentation: Doctor Who and musical sound design' in Butler, David (ed.), *Time and Relative Dissertations in Space Manchester* (Manchester, Manchester University Press, 2007).

DWAS/Vincent-Rudzki, Jan. 'The Deadly Assassin', *TARDIS*. Vol. II, No. 1; January/February 1977. Quoted in Celestial Toyroom, October 1991.

DWAS/Blows, Gordon. 'Editorial: Today's Face of Evil' in *TARDIS*. Vol. 3, No. 4. Published by the DWAS, July/August 1978.

DWAS/French, Gavin. 'Astronomy of Doctor Who: Voga', *TARDIS*. Vol. 4, No. 5; 1979.

DWAS/Dollin, Tim. 'Teleview: City of Death' in *TARDIS*. Vol. 4, No. 6; 1979.

DWAS/Peel, John. 'Teleview' in *TARDIS*. Vol. 5, No. 1; 1980.

DWAS. *Celestial Toyroom*, February 1982.

DWAS/Saunders, David. 'Co-Ordinators Corner' *Celestial Toyroom*. January 1984.

DWAS. *Celestial Toyroom* February 1984.

—— May 1984.

—— June 1984.

—— September 1984.

—— October 1984.

—— February 1985.

DWAS. *The CT Advertiser*. April 1985.

Eco, Umberto. *Travels in Hyper-Reality* (Picador, London, 1986).

Fiske, John. 'Dr. Who, Ideology and the Reading of a Popular Narrative Text', *The Australian Journal of Screen Theory* No. 14; 1983, pp. 60–100.

—— *Television Culture* (Methuen, London/New York, 1987).

Fleming, John. 'The New Dr Who', *Starburst*. No. 27; September/October 1980.

Freeman, John. 'Back to the TARDIS', *In-Vision*. Issue 109; October 2003.

Guerrier, Simon. *Bernice Summerfield: The Inside Story* (Big Finish Publishing, Maidenhead, 2009).

Gwenllian Jones, Sarah. 'Web Wars: Online Fandom and Studio Censorship' in Jancovich, Mark and James Lyons (eds.). *Quality Popular television London* (British film institute, 2003), pp. 163–77.

Haining, Peter. *Doctor Who – A Celebration: Two Decades Through Time and Space.* (W. H. Allen, London, 1983).

Heath, Adrian. *Doctor Who: Brain Teasers and Mind Benders* (London, Target, 1984).

Henley, Dennis E. 'From Flickering Image to Printed Page', *Fantasy Empire*. No. 1; July 1981 (New Media Publishing, Largo, Florida), pp. 36–42.

Hills, Matt. *Fan Cultures* (London, Routledge, 2002).

—— *Triumph of a Time Lord: Regenerating Doctor Who in the Twenty-First Century* (I.B.Tauris, London, 2010).

Horne, Mark. 'Doctor Who in War with Planet Maggie' *The Sunday Times,* 14 February 2010.

Howe, David J. and Stephen James Walker. *Doctor Who: The Television Companion* (BBC Worldwide, London, 1998).

Howe, David J. and Arnold T. Blumberg. *Howe's Transcendental Toybox* (Telos/ATB Publishing, 2000).

Howe, David J. and Tim Neal. *The Target Book* (Telos, Tolworth, 2007).

Hulke, Malcolm and Terrance Dicks. *The Making of Doctor Who* (Pan Books, London, 1973).

In-Vision: *Warriors' Gate.* Issue 50; 1994 (Doctor Who fanzine).

Jenkins, Henry. *Textual Poachers: Television Fans and Participatory Culture* (Routledge, New York/ London, 1992).

Laycock, Michael. 'Paradigm Rift' *Skaro 13*, Summer 1997. Published in Bath.

Lofficier, Jean-Marc. *The Doctor Who Programme Guide Volume 1: The Programmes* (Target, London, 1981).

McKee, Alan. 'Which is the Best Doctor Who Story? A Case Study in Value Judgements Outside', *The Academy' Intensities: The Journal of Cult Media.* No. 1; 2001. Find it now at intensities.org/essaysMcKee.pdf.

—— 'Why is 'City of Death' the Best Doctor Who story?' Butler, David (ed.), *Time and Relative Dissertations in Space Manchester* (Manchester, Manchester University Press, 2007).

Milton, Mary. 'Ian Marter Interview', *Paradise Lost*. Issue 1; Swindon, 1984.

Newman, Kim. *Doctor Who*. (London, BFI, 2005).

Newman, Philip. 'Sid Sutton Interview', *The Frame*. Issue 21/22; Spring/Summer, 1992 (Tolworth).

Parkin, Lance. *Doctor Who: A History of the Universe* (London, Virgin, 1996).

—— 'Canonicity Matters: Defining the Doctor Who Canon' Butler, David (ed.). *Time and Relative Dissertations In Space* (Manchester, Manchester University Press, 2007), p. 249.

—— *Time Unincorporated: The Doctor Who Fanzine Archives* (Des Moines, Mad Norwegian Press, 2009).

Parsons, Paul. *The Science of Doctor Who* (Icon Books, London, 2007).

Richardson, David. '20 Minutes', *Skaro*. Vol. 3, No. 2; November, 1982. Published in Bath, pp. 24/5.

Rickard, Graham. *A Day With a TV Producer* (Wayland Publishers, Hove, 1980).

Road, Alan. *Doctor Who: The Making of a Television Series* (André Deutsch, London, 1983).

Roberts, Gareth. '1993', *Skaro*. Vol. 2, No. 8; Autumn 1993.

—— 'Strange Love', *Doctor Who Magazine*. Issue 351; 5 January 2005.

Robins, Tim. 'Who Wars', *The Frame*. 15, August 1990 (Tolworth), pp. 20–23.

Robinson, Nigel. *The Doctor Who Quiz Book* (Target, London, 1981).

—— *The Doctor Who Crossword Book* (Target, London, 1982).

—— *The Second Doctor Who Quiz Book* (Target, London, 1983).

—— *The Third Doctor Who Quiz Book* (Target, London, 1985).

Skaro. 'Working for the Yankee Dollar', *Skaro*. Vol. IV, No. 1.

—— 'Review of Planet of Evil', *Skaro*. Vol. IV, No. 1; 1983.

—— 'No Confidence' (Editorial) *Skaro*. Vol. IV, No. 2. December/January 1983/4.

Smith, Dale. 'Broader and Deeper: the lineage and impact of the Timewyrm series', Butler, David (ed.). *Time and Relative dissertations in Space: Critical Perspectives on Doctor Who* (Manchester, Manchester University Press, 2007).

Spectrox. VIII, p. 11. The 'zine would appear to have been published in 1989 or 90.

Thacker, Anthony. *Behind the Sofa: A Closer Look at Doctor Who* (Kingsway Publications, Eastbourne, 2006).

Topping, Keith. *Inside Bartlett's White House: An Unauthorised and Unofficial Guide To The West Wing* (Virgin, London, 2002).

Toth, Kathleen. 'JN-T Working for The Yankee Dollar' *Doctor Who Bulletin Summer Special*, July 1986.

Tulloch, John. and Alvarado, Manuel. *Doctor Who: The Unfolding Text* (MacMillan, London, 1983).

Tulloch, John. *Television Drama: Agency, Audience and Myth* (Routledge, London/ New York, 1990).

Tulloch, John and Henry Jenkins. *Science Fiction Audiences: Watching Doctor Who and Star Trek* (London, Routledge, 1995).

Walker, Stephen James. *Talkback: The Unofficial and Unauthorised Doctor Who Interview Book Vol one: The Sixties* (Telos, Tolworth, 2006).

—— *Talkback: The Unofficial and Unauthorised Doctor Who Interview Book Volume Three: The Eighties* (Telos,Tolworth, 2007).

White, Michael. *A Teaspoon and an Open Mind: The Science of Doctor Who* (Penguin Books, London, 2006).

Wood, Tat. and Lawrence Miles. *About Time* (Des Moines, Mad Norwegian Press, 7 volumes, 2004 – continuing).

DVD

Doctor Who is released on DVD by 2Entertain, a company part-owned by the BBC. The discs contain numerous informative features and commentaries. As this book goes to press, the BBC has announced the end of the 2Entertain branding. Those used as research in the course of this book are listed here.

Doctor Who: Arc of Infinity. BBC DVD 2327B.
Doctor Who: The Curse of Fenric. BBC DVD 1154.
Doctor Who: The Leisure Hive. BBC DVD 1351.
Doctor Who: Survival. BBC DVD 1834.

INDEX